# PRACTICAL ENGLISH

## Volume Two

# PRACTICAL
# ENGLISH

by
Madeline Semmelmeyer
*Former Supervisor of Languages, Chicago Public Schools,
and Lecturer in Education: Chicago Teachers Review School,
Roosevelt University, and National College of Education.*

Edited by
Donald O. Bolander
*Director of Education, Career Institute*

A Two Volume Course
Containing 27 Self-graded Units
on GRAMMAR, CORRECT USAGE, and PUNCTUATION

*Career Institute*
30 East Adams Street • Chicago 3, Illinois

**TWO VOLUME EDITION 1963/2**
Copyright 1955, by
**CAREER INSTITUTE, Inc.**
30 East Adams Street
Chicago 3, Illinois

Reprinted 1966

Printed in Great **Britain**
by
Henry Garnett & Co. Ltd., Rotherham and London

# TABLE OF CONTENTS
## Volume Two

Note: A *Glossary of Terms* and a *Comprehensive Index* are contained at the back of Volume 1.

UNIT 14: THE TENSES OF VERBS

The Six Tenses, 5 • The Simple Tenses, 6 • The Perfect Tenses, 8 • The Verb "To Be," 11 • Progressive Forms of Verbs, 16 • Emphatic Forms of the Verb, 18 • The Use of "Shall" and "Will" — "Should" and "Would," 20 • Mixed Tenses, 24 • The "Of" Error, 25 • Summary, 26

UNIT 15: VERBS: VOICE AND MOOD

Active and Passive Voice, 5 • How The Passive Voice is Formed, 8 • Six Tenses of the Verb "Call" — Passive Voice, 9 • Six Tenses of the Verb "Know" Passive Voice, 11 • When to Use the Passive Voice, 14 • Mood of Verbs, 17 • Subjunctive Forms of Verb "To Be," 18 • Uses of the Subjunctive Mood, 20 • Summary, 22

UNIT 16: AGREEMENT OF SUBJECT AND VERB

Agreement in Person and Number, 5 • Agreement of Verb With Compound Subject, 6 • Agreement of Verb With Collective Nouns, 10 • Intervening Phrases, 12 • Agreement of Subject With Contractions, 14 • Agreement of Verb With Indefinite Pronouns, 16 • Special Cases of Agreement, 19 • Summary, 22

UNIT 17: PREPOSITIONAL PHRASES

Adjective Phrases, 6 • Commonly Used Prepositions, 7 • Adverbial Phrases, 9 • Compound or Phrasal Prepositions, 11 • Pronouns Used as Objects of Prepositions, 13 • Diagramming the Prepositional Phrase, 15 • The Correct Use of Prepositions, 18 • Position of the Preposition, 21 • Summary, 23

UNIT 18: THE COMPOUND SENTENCE

Kinds of Clauses, 5 • The Simple Sentence, 7 • The Compound Sentence, 9 • Co-Ordinate Conjunctions, 10 • Use of the Semicolon in the Compound Sentence, 13 • The Comma Fault, 13 • The Run-On Sentence, 15 • Transitional Words, 18 • Diagramming the Compound Sentence, 21 • Summary, 23

*UNIT 19:* THE COMPLEX SENTENCE—ADJECTIVE CLAUSES

The Complex Sentence, 5 • Kinds of Subordinate Clauses, 6 • Adjective Clauses, 7 • Adjective Clauses Introduced by Relative Adverbs, 10 • "Who" and "Whom" in Subordinate Clauses, 12 • Restrictive and Non-restrictive Clauses, 14 • Diagramming the Complex Sentence, 17 • Summary, 21

*UNIT 20:* ADVERBIAL CLAUSES

Subordinate Conjunctions, 5 • Words Used as Subordinate Conjunctions, 6 • Kinds of Adverbial Clauses, 8 • Clauses of Degree, 9 • Position of the Adverbial Clause, 10 • Clauses of Comparison, 13 • "As—As" and "Not So—As" in Comparisons, 14 • Incorrect Use of "Like" in Clauses, 15 • Diagramming the Adverbial Clause, 20 • Summary 22

*UNIT 21:* NOUN CLAUSES

Function of the Noun Clause, 5 • Omission of the Connecting Word, 9 • The Noun Clause Used as an Appositive, 11 • The Noun Clause and the Introductory, "It," 12 • Words That Introduce Noun Clauses, 14 • Diagramming the Noun Clause, 18 • Summary, 23

*UNIT 22:* PARTICIPLES

The Nature of Verbals, 5 • Forms of the Participle, 8 • The Participial Phrase, 12 • Modifiers of Participles, 12 • Complements of Participles, 13 • Participles Used in Independent Constructions, 14 • Dangling Participles, 16 • Misplaced Modifiers, 17 • Participles Used in Verb Phrases, 19 • Diagramming the Participial Phrase, 22 • Summary, 25

*UNIT 23:* GERUNDS

Nature of the Gerund, 5 • The Gerund Phrase, 7 • Complements of Gerunds, 7 • Adverbial Modifiers of Gerunds, 8 • Adjective Modifiers of Gerunds, 11 • The Possessive Case Before the Gerund, 12 • The Dangling Gerund, 14 • Diagramming the Gerund, 17 • Diagramming the Gerund Phrase, 19 • Summary, 22

*UNIT 24:* INFINITIVES

Nature of the Infinitive, 5 • Uses of the Infinitive, 6 • Infinitives Used as Adjectives, 8 • Infinitives Used as Adverbs, 9 • Complements of Infinitives, 12 • Modifiers of Infinitives, 13 • The Infinitive Phrase, 14 • The Omission of the Sign "To," 16 • Summary, 18

## UNIT 25: PROBLEMS IN THE USE OF INFINITIVES

The Infinitive Clause, 5 • Verb "To Be" in an Infinitive Clause, 8 • The Split Infinitive, 11 • Special Uses of the Infinitive, 14 • The Three-Sided Character of the Infinitive, 16 • Diagramming Infinitives, 17 • Summary, 23

## UNIT 26: COMPREHENSIVE REVIEW—MASTERY TESTS

Parts of Speech, 6 • Subject and Predicate, 7 • Complements of Verbs, 8 • Kinds of Sentences, 9 • Verb Forms, 10 • Comparison of Adjectives and Adverbs, 11 • Agreement of Subject and Verb, 12 • Agreement of Pronoun With Antecedent, 13 • Identifying Phrases, 14 • Correct Case of Pronouns, 15 • Subordinate Clauses, 16 • Identifying Participles, Gerunds, and Infinitives, 17 • Plurals of Nouns, 18 • Capital Letters, 19 • Correct Usage, 20

## UNIT 27: PUNCTUATION REVIEW

Open and Closed Punctuation, 5 • The Period, 6 • The Comma, 7 • The Semicolon, 17 • The Colon, 20 • Parentheses, 21 • The Dash, 22 • Brackets, 25 • The Question Mark, 25 • The Exclamation Mark, 26 • Quotation Marks, 27 • Single Quotation Marks, 28 • The Apostrophe, 29

**Practical English Grammar**

## OUTLINE OF UNIT FOURTEEN

# THE TENSES OF VERBS

Page

1. THE SIX TENSES ................................................................. 5

2. THE SIMPLE TENSES.............................................................. 6

3. THE PERFECT TENSES ........................................................ 8

4. THE VERB "TO BE"................................................................. 11

5. PROGRESSIVE FORMS OF VERBS.................................... 16

6. EMPHATIC FORMS OF THE VERB................................ 18

7. THE USE OF "SHALL" AND "WILL"—
   "Should" and "Would"................................................................. 20

8. MIXED TENSES ................................................................... 24

9. THE "OF" ERROR .............................................................. 25

10. SUMMARY OF GRAMMAR UNIT FOURTEEN............. 26

*Self-Grading Assignments* ...................................................... 27

*Progress Test Fourteen* ............................................................ 30

*Key to Correct Answers* ........................................................... 32

# THE TENSES OF VERBS

## THE SIX TENSES

A VERB is the most important word in any sentence because more constructions depend upon the verb than upon any other part of speech. Verbs have a number of properties which other parts of speech do not have. One of the properties that belongs exclusively to verbs and verb forms is tense.

In Grammar Unit 12 you learned that in grammar *tense* means *time*. Verbs have **six tenses** which show differences in the time of *action* or the time of the *state of being* or *condition* (linking verbs).

I *see* a robin on the fence. (**present** time)

I *saw* a robin on the fence yesterday. (**past** time)

I *shall see* a number of birds when I go to the woods. (**future** time)

These sentences do not mean the same thing. The meaning depends to a large extent upon the verb form that is used; that is, the verb form that is used to show the *time* of the action.

The first sentence means that the action expressed by the verb *see* is going on now. The second sentence means that the action expressed by the verb *saw* happened at some time in the past (yesterday). The third sentence means that the action expressed by the verb *shall see* will occur at some future time.

The verbs used in the three sentences are forms of the verb *see*. The verb *see* in the first sentence is the form used in the present tense. It expresses or denotes *present time*. The verb *saw* in the second sentence is the form used to express *past time*. The verb *shall see* is the form used to express *future time*.

Remember, there are six tenses in English. The three tenses which you have just studied are called the **simple tenses.** The other three tenses are called the **perfect tenses.** The only difference between the simple tenses and the perfect tenses is that the perfect tenses include the idea of completion. In grammar, the word *perfect* refers to an action or state of being that is completed at the time of speaking or writing.

| **Simple Tenses** | **Perfect Tenses** |
|---|---|
| 1. *present* tense | 4. *present perfect* tense |
| 2. *past* tense | 5. *past perfect* tense |
| 3. *future* tense | 6. *future perfect* tense |

## THE SIMPLE TENSES

The present tense denotes *present time.* It is also used to express *habitual action,* or to express an idea that is *generally accepted as true.*

I hear the bell. (present time)
present tense

Oscar works in an airplane factory. (habitual action)
present tense

"Honesty is the best policy." (generally accepted truth)
present tense

The present tense is often used to express *future time.* Examine the following sentences carefully. In all of them the present tense expresses a future idea:

If it rains, we shall not go to the woods.
present tense

If the bill passes, the tax will be removed.
present tense

Our lease on the factory expires tomorrow.
present tense

The past tense denotes *past time.* The past tense of **regular verbs** is formed by adding *d* or *ed* to the present tense form: call, call*ed;* dive, div*ed*. Sometimes the *d* at the end of the present tense form changes to *t* in the past tense: build, buil*t*.

> I <u>mailed</u> the letter yesterday. (addition of *ed*)
> <sub>past tense</sub>

> We <u>dived</u> into the pool. (addition of *d*)
> <sub>past tense</sub>

> The hunter <u>built</u> a cabin in the woods. (change of *d* to *t*)
> <sub>past tense</sub>

The past tense of **irregular verbs** is formed in various ways. Sometimes there is a change in the vowel: s*i*ng, s*a*ng; sw*i*m, sw*a*m; beg*i*n, beg*a*n; dr*i*ve, dr*o*ve; br*ea*k, br*o*ke. Sometimes the same form is used in the past tense and in the present tense: bid, bid; hurt, hurt; cut, cut; slit, slit.

The future tense denotes *future time*. The future tense is formed by combining the auxiliary *shall* or *will* with the present tense form of the verb. Use *shall* with the pronouns *I* and *we*. Use *will* with the pronouns *you, he, she, it, they.*

> I *shall see* you tomorrow. (*shall*—first person)

> I am sure that you *will be* late. (*will*—second person)

> The speaker *will arrive* at seven. (*will*—third person)

To express future time, use *shall* in the first person and *will* in the second and third persons.

### EXERCISE 1

Underline the **verbs** in the following sentences. On the line to the right, indicate the tense of the verb: *present, past,* or *future tense.* Some sentences have two verbs. Underline both.

1. Jerry met our guests at the station.　　　1. ................

2. Will you help me translate this letter?　　2. ................

3. The conference begins at eight o'clock.　　3. ................

4. Our engineers will install the new machinery.　4. ................

5.  Are you a member of the Camera Club?          5. ................

6.  The milk became sour over night.              6. ................

7.  The detective examined the room carefully.    7. ................

8.  If he comes, I shall give him your letter.    8. ................

9.  Were you in the parade yesterday?             9. ................

10. Who will start the discussion?                10. ................

11. I listen to the same commentator every evening. 11. ................

12. What are you doing?                           12. ................

13. He believes that the manager will resign.     13. ................

14. The cake seems fresh.                          14. ................

15. We shall send the goods promptly.              15. ................

Note: *The correct answers to exercises will be found at the back of this booklet. Correct your mistakes and, if necessary, re-read the text material before going on to the next section.*

## THE PERFECT TENSES

You can remember the *perfect tenses* easily, if you remember that the word **perfect** is always used in identifying them. The three perfect tenses are the *present perfect tense*, the *past perfect tense*, and the *future perfect tense*.

The present perfect tense denotes *action that is completed* at the time of speaking or writing. It may also indicate action that is *continuing into the present.*

The present perfect tense is formed by combining the auxiliary *have* or *has* with the past participle of the principal verb. The auxiliary *has* is always used in the third person singular: He *has spoken* to the manager.

I have seen three of Shaw's plays. (*have seen*—first person)
<u>present perfect</u>

You have earned a promotion. (*have earned*—second person)
<u>present perfect</u>

John has washed the car. (*has washed*—third person)
<u>present perfect</u>

In the first sentence, the verb phrase is *have seen.* It is in the present perfect tense. The verb phrase is made up of the auxiliary *have* and the past participle of the verb *see,* which is *seen* (*have seen*). In the third sentence, the auxiliary *has* is used instead of *have* (*has washed*).

The past perfect tense denotes *action that was completed* before some definite time in the past. The past perfect tense is formed by combining the auxiliary *had* with the past participle of the principal verb: *had walked, had known, had given, had drunk, had become, had been,* etc.

By the time the officer arrived, the thief had disappeared.
<u>past tense</u>                <u>past perfect</u>

I liked the speaker better after I had heard him the second time.
<u>past tense</u>                <u>past perfect</u>

The agent had sold all the tickets before I applied for mine.
<u>past perfect</u>                <u>past tense</u>

The future perfect tense denotes *action that will be completed* at some definite time in the future. The future perfect tense is seldom used in informal speaking or writing.

The future perfect tense is formed by combining the auxiliaries *shall have* or *will have* with the past participle of the principal verb. *Shall have* is used in the first person, and *will have* in the second and third persons.

My friend will have sailed before I reach the pier.
<u>future perfect</u>

By January, the committee will have completed the investigation.
<u>future perfect</u>

I shall have crossed the river three times before noon.
<u>future perfect</u>

Many verb errors are made because the writer or speaker is not familiar with the forms for the past tense and the past participle. Whenever you are not sure of one of these forms, consult the tables in Grammar Unit 12. If the verb you are interested in is not listed, consult a reliable, up-to-date dictionary. You will find these forms listed after the verb.

You can also avoid verb errors if you know the auxiliaries that indicate the tense:

> *shall* and *will* for the future tense
>
> *have* and *has* for the present perfect tense
>
> *had* for the past perfect tense
>
> *shall have* or *will have* for the future perfect tense

### EXERCISE 2

Underline the **verbs** in the following sentences that are in the *present perfect tense,* the *past perfect tense,* or the *future perfect tense.* Indicate the **tense** on the line to the right. Do not underline the simple tenses: present tense, past tense, future tense.

1. The committee has published its final report.     1. ..................

2. By next year, I shall have met the requirements for college.     2. ..................

3. What have they done with the new fixtures?     3. ..................

4. The bookkeeper will have corrected the error by the time he is ready to leave.     4. ..................

5. The river has risen several feet.     5. ..................

6. He has held that office for twenty years.     6. ..................

7. The enemy had already bombed many of the public buildings.     7. ..................

8. The clerks have not always obeyed the regulations.

8. ................

9. Arnold had completed his plans before we arrived.

9. ................

10. The auditor will have finished his third report by next week.

10. ................

11. By the time we arrived, the rain had stopped.

11. ................

12. We have received several letters from that firm.

12. ................

13. What books have you read recently?

13. ................

14. Pete has always wanted to be an engineer.

14. ................

15. He will have earned ten thousand dollars by January first.

15. ................

## THE VERB "TO BE"

Every person should be thoroughly familiar with the forms of the verb **to be.** It is the most irregular, and also the most important verb in the English language. The verb *to be* is used as an independent verb, and is also used as an auxiliary verb. The entire passive voice and all the progressive forms of other verbs are formed by using the verb *to be* as an auxiliary or helping verb. You should become familiar with the forms for the six tenses of this important verb.

On the following pages you will find reference tables for the tenses of three verbs; the verb *to be,* the regular verb *call,* and the irregular verb *ring.* Study these tables carefully before doing Exercise 3.

### REFERENCE TABLE

## SIX TENSES OF THE VERB "TO BE"

### PRESENT TENSE

| Singular | | Plural |
|---|---|---|
| First person: | I am | we are |
| Second person: | you are | you are |
| Third person: | he, she, it is | they are |

### PAST TENSE

| | | |
|---|---|---|
| First person: | I was | we were |
| Second person: | you were | you were |
| Third person: | he, she, it was | they were |

### FUTURE TENSE

| | | |
|---|---|---|
| First person: | I *shall* be | we *shall* be |
| Second person: | you *will* be | you *will* be |
| Third person: | he, she, it *will* be | they *will* be |

### PRESENT PERFECT TENSE

| | | |
|---|---|---|
| First person: | I *have* been | we *have* been |
| Second person: | you *have* been | you *have* been |
| Third person: | he, she, it *has* been | they *have* been |

### PAST PERFECT TENSE

| | | |
|---|---|---|
| First person: | I *had* been | we *had* been |
| Second person: | you *had* been | you *had* been |
| Third person: | he, she, it *had* been | they *had* been |

### FUTURE PERFECT TENSE

| | | |
|---|---|---|
| First person: | I *shall have* been | we *shall have* been |
| Second person: | you *will have* been | you *will have* been |
| Third person: | he, she, it *will have* been | they *will have* been |

## REFERENCE TABLE

## THE SIX TENSES OF A REGULAR VERB

## VERB "CALL"—ACTIVE VOICE

### PRESENT TENSE

| **Singular** | | **Plural** |
|---|---|---|
| *First person*: | I call | we call |
| *Second person*: | you call | you call |
| *Third person*: | he, she, it *calls* | they call |

### PAST TENSE

| | | |
|---|---|---|
| *First person*: | I call*ed* | we call*ed* |
| *Second person*: | you call*ed* | you call*ed* |
| *Third person*: | he, she, it call*ed* | they call*ed* |

### FUTURE TENSE

| | | |
|---|---|---|
| *First person*: | I *shall* call | we *shall* call |
| *Second person*: | you *will* call | you *will* call |
| *Third person*: | he, she, it *will* call | they *will* call |

### PRESENT PERFECT TENSE

| | | |
|---|---|---|
| *First person*: | I *have* called | we *have* called |
| *Second person*: | you *have* called | you *have* called |
| *Third person*: | he, she, it *has* called | they *have* called |

### PAST PERFECT TENSE

| | | |
|---|---|---|
| *First person*: | I *had* called | we *had* called |
| *Second person*: | you *had* called | you *had* called |
| *Third person*: | he, she, it *had* called | they *had* called |

### FUTURE PERFECT TENSE

| | | |
|---|---|---|
| *First person*: | I *shall have* called | we *shall have* called |
| *Second person*: | you *will have* called | you *will have* called |
| *Third person*: | he, she, it, *will have* called | they *will have* called |

## REFERENCE TABLE

## THE SIX TENSES OF AN IRREGULAR VERB

## VERB "RING"—ACTIVE VOICE

### PRESENT TENSE

| **Singular** | | **Plural** |
|---|---|---|
| *First person*: | I ring | we ring |
| *Second person*: | you ring | you ring |
| *Third person*: | he, she, it *rings* | they ring |

### PAST TENSE

| | | |
|---|---|---|
| *First person*: | I rang | we rang |
| *Second person*: | you rang | you rang |
| *Third person*: | he, she, it rang | they rang |

### FUTURE TENSE

| | | |
|---|---|---|
| *First person*: | I *shall* ring | we *shall* ring |
| *Second person*: | you *will* ring | you *will* ring |
| *Third person*: | he, she, it *will* ring | they *will* ring |

### PRESENT PERFECT TENSE

| | | |
|---|---|---|
| *First person*: | I have rung | we have rung |
| *Second person*: | you have rung | you have rung |
| *Third person*: | he, she, it has rung | they have rung |

### PAST PERFECT TENSE

| | | |
|---|---|---|
| *First person*: | I had rung | we had rung |
| *Second person*: | you had rung | you had rung |
| *Third person*: | he, she, it had rung | they had rung |

### FUTURE PERFECT TENSE

| | | |
|---|---|---|
| *First person*: | I shall have rung | we shall have rung |
| *Second person*: | you will have rung | you will have rung |
| *Third person*: | he, she, it will have rung | they will have rung |

## EXERCISE 3

On the lines to the right indicate the **tenses** of the following verbs: *present, past, future, present perfect, past perfect,* or *future perfect.*

| | | | |
|---|---|---|---|
| 1. has sung | 1. ............... | 26. had chosen | 26. ............... |
| 2. will have rung | 2. ............... | 27. shall be | 27. ............... |
| 3. had been | 3. ............... | 28. had gone | 28. ............... |
| 4. seemed | 4. ............... | 29. became | 29. ............... |
| 5. had swum | 5. ............... | 30. had eaten | 30. ............... |
| 6. knew | 6. ............... | 31. grows | 31. ............... |
| 7. shall have walked | 7. ............... | 32. thought | 32. ............... |
| 8. has sunk | 8. ............... | 33. sat | 33. ............... |
| 9. am | 9. ............... | 34. have proved | 34. ............... |
| 10. had drunk | 10. ............... | 35. laid | 35. ............... |
| 11. grew | 11. ............... | 36. dived | 36. ............... |
| 12. will have taken | 12. ............... | 37. has risen | 37. ............... |
| 13. saw | 13. ............... | 38. flows | 38. ............... |
| 14. have done | 14. ............... | 39. had lain | 39. ............... |
| 15. chose | 15. ............... | 40. rose | 40. ............... |
| 16. shall have driven | 16. ............... | 41. had hidden | 41. ............... |
| 17. will have led | 17. ............... | 42. shrank | 42. ............... |
| 18. has | 18. ............... | 43. swung | 43. ............... |
| 19. began | 19. ............... | 44. fits | 44. ............... |
| 20. have broken | 20. ............... | 45. lost | 45. ............... |
| 21. forgot | 21. ............... | 46. has wrung | 46. ............... |
| 22. looks | 22. ............... | 47. tore | 47. ............... |
| 23. shall have taught | 23. ............... | 48. shone | 48. ............... |
| 24. were | 24. ............... | 49. has sprung | 49. ............... |
| 25. will lay | 25. ............... | 50. freezes | 50. ............... |

## PROGRESSIVE FORMS OF VERBS

In addition to the forms which have already been given to show tense, a verb has special forms to show that the *action is continuing*. These forms are called the **progressive forms** of a verb. The *progressive forms* are used to show that an action is *continuing* or *progressing* at the time indicated by a particular tense.

I am studying English. (The action is continuing.)
<u>progressive form</u>

He is planning a trip to Mexico. (The action is continuing.)
<u>progressive form</u>

The progressive form of a verb is made up by using some form of the verb *to be* with the *ing* form of the principal verb. The form of a verb that ends in *ing* is called the **present participle.**

In the first sentence, the progressive form of the verb is *am studying*. It is made up of a form of the verb *to be,* which is *am,* and the present participle of the principal verb, which is *studying.* In the second sentence, the progressive form of the verb, *is planning,* is made up in a similar way.

The following are the progressive forms of the verb *call* for the six tenses (first person, singular).

I *am calling* you. (present progressive)

I *was calling* you. (past progressive.)

I *shall be calling* you. (future progressive)

I *have been calling* you. (present perfect progressive)

I *had been calling* you. (past perfect progressive)

I *shall have been calling* you. (future perfect progressive)

The present tense, progressive form often expresses a future idea. The verb *to go* is commonly used in this way:

I *am going* to New York next week. (in the future)

He *is going* to buy a new home in the suburbs. (in the future)

## REFERENCE TABLE

## VERB "CALL"

### PROGRESSIVE FORMS—ACTIVE VOICE

#### PRESENT TENSE

| **Singular** | | **Plural** |
|---|---|---|
| *First person*: | I *am* calling | we *are* calling |
| *Second person*: | you *are* calling | you *are* calling |
| *Third person*: | he, she, it *is* calling | they *are* calling |

#### PAST TENSE

| | | |
|---|---|---|
| *First person*: | I *was* calling | we *were* calling |
| *Second person*: | you *were* calling | you *were* calling |
| *Third person*: | he, she, it *was* calling | they *were* calling |

#### FUTURE TENSE

| | | |
|---|---|---|
| *First person*: | I *shall be* calling | we *shall be* calling |
| *Second person*: | you *will be* calling | you *will be* calling |
| *Third person*: | he, she, it *will be* calling | they *will be* calling |

#### PRESENT PERFECT TENSE

| | | |
|---|---|---|
| *First person*: | I *have been* calling | we *have been* calling |
| *Second person*: | you *have been* calling | you *have been* calling |
| *Third person*: | he, she, it *has been* calling | they *have been* calling |

#### PAST PERFECT TENSE

| | | |
|---|---|---|
| *First person*: | I *had been* calling | we *had been* calling |
| *Second person*: | you *had been* calling | you *had been* calling |
| *Third person*: | he, she, it *had been* calling | they *had been* calling |

#### FUTURE PERFECT TENSE

| | | |
|---|---|---|
| *First person*: | I *shall have been* calling | we *shall have been* calling |
| *Second person*: | you *will have been* calling | you *will have been* calling |
| *Third person*: | he, she, it *will have been* calling | they *will have been* calling |

## EMPHATIC FORMS OF THE VERB

The **emphatic forms** of a verb are often used to give greater emphasis to the idea expressed by the verb. The auxiliaries *do, does,* and *did* are used to give this additional emphasis. The emphatic forms are used in only two tenses, the *present tense* and the *past tense.*

I do agree with you. (present tense)
emphatic form

Jane did send the letter. (past tense)
emphatic form

The editor does need to know the facts. (present tense)
emphatic form

### EMPHATIC FORMS—*PRESENT TENSE*

| Singular | | Plural |
|---|---|---|
| *First person*: | I *do* call | we *do* call |
| *Second person*: | you *do* call | you *do* call |
| *Third person*: | he *does* call | they *do* call |

### EMPHATIC FORMS—*PAST TENSE*

| | | |
|---|---|---|
| *First person*: | I *did* call | we *did* call |
| *Second person*: | you *did* call | you *did* call |
| *Third person*: | he *did* call | they *did* call |

When *do, does,* and *did* are used in questions, the form is not used for emphasis. The use of *do, does,* and *did* in questions is an idiomatic way of asking questions in English. In the following questions *do, does,* and *did* are not the emphatic form of the verb:

Did he buy that hat last week?

Do you know her?

Does he want to pay the bill now?

## EXERCISE 4

Underline the **verbs** in the following sentences. On the line to the right, indicate the form of the verb by using **P.** for the *progressive form* or **E.** for the *emphatic form.* Classify those verbs that do not belong in either group as *regular form* by using **R.**

Example: John <u>has completed</u> the assignment.    **R.** (regular form)

1. The men are repairing the walk.      1. ................

2. You do make errors in addition.      2. ................

3. I am still attending the same series of lectures.      3. ................

4. Are you writing a book on atomic energy?      4. ................

5. The men did the work too hurriedly.      5. ................

6. I shall be traveling in Cuba all winter.      6. ................

7. We are making plans for an extended trip.      7. ................

8. Were you ill last week?      8. ................

9. I do know the answer to that question.      9. ................

10. The papers are giving him too much publicity.      10. ................

11. Have you seen my golf clubs anywhere?      11. ................

12. She did mail that letter to you.      12. ................

13. The carpenters have been building an addition to the stadium.      13. ................

14. The plumber has stopped the leak in the pipe.      14. ................

15. The picture has been hanging in the Art Institute.      15. ................

## THE USE OF SHALL AND WILL

Many of the precise distinctions concerning the use of *shall* and *will* are rapidly passing out of informal speaking and writing. Careful writers, however, still observe some of these distinctions. The following are some of the distinctions that are most generally observed:

### Simple Futurity

Use *shall* in the first person and *will* in the second and third persons to express **simple futurity**. Simple futurity means anticipation or expectation of what is likely to happen, or what one is likely to do. It follows the regular forms for the future tense:

| | | |
|---|---|---|
| *First person*: | I *shall* go | we *shall* go |
| *Second person*: | you *will* go | you *will* go |
| *Third person*: | he *will* go | they *will* go |

### Determination, Threat, Promise

If you want to express determination, compulsion, threat, or promise (willingness to do something), reverse the order of *shall* and *will*. Use *will* in the first person, and *shall* in the second and third persons.

| | | |
|---|---|---|
| *First person*: | I *will* go | we *will* go |
| *Second person*: | you *shall* go | you *shall* go |
| *Third person*: | he *shall* go | they *shall* go |

### Special Cases

When *shall* and *will* are followed by such expressions as *be glad, be sorry, be happy, be delighted, be pleased,* etc., use *shall* in the first person, and *will* in the second and third persons. If *will* is used in the first person, it would mean that you are determined *to be glad, sorry, delighted,* etc. If *shall* is used in the second and third persons, it would mean that you are compelling someone *to be glad, sorry,* etc. The following are the accepted ways of using such expressions:

I shall be glad to see you. (not *will*)
<small>first person</small>

We shall be delighted to help you. (not *will*)
<small>first person</small>

You will be sorry to learn of his misfortune. (not *shall*)
<small>second person</small>

He will be pleased to see you at four. (not *shall*)
<small>third person</small>

In giving courteous commands, you should use *will* in the second and third persons instead of *shall.* This is the form that is generally followed in giving military orders and instructions:

Corporal Smith *will report* to Captain Allen. (not *shall report*)

You *will hand* in your report on Wednesday. (not *shall*)

The meeting *will come* to order. (not *shall*)

Mr. Ames, you *will meet* with the committee today. (not *shall*)

## SHOULD AND WOULD

*Should* is the past tense of *shall* and in general, follows the same rules that apply to the use of *shall. Would* is the past tense of *will* and follows the same rules that apply to the use of *will.*

Both *should* and *would* have special uses. *Would* is used in all three persons to express *habitual* or *customary* action. *Should* is often used in all three persons to express *obligation. Ought* and *should* both express obligation and are used interchangeably.

Every evening we *would play* cards for hours. (*habitual action*)

You *should read* something worth while every day. (*obligation*)

You *ought to read* something worth while every day. (*obligation*)

Study the following sentences carefully. Note especially the explanations given in parentheses. This will help you understand the distinctions which have been made in the preceding discussion:

I shall go to the theater this evening. (*simple futurity—expectation*)
first person

I will not see him today. (*determination* on the part of the speaker)
first person

You will enjoy meeting him. (*simple futurity* or *expectation*)
second person

He will enter Harvard in September. (*simple futurity*)
third person

I will accompany you to the clinic. (*promise—willingness*)
first person

He shall report to the judge every month. (*I am determined* that
third person
he shall.)

You shall have any assistance that you may need. (*I am determined*
second person
that you shall.)

We shall be pleased to grant you an interview. (*simple futurity*)
first person

You would drown if you ventured out in deep water. (*simple*
second person
*futurity*)

He would drown if he ventured out in deep water. (*simple*
third person
*futurity*)

We should be very happy if you would call for us. (*simple futurity*)
first person                              second person

I should be the first one to volunteer. (*obligation*)
first person

You should read good books. (*obligation*)
second person

They should offer their services to the committee. (*obligation*)
third person

## EXERCISE 5

Fill in the blank spaces with the auxiliary *shall or will*. On the line to the right, indicate whether the auxiliary is used to express *simple futurity, determination, threat, promise,* or a *courteous command.*

1. I............leave for New York tomorrow.      1. ..................

2. He............represent us at the convention.      2. ..................

3. You............receive the order within a week.      3. ..................

4. I............employ him in spite of all opposition.      4. ..................

5. Harvey............not go back to college this fall.      5. ..................

6. We............be happy to grant you an interview.      6. ..................

7. Sergeant Jones, you............report to the colonel at twelve o'clock.      7. ..................

8. They............pay the damages. The accident was their fault.      8. ..................

9. You............be glad to learn that you have won a prize.      9. ..................

10. Mr. Hanson............have charge of this department.      10. ..................

11. We............demand prompt payment in the future.      11. ..................

12. I............do everything in my power to help you.      12. ..................

13. She............pay dearly for those remarks.      13. ..................

14. The meeting............please come to order.      14. ..................

15. We positively............not lower our prices.      15. ..................

## MIXED TENSES

Unless there is a good reason for making a change, the tenses of the verbs in a sentence or in a paragraph should agree. If you start out with a verb in the *past tense*, you should not change to another verb in the *present tense*. If you start with a verb in the *present tense*, you should not change to the *past tense*.

*Tense* means *time*, and when you change the tense, you also change the time. Tenses must be consistent; that is, there must be a logical sequence of time. It is illogical to shift from one tense to another tense. Study the following illustrations carefully:

Dr. Smith *examined* the patient and *calls* the nurse. (*incorrect*)

In this sentence, the verb *examined* is in the past tense. It is followed by the verb *calls* which is in the present tense. There is a shift from the past tense to the present tense. Both verbs should be in the past tense or both verbs should be in the present tense.

Dr. Smith examines the patient and calls the nurse. (*correct*)
present           present

*or*

Dr. Smith examined the patient and called the nurse. (*correct*)
past           past


I went into the hall and there I see a strange man. (*incorrect*)
past           present

I went into the hall and there I saw a strange man. (*correct*)
past           past


The officer stopped the car and speaks to the driver. (*incorrect*)
past           present

The officer stopped the car and spoke to the driver. (*correct*)
past           past

## THE "OF" ERROR

Careless speakers and writers often use the preposition *of* in place of the auxiliary verb *have*. The word *of* is a preposition and should never be used as part of a verb phrase.

The *"of"* error is generally caused by the use of contractions or by careless enunciation on the part of a speaker. The mistake is commonly made after the words *could, might, ought to, should,* and *would.* When *have* is used following any of these words, and the two words are contracted, the resulting combination sounds as if *of* were being used rather than *have: could've* sounds like *could of, should've* sounds like *should of,* etc.

Since in speech the contracted form of *have* cannot readily be distinguished from *of,* many persons have the mistaken belief that *of* is the word being said and that it is the correct word to use. As a result they carry over the mistake from their speech into their writing, and never know they are in error. To avoid making the *"of"* error when you are speaking, never contract *have* to *'ve.*

Study the following examples. The preposition *of* should never be used in place of *have* as part of a verb phrase.

We should *of* been more careful. (*incorrect*)

We should *have* been more careful. (*correct*)


He must *of* taken it. (*incorrect*)

He must *have* taken it. (*correct*)


They might *of* notified us. (*incorrect*)

They might *have* notified us. (*correct*)


I should *of* prepared the report. (*incorrect*)

I should *have* prepared the report. (*correct*)

## SUMMARY OF GRAMMAR UNIT FOURTEEN

In grammar, *tense* means *time.* The tense of a verb indicates the time of the action or the time of the state of condition (linking verb).

There are six tenses in English: *present* tense, *past* tense, *future* tense, *present perfect* tense, *past perfect* tense, and *future perfect* tense.

The *present tense* indicates present time: I *know* him.

The *past tense* indicates past time: John *was* ill yesterday.

The *future tense* indicates future time: I *shall see* you tomorrow.

The *present perfect tense* indicates an action that is completed at the time of speaking or writing:

I *have called* him twice today.

The *past perfect tense* indicates an action that was completed before some definite time in the past:

At the meeting, I recognized a delegate whom I *had met* in Boston.

The *future perfect tense* indicates an action that will be completed at some definite time in the future. The future perfect tense expresses the relation between two future times:

You will understand the subject of tense when you *will have finished* this unit.

The *progressive form* of the verb is the form that is used to indicate that the action is continuing at the time indicated by the tense:

We *have been planning* to go to Europe.

The *emphatic form* of the verb is used to give added emphasis to a statement:

I *did write* that letter.

## SELF-GRADING ASSIGNMENT 1

Directions: Underline the **verb** or **verb phrase** in each of the following sentences. Indicate the *tense* of the verb on the line to the right.

Example: You <u>have broken</u> the entire set.                *present perfect.*
......................

1. The pen lies on your desk in the library.            1. ...................

2. My uncle has lived in that house for fifty years.    2. ...................

3. The speaker became very nervous.                     3. ...................

4. I shall remain in England for several years.         4. ...................

5. Will the solution of the problem be difficult?       5. ...................

6. By tomorrow, I shall have lived here six years.      6. ...................

7. Who dived for shells yesterday?                      7. ...................

8. The water flowed through a hole in the dike.         8. ...................

9. She has taken part in the contest every year.        9. ...................

10. I had already examined the papers.                 10. ...................

11. He gets an adequate income from his
    investments.                                        11. ...................

12. The officers went to a convention yesterday.       12. ...................

13. I shall not leave until ten o'clock.               13. ...................

14. What policy had he followed during that period?    14. ...................

15. Have you spoken to the manager about a
    promotion?                                          15. ...................

*Caution: Check your answers to each assignment with the answer key at the back of the booklet before proceeding with the next assignment.*

## SELF-GRADING ASSIGNMENT 2

Directions: Fill in the blank in the following sentences with the *form of the verb* called for in the parentheses that follow each sentence.

Example: Alice............a novel. (present perfect of *write*)

Alice *has written* a novel.

1.  A pipe in the cellar............yesterday. (past tense of *burst*)

2.  We............many miles before the sun sets. (future perfect of *ride*)

3.  The men............a new cement walk in front of the library. (past tense of *lay*)

4.  He............across the channel four times. (present perfect of *swim*)

5.  We............a large sum of money for the hospital. (past tense of *raise*)

6.  He............to the library every day. (present tense of *go*)

7.  They............down the old tower. (present perfect of *tear*)

8.  The speaker............to the occasion. (past tense of *rise*)

9.  They............to clear the hall before I came in. (past perfect of *begin*)

10. I............to do my best work for you. (present perfect of *strive*)

11. ............you one of the ushers? (past tense of the verb *to be*)

12. The artist............an interesting cartoon. (present perfect of *draw*)

13. She............the money in a book. (past tense of *hide*)

14. The wind............hard all day. (past tense of *blow*)

15. He............two competent assistants. (present tense of *have*)

## SELF-GRADING ASSIGNMENT 3

Directions: Cross out the **verbs** that are used incorrectly. Write the correct form above the incorrect form. Two sentences are correct.

> *shall*
> Example: I ~~will~~ need a heavier coat.

1. You might of spoken sooner.

2. They shall miss the train if they don't hurry.

3. You should of seen the way the team played yesterday.

4. We will probably leave on the six o'clock train.

5. The old man walked down the road, stops suddenly, and then turns back.

6. I will be glad to wait for you at the club.

7. They will pay the rent or move at once.

8. Mother shall expect you at six o'clock.

9. I will certainly sue him for the damage to my car.

10. He will sail for France on Monday.

11. I will be pleased to grant your request.

12. Sergeant Lee, you shall report to headquarters tomorrow.

13. I shall do everything in my power to help you.

14. He must of written that letter last week.

15. My aunt spent the holidays with us and enjoys the festivities.

## PROGRESS TEST FOURTEEN

This progress test should not be taken until a day or two after you have completed the assignments. The score you make on the test will then more clearly reflect your understanding of the material in the unit.

### A.

Directions: Cross out the incorrect forms of the **verbs.** Write the correct form above the incorrect form. On the line to the right, indicate the *tense* that is required in the sentence.    *(24 points)*

Example: She has ~~proven~~ the problem.    *present perfect*

*proved*

1. There was twenty people at the meeting.    1. ................

2. The campers have went to the woods.    2. ................

3. Yesterday I done the entire assignment.    3. ................

4. The waitress give me an extra cup of coffee.    4. ................

5. I have broke my new watch.    5. ................

6. All the guests begun to cheer when the ambassador entered.    6. ................

7. The birds have flowed to the South.    7. ................

8. We wasn't ready when the alarm rung.    8. ................

9. The audience drownded the speaker's voice.    9. ................

10. The sun shined every day last week.    10. ................

11. What credentials has he brung with him?    11. ................

12. Each one drunk his favorite beverage.    12. ................

**B.**

Directions: Change the tenses of the verbs whenever necessary to make them *consistent*. Cross out the incorrect form and write the correct form above it. You must decide, first of all, whether the verbs should be in the *present tense* or in the *past tense*. (*25 points*)

One of the most unusual thrills I ever experienced is the one I receive when my fishing rod is almost jerked out of my hands. We are two miles off Strawberry Island on a rough lake. My friend was laboriously rowing toward our camp on the mainland. We are tired and hungry, and it is long past supper time. It is necessary to alternate at the oars because the waves make it difficult to row.

One of us maneuvers the boat, while the other trolled. It is my turn to troll, but my thoughts are on reaching camp, and not on catching fish. My attention was devoted to dodging the spray, when the "strike" comes. There is a jolt and a heavy, jerky pull. The battle is on. My hands are full. Camp, clothes, and supper are forgotten.

Nervously I pull the fish in as fast as I can manipulate the reel. It is hard work, for I had over a hundred yards of line to take in. I have to keep reeling the fish in, for the slightest pause offers him a chance to escape.

My arms ache as the gray-spotted fish hove into view. Lifting the slippery battler into the boat, I end its struggles with a knife. He weighs only five pounds, but he feels like a muskellunge.

## ANSWER KEY

for

## EXERCISES, ASSIGNMENTS, AND PROGRESS TEST

### Grammar Unit Fourteen

---

### CORRECT ANSWERS TO EXERCISE 1

Verbs are printed in **heavy type.**

Tense

1. Jerry **met** our guests at the station.     1. *past*

2. **Will** you **help** me translate this letter?     2. *future*

3. The conference **begins** at eight o'clock.     3. *present*

4. Our engineeers **will install** the new machinery.     4. *future*

5. **Are** you a member of the Camera Club?     5. *present*

6. The milk **became** sour over night.     6. *past*

7. The detective **examined** the room carefully.     7. *past*

8. If he **comes,** I **shall give** him your letter.     8. **comes**—*present*
    **shall give**—*future*

9. **Were** you in the parade yesterday?     9. *past*

10. Who **will start** the discussion?     10. *future*

11. I **listen** to the same commentator every evening.     11. *present*

12. What **are** you **doing?**     12. *present*

13. He **believes** that the manager **will resign.**     13. **believes**—*present*
    **will resign**—*future*

14. The cake **seems** fresh.     14. *present*

15. We **shall send** the goods promptly.     15. *future*

## CORRECT ANSWERS TO EXERCISE 2

Verbs are printed in **heavy type.**

**Tense**

1. The committee **has published** its final report.
   1. *present perfect*

2. By next year, I **shall have met** the requirements for college.
   2. *future perfect*

3. What **have** they **done** with the new fixtures?
   3. *present perfect*

4. The bookkeeper **will have corrected** the error by the time he is ready to leave.
   4. *future perfect*

5. The river **has risen** several feet.
   5. *present perfect*

6. He **has held** that office for twenty years.
   6. *present perfect*

7. The enemy **had** already **bombed** many of the public buildings.
   7. *past perfect*

8. The clerks **have** not always **obeyed** the regulations.
   8. *present perfect*

9. Arnold **had completed** his plans before we arrived.
   9. *past perfect*

10. The auditor **will have finished** his third report by next week.
    10. *future perfect*

11. By the time we arrived, the rain **had stopped.**
    11. *past perfect*

12. We **have received** several letters from that firm.
    12. *present perfect*

13. What books **have** you **read** recently?
    13. *present perfect*

14. Pete **has** always **wanted** to be an engineer.
    14. *present perfect*

15. He **will have earned** ten thousand dollars by January first.
    15. *future perfect*

## CORRECT ANSWERS TO EXERCISE 3

1. present perfect
2. future perfect
3. past perfect
4. past
5. past perfect
6. past
7. future perfect
8. present perfect
9. present
10. past perfect
11. past
12. future perfect
13. past
14. present perfect
15. past
16. future perfect
17. future perfect
18. present
19. past
20. present perfect
21. past
22. present
23. future perfect
24. past
25. future

26. past perfect
27. future
28. past perfect
29. past
30. past perfect
31. present
32. past
33. past
34. present perfect
35. past
36. past
37. present perfect
38. present
39. past perfect
40. past
41. past perfect
42. past
43. past
44. present
45. past
46. present perfect
47. past
48. past
49. present perfect
50. present

## CORRECT ANSWERS TO EXERCISE 4

Verbs are printed in **heavy type.**

| | Form |
|---|---|
| 1. The men **are repairing** the walk. | 1. *progressive* |
| 2. You **do make** errors in addition. | 2. *emphatic* |
| 3. I **am** still **attending** the same series of lectures. | 3. *progressive* |
| 4. **Are** you **writing** a book on atomic energy? | 4. *progressive* |

5. The men *did* the work too hurriedly.     5. *regular*

6. I *shall be traveling* in Cuba all winter.     6. *progressive*

7. We *are making* plans for an extended trip.     7. *progressive*

8. *Were* you ill last week?     8. *regular*

9. I *do know* the answer to that question.     9. *emphatic*

10. The papers *are giving* him too much publicity.     10. *progressive*

11. *Have* you *seen* my golf clubs anywhere?     11. *regular*

12. She *did mail* that letter to you.     12. *emphatic*

13. The carpenters *have been building* an addition to the stadium.     13. *progressive*

14. The plumber *has stopped* the leak in the pipe.     14. *regular*

15. The picture *has been hanging* in the Art Institute.     15. *progressive*

## CORRECT ANSWERS TO EXERCISE 5

Correct forms are printed in **heavy type.**

**Expresses**

1. I **shall leave** for New York tomorrow.     1. *simple futurity*

2. He **will represent** us at the convention.     2. *simple futurity*

3. You **will receive** the order within a week.     3. *simple futurity.*

4. I **will employ** him in spite of all opposition.     4. *determination*

5. Harvey **will** not **go** back to college this fall.     5. *expectation or simple futurity*

6. We **shall be** happy to grant you an interview.     6. *simple futurity*

7. Sergeant Jones, you **will report** to the colonel at twelve o'clock.     7. *courteous command*

8. They **shall pay** the damages. The accident was their fault.     8. *determination*

9. You **will be** glad to learn that you have won a prize.     9. *simple futurity*

10. Mr. Hanson **will have** charge of this department.     10. *simple futurity*

11. We **will demand** prompt payment in the future.

    11. *determination*

12. I **will do** everything in my power to help you.

    12. *promise—willingness*

13. She **shall pay** dearly for those remarks.

    13. *determination*

14. The meeting **will** please **come** to order.

    14. *courteous command*

15. We positively **will** not **lower** our prices.

    15. *determination*

## CORRECT ANSWERS TO ASSIGNMENT 1

1. lies—*present tense*
2. has lived—*present perfect*
3. became—*past tense*
4. shall remain—*future tense*
5. Will be—*future tense*
6. shall have lived—*future perfect*
7. dived—*past tense*
8. flowed—*past tense*
9. has taken—*present perfect*
10. had examined—*past perfect*
11. gets—*present tense*
12. went—*past tense*
13. shall leave—*future tense*
14. had followed—*past perfect*
15. Have spoken—*present perfect*

## CORRECT ANSWERS TO ASSIGNMENT 2

1. burst
2. shall have ridden
3. laid
4. has swum
5. raised
6. goes
7. have torn
8. rose
9. had begun
10. have striven
11. Were
12. has drawn
13. hid
14. blew
15. has

## CORRECT ANSWERS TO ASSIGNMENT 3

Correct verb is printed in **heavy type.**

1. You might **have** spoken sooner.

2. They **will** miss the train if they don't hurry.

3. You should **have** seen the way the team played yesterday.

4. We **shall** probably leave on the six o'clock train.

5. The old man walked down the road, **stopped** suddenly, and then **turned** back.

6. I **shall** be glad to wait for you at the club.

7. They **shall** pay the rent or move at once.

8. Mother **will** expect you at six o'clock.

9. I will certainly sue him for the damage to my car. *(correct)*

10. He will sail for France on Monday. *(correct)*

11. I **shall** be pleased to grant your request.

12. Sergeant Lee, you **will** report to headquarters tomorrow.

13. I **will** do everything in my power to help you.

14. He must **have** written that letter last week.

15. My aunt spent the holidays with us and **enjoyed** the festivities.

## CORRECT ANSWERS TO PROGRESS TEST FOURTEEN

### A.—(24 *points*)

|  | Tense |
|---|---|
| 1. There **were** twenty people at the meeting. | 1. *past tense* |
| 2. The campers **have gone** to the woods. | 2. *present perfect* |
| 3. Yesterday I **did** the entire assignment. | 3. *past tense* |
| 4. The waitress **gave** me an extra cup of coffee. | 4. *past tense* |
| 5. I **have broken** my new watch. | 5. *present perfect* |
| 6. All the guests **began** to cheer when the ambassador entered. | 6. *past tense* |
| 7. The birds **have flown** to the South. | 7. *present perfect* |

8. We **weren't** ready when the alarm **rang**.

8. **weren't**—*past tense*
**rang**—*past tense*

9. The audience **drowned** the speaker's voice.

9. *past tense*

10. The sun **shone** every day last week.

10. *past tense*

11. What credentials **has** he **brought** with him?

11. *present perfect*

12. Each one **drank** his favorite beverage.

12. *past tense*

## B.—(25 points)

*This article should be written in the past tense.* The verbs that have been corrected are printed in **heavy type.**

One of the most unusual thrills I ever experienced **was** the one I **received** when my fishing rod **was** almost jerked out of my hands. We **were** two miles off Strawberry Island on a rough lake. My friend was laboriously rowing toward our camp on the mainland. We **were** tired and hungry, and it **was** long past supper time. It **was** necessary to alternate at the oars because the waves **made** it difficult to row.

One of us **maneuvered** the boat, while the other trolled. It **was** my turn to troll, but my thoughts **were** on reaching camp, and not on catching fish. My attention was devoted to dodging the spray when the "strike" **came**. There **was** a jolt and a heavy, jerky pull. The battle **was** on. My hands **were** full. Camp, clothes, and supper **were** forgotten.

Nervously I **pulled** the fish in as fast as I **could** manipulate the reel. It **was** hard work, for I had over a hundred yards of line to take in. I **had** to keep reeling the fish in, for the slightest pause **offered** him a chance to escape.

My arms **ached** as the gray-spotted fish hove into view. Lifting the slippery battler into the boat, I **ended** its struggles with a knife. He **weighed** only five pounds, but he **felt** like a muskellunge.

## HOW TO OBTAIN YOUR SCORE

*The test totals 49 points. To obtain your score, divide the number of your correct answers by 49. The answer will be your score on this test. For example, if you have 44 points correct, your score is 44 divided by 49 or 90 per cent. In other words, your score on this test is 90. You can obtain your score on any of the excercises or assignments by following the same procedure.*

**Practical English Grammar**

## OUTLINE OF UNIT FIFTEEN

# VERBS: VOICE AND MOOD

Page

1. ACTIVE AND PASSIVE VOICE..................................... 5

2. HOW THE PASSIVE VOICE IS FORMED........................... 8

3. SIX TENSES OF THE VERB "CALL"—PASSIVE VOICE........ 9

4. SIX TENSES OF THE VERB "KNOW"—PASSIVE VOICE.... 11

5. WHEN TO USE THE PASSIVE VOICE............................... 14

6. MOOD OF VERBS ................................................... 17

7. SUBJUNCTIVE FORMS OF VERB "TO BE"...................... 18

8. USES OF THE SUBJUNCTIVE MOOD............................... 20

9. SUMMARY OF GRAMMAR UNIT FIFTEEN...................... 22

Self-Grading Assignments ............................................. 23

Progress Test Fifteen .................................................... 26

Key to Correct Answers................................................. 28

# VERBS: VOICE AND MOOD

IN UNIT FOURTEEN you learned that verbs have six tenses. You also learned that you must be familiar with the various changes that occur in the form of the verb to express variations in time. In this unit you will learn about certain changes that occur in the form of the verb which make it possible to tell whether the subject is acting or is acted upon.

## ACTIVE AND PASSIVE VOICE

A verb not only undergoes certain changes to show *tense,* or the time of the action, but it changes in form to show *voice.* **Voice** is a grammatical term which is used to *tell whether the subject of the sentence is acting or is receiving the action expressed by the verb.*

When the subject is acting, we say that the subject is the *doer.* When the subject is receiving the action, we say that the subject is the *receiver.* If you keep these two terms, *doer* and *receiver,* in mind, you will have no difficulty in understanding what *voice* means in grammar.

Study the following sentences carefully. Note the changes that occur in the form of the verb. Note the change that occurs in the subject of the sentence:

Ned washed the car. (*Ned* is the *doer* of the action.)

The car was washed by Ned. (*Car* is the *receiver* of the action.)

In the first sentence, the subject is *Ned.* He is the *doer,* the one who is performing the action expressed by the verb *washed.* The *car* is receiving the action. In grammar we say that the verb in this sentence is in the **active voice** because the subject is the *doer,* or is doing the washing. The car is the *receiver* of the action.

The second sentence is written in the reverse order. The subject is now the receiver of the action instead of the doer. In order to express this idea, it was necessary to use another verb form, *was washed*. What happened to *Ned*, the doer? *Ned* is still in the sentence but is now in a phrase introduced by the preposition *by*.

The verb *was washed* is in the **passive voice** because it represents the subject of the sentence as the receiver of the action. In other words, the subject is not acting, but is *passive*. The doer, or the actor, appears in a phrase introduced by the preposition *by*.

A verb in the passive voice is *never* a simple verb. It is always a verb phrase. In the sentence, *Our car was stolen yesterday*, the verb *was stolen* is in the *passive voice*. The subject is the receiver of the action. Since the doer is unknown, the "*by* phrase" is omitted. But we know that it was stolen by someone. If we discover who stole the car, the doer might be added to the sentence:

Our car was stolen yesterday by two <u>strangers.</u>
　　　<u>receiver</u>　　　　　　　　　　　　doer

If a verb is in the **active voice,** *the subject is the doer of the action.* If a verb is in the **passive voice,** *the subject is the receiver of the action.* When a verb is in the passive voice, the doer is often omitted. Sometimes the doer is unknown, and sometimes the doer is so evident that it is not necessary to include the "*by* phrase."

### EXERCISE 1

Underline the **doer** and the **receiver** in the following sentences. Write **D.** under the word that names the *doer* and **R.** under the word that names the *receiver*. On the line to the right, indicate whether the verb is in the *active voice* or in the *passive voice*.

*Active voice*—subject is the *doer* of the action.

*Passive voice*—subject is the *receiver* of the action.

Example: <u>He</u> was hired by the <u>director.</u>　　　　*passive*
　　　　　R.　　　　　　　　　　D.　　　　　　　.................

1. The hunter killed the deer.　　　　　　1. .................

2. The deer was killed by the hunter.　　　2. .................

3.  John struck James.                               3. ...................

4.  James was struck by John.                        4. ...................

5.  The car was repaired by the mechanic.            5. ...................

6.  We finished the test yesterday.                  6. ...................

7.  John was sent to New York by the manager.        7. ...................

8.  Her beautiful mink coat was stolen by the maid.  8. ...................

9.  We found an apartment in a good neighborhood.    9. ...................

10. Coffee is raised in Brazil by the planters.      10. ...................

11. The officers searched the ship.                  11. ...................

12. The broken bone was set by the doctor.           12. ...................

13. The doctor set the broken bone.                  13. ...................

14. The snow covered the trees and the bushes.       14. ...................

15. The lawn was mowed by John and his father.       15. ...................

Note: *The correct answers to exercises will be found at the back of this booklet. Correct your mistakes and, if necessary, re-read the text material before going on to the next section.*

## HOW THE PASSIVE VOICE IS FORMED

You cannot express an idea in the passive voice without using an auxiliary or helping verb. The verb *to be* is the auxiliary verb that is used to help form the six tenses of the passive voice. If you are familiar with the conjugation of the verb *to be,* you will have no difficulty in forming the passive voice of any verb that takes an object.

The passive voice is formed by combining the verb *to be* with the **past participle** of the principal verb. The principal verb is the verb that names the action.

The verb *was washed* in the sentence, *The car was washed by Ned,* is made up of the auxiliary verb *was,* which is a form of the verb *to be.* The *past participle* of the principal verb is added to the auxiliary *was.* The past participle of the verb *wash* is *washed.* The verb phrase is *was washed.* It is a verb phrase in the passive voice.

The verb phrases in the following sentences are in the passive voice. They are formed by combining some form of the verb *to be* with the past participle of the principal verb, or the verb that names the action.

The plans <u>will be made</u> by the general.
<small>passive voice</small>

Trees <u>have been planted</u> in the park by the commissioners.
<small>passive voice</small>

The verb in the first sentence is *will be made.* It is made up of the auxiliary *will be,* which is a form of the verb *to be,* and the past participle of the verb *make,* which is *made* (*will be made*).

The verb in the second sentence is *have been planted.* It is made up of the auxiliary verb *have been,* which is a form of the verb *to be* and the past participle of the verb *plant* (*planted*).

The six tenses of the verb *call* given in Unit Fourteen are the forms for the *active voice.* The forms for the *passive voice* follow. If you examine these forms carefully, you will see that the tenses follow the regular conjugation of the verb *to be.* The past participle of the verb *call* (*called*) is added to the forms of the verb *to be.*

**Reference Table**

## SIX TENSES OF THE VERB "CALL"

### PASSIVE VOICE

#### Present Tense

|  | Singular | Plural |
|---|---|---|
| *First person:* | I *am* called | we *are* called |
| *Second person:* | you *are* called | you *are* called |
| *Third person:* | he *is* called | they *are* called |

#### Past Tense

| | | |
|---|---|---|
| *First person:* | I *was* called | we *were* called |
| *Second person:* | you *were* called | you *were* called |
| *Third person:* | he *was* called | they *were* called |

#### Future Tense

| | | |
|---|---|---|
| *First person:* | I *shall be* called | we *shall be* called |
| *Second person:* | you *will be* called | you *will be* called |
| *Third person:* | he *will be* called | they *will be* called |

#### Present Perfect Tense

| | | |
|---|---|---|
| *First person:* | I *have been* called | we *have been* called |
| *Second person:* | you *have been* called | you *have been* called |
| *Third person:* | he *has been* called | they *have been* called |

#### Past Perfect Tense

| | | |
|---|---|---|
| *First person:* | I *had been* called | we *had been* called |
| *Second person:* | you *had been* called | you *had been* called |
| *Third person:* | he *had been* called | they *had been* called |

#### Future Perfect Tense

| | | |
|---|---|---|
| *First person:* | I *shall have been* called | we *shall have been* called |
| *Second person:* | you *will have been* called | you *will have been* called |
| *Third person:* | he *will have been* called | they *will have been* called |

## EXERCISE 2

Rewrite the following sentences, changing the form of the verb from the *active voice* to the *passive voice*. Make any other changes that are necessary. Underline the **verb** in the *passive voice*.

Example: The librarian read the book. (*active voice*)

The book <u>was read</u> by the librarian. (*passive voice*)

1. Fred wrote an article about our trip.

2. We appreciate your courtesy.

3. The judge pronounced the sentence.

4. John will accept the position.

5. The stenographer has written the letter.

6. We adopted his recommendations.

7. The physician will set the broken arm.

8. I have placed the package on the table.

9. The committee has sent out the invitations.

10. Marian designs dresses for actresses.

11. The manager recently employed ten men.

12. The pilot inspected the plane.

13. The explorers have obtained the necessary supplies.

14. The women served the refreshments.

15. The engineers have just built a new bridge.

## Reference Table

## SIX TENSES OF THE IRREGULAR VERB "KNOW"

## PASSIVE VOICE

### Present Tense

|  | Singular | Plural |
|---|---|---|
| *First person*: | I *am* known | we *are* known |
| *Second person*: | you *are* known | you *are* known |
| *Third person*: | he *is* known | they *are* known |

### Past Tense

| *First person*: | I *was* known | we *were* known |
|---|---|---|
| *Second person*: | you *were* known | you *were* known |
| *Third person*: | he *was* known | they *were* known |

### Future Tense

| *First person*: | I *shall be* known | we *shall be* known |
|---|---|---|
| *Second person*: | you *will be* known | you *will be* known |
| *Third person*: | he *will be* known | they *will be* known |

### Present Perfect Tense

| *First person*: | I *have been* known | we *have been* known |
|---|---|---|
| *Second person*: | you *have been* known | you *have been* known |
| *Third person*: | he *has been* known | they *have been* known |

### Past Perfect Tense

| *First person*: | I *had been* known | we *had been* known |
|---|---|---|
| *Second person*: | you *had been* known | you *had been* known |
| *Third person*: | he *had been* known | they *had been* known |

### Future Perfect Tense

| *First person*: | I *shall have been* known | we *shall have been* known |
|---|---|---|
| *Second person*: | you *will have been* known | you *will have been* known |
| *Third person*: | he *will have been* known | they *will have been* known |

## EXERCISE 3

Rewrite the following sentences changing the form of the verb from the *passive voice* to the *active voice*. Make any other changes that are necessary. Underline the **verb** in the *active voice*.

Example: The book was written by a chemist. (*passive voice*)

A chemist <u>wrote</u> the book. (*active voice*)

1.  A meeting was planned by the diplomats.

2.  The boy has been given emergency treatment by the doctor.

3.  I am called every morning at six o'clock by my sister.

4.  Many objections to the plan have been raised by the men.

5.  The books will be audited by the examiners.

6.  Oil was discovered on the land by a scientist.

7.  The coach was consulted by the players.

8.  A meeting has been arranged by the manager.

9.  The soldier was protected by a metal helmet.

10. An important part in the play was given to Mary by the producer.

11. The farm will be sold by the owner.

12. Results of the election will be broadcast by WGN.

13. A number of books were ordered by the librarian.

14. That beautiful rug was woven by the Indians.

15. The records were copied by the clerks.

## EXERCISE 4

Underline the **verbs** in the following sentences. On the line to the right, indicate whether the verb is in the *active* voice or the *passive* voice.

Example: Her suit <u>was designed</u> by Dior.      *passive voice*
.....................

1. Mr. Jones bought his camera in New York.     1. ...................

2. The story was written by the news editor.     2. ...................

3. Men of different races delivered speeches.     3. ...................

4. He blazed a new trail for the air mail.     4. ...................

5. Many interesting stories were related by the travelers.     5. ...................

6. The actors will be entertained by the Drama League.     6. ...................

7. The date of the meeting was set by the president.     7. ...................

8. I have not seen him at the bank lately.     8. ...................

9. The radio script was written by Norman.     9. ...................

10. Reunions have been planned by the alumni.     10. ...................

11. The packages were handled with care by the driver.     11. ...................

12. The letters were examined by the postal authorities.     12. ...................

13. The agent authorized the use of the building.     13. ...................

14. Crowds cheered the soldiers.     14. ...................

15. A cover had been placed on the table.     15. ...................

## WHEN TO USE THE PASSIVE VOICE

Since you may show that the subject is either the doer or the receiver of the action, the question naturally arises, "Which form is better?" If you read the sentences in Exercise 3 carefully, you will readily see that the use of the passive voice often results in a roundabout, awkward method of expression.

In the large majority of cases the *active voice is the better form to use.* Never use the passive voice, either in speaking or writing, when the active voice would be more natural or more direct. The following illustrations show clearly that the active voice would be more natural and more direct than the passive voice.

The concert was enjoyed by us. (*passive voice*)

We enjoyed the concert. (*active voice*)

Your order was sent by us by express today. (*passive voice*)

We sent your order by express today. (*active voice*)

The stranger was barked at by a dog. (*passive voice*)

A dog barked at the stranger. (*active voice*)

As a rule, the active voice is preferred for business writing, and for any other form of writing that requires the direct approach. The use of the *active voice increases vividness.* The passive voice expresses reversed action, since the receiver comes before the doer. Active verbs are often used in newspaper headlines because they are more vivid and take less space. The following headlines are all in the active voice:

**"Bushman Gets Out of Cage"**

**"White Sox Capture First Title"**

**"Urges France to Begin Defense Plan"**

**"Governor Advises Aid for Workers"**

The passive voice is generally used when the subject of the sentence is *indefinite, general,* or *unimportant.* In the sentence, *They mine coal in Pennsylvania,* the subject is so indefinite that it is not clear what is meant by *they.* It might mean the miners, the people, or the companies. This sentence, and sentences like it, are improved by putting the verb in the passive voice.

> They *mine* coal in Pennsylvania. (*poor*)
>
> Coal *is mined* in Pennsylvania. (*better*)
>
> They *grow* wheat in many of our states. (*poor*)
>
> Wheat *is grown* in many of our states. (*better*)
>
> They *use* tractors on some farms. (*poor*)
>
> Tractors *are used* on some farms. (*better*)

The passive voice is also used when *what was done* is more important than the doer of the action. Study the following sentences:

> The play, "Man and Superman," *was written* by Shaw. (*passive*)
>
> Shaw *wrote* the play "Man and Superman." (*active*)
>
> America *was discovered* by Columbus. (*passive*)
>
> Columbus *discovered* America. (*active*)

In the first sentence, if you wish to emphasize the play more than the author, put the verb in the passive voice. In the third sentence, if you wish to emphasize the discovery more than the discoverer, put the verb in the passive voice.

The use of the passive voice is generally used when you want to emphasize the *receiver* rather than the *doer.* However, in the great majority of cases the active voice is more effective than the passive voice.

**EXERCISE 5**

The following pairs of sentences are written in the active voice and in the passive voice. Write the word *better* after the sentence that expresses the idea in the better form.

Example: They grow orchids in Brazil.

Orchids are grown in Brazil. (*better*)

1. A number of planes were seen flying overhead by the officers.
   The officers saw a number of planes flying overhead.

2. A famous bone specialist set the broken arm.
   The broken arm was set by a famous bone specialist.

3. I knew that professor of physics at college.
   That professor of physics was known by me at college.

4. They sell men's hats in this department.
   Men's hats are sold in this department.

5. An umbrella has been left in the hall by someone.
   Someone has left an umbrella in the hall.

6. Our salary checks were given to us by the bookkeeper.
   The bookkeeper gave us our salary checks.

7. Our car has been repaired by the garage mechanic.
   The garage mechanic has repaired our car.

8. The members of the club elected Mr. Allerton president.
   Mr. Allerton was elected president by the members of the club.

9. The inspector examined the boiler carefully.
   The boiler was examined carefully by the inspector.

10. They use tractors on many of our modern farms.
    Tractors are used on many of our modern farms.

## MOOD OF VERBS

In addition to tense and voice, verbs have another property which *is* called **mood** (or *mode*). The word *mood* comes from a Latin word which means *manner*. When we apply the term mood to verbs, we mean *the manner in which the verb expresses the action or state of being.*

There are three moods in English, the *indicative mood*, the *imperative mood*, and the *subjunctive mood*. The *indicative mood* is used *to make statements* and *to ask questions*. Most of the verbs that you commonly use are in the indicative mood.

> The stenographer wrote the letter. (*statement of fact*)
> indicative mood

> Did you hear the President's address? (*question*)
> indicative mood

The imperative mood is used to *express a command* or *a request*. The imperative mood is found only in the present tense, second person. The subject is always the pronoun *you*, which is seldom expressed.

> Come here at once! (*command*)
> imperative mood

> Close the door, Jane. (*request*)
> imperative mood

The subjunctive mood is used to *express a wish* or *a condition which is contrary to fact*. By contrary to fact we mean something which is not true. A contrary to fact condition is usually introduced by the word *if* or *as if*.

> If he were here, I would give him the keys. (*He is not here.*)
> subjunctive mood

> I wish I were in Florida. (*expresses a wish*)
> subjunctive mood

The indicative and the imperative moods do not present any problems in English. The verb has the same form to express a statement or to ask a question. You can identify the imperative mood easily because the subject is *you*, which is usually understood. The imperative mood always expresses a command or a request.

Although most of the forms for the subjunctive have disappeared from our language, there are a few forms left that you should be able to recognize and to use. The verb *to be* still retains more of the subjunctive forms than any other verb. Compare the following indicative and subjunctive forms of the verb *to be*:

## Reference Table

## SUBJUNCTIVE FORMS OF VERB "TO BE"

| Indicative Mood | | Subjunctive Mood | |
|---|---|---|---|

### Present Tense—Singular and Plural

| *First person*: | I am | we are | (If) I *be* | (If) we *be* |
|---|---|---|---|---|
| *Second person*: | you are | you are | (If) you *be* | (If) you *be* |
| *Third person*: | he is | they are | (If) he *be* | (If) they *be* |

### Past Tense—Singular

| *First person*: | I was | (If) I *were* |
|---|---|---|
| *Second person*: | you were | (If) you were |
| *Third person*: | he was | (If) he *were* |

### Present Perfect Tense—Singular

| *First person*: | I have been | (If) I have been |
|---|---|---|
| *Second person*: | you have been | (If) you have been |
| *Third person*: | he has been | (If) he *have* been |

The subjunctive with *be* (present tense) is almost never used in informal speaking and writing. The subjunctive form *have been* instead of *has been* is also passing out of use.

In the preceding table, the forms for the subjunctive that are different from the indicative are printed in *italics;* that is, *be* in the present tense; *were* in the past tense, first person, singular, and third person, singular; *have* in the present perfect tense, third person, singular.

There is only one change that occurs in the subjunctive in the case of other verbs. In the present tense, third person, singular, the *s* is dropped in the subjunctive.

The verb *have* has only one form in the subjunctive that is different from the indicative. In the present tense, third person, singular, *have* is used in place of *has*:

If he *have* the time, he will meet with you. (subjunctive)

He *has* the time, and he will meet with you. (indicative)

If he fail— (not *fails*)

If he keep— (not *keeps*)

If he find— (not *finds*)

If he have— (not *has*)

If he call— (not *calls*)

The word *if* is not a part of the subjunctive. The forms for the subjunctive are usually given with the word *if* because the group of words in which the subjunctive is used is very frequently introduced by the word *if.*

Although the subjunctive mood is rapidly passing out of use in informal speaking and writing, there are certain uses that are still observed by discriminating writers and speakers. The subjunctive expressing a *wish* and the subjunctive in a *contrary to fact condition* are two of these uses.

## USES OF THE SUBJUNCTIVE MOOD

You have just learned that careful writers and speakers use the subjunctive to express a wish, a condition that is contrary to fact (not true), and a condition of uncertainty (it may be true or not true). Sometimes careful writers and speakers also use the subjunctive *in making a suggestion, in making a demand,* or *in expressing a need.*

I wish I *were* a millionaire. (wish)

If I *were* you, I should give up the contest. (contrary to fact)

If this plan *fail,* we shall give up the project. (condition of uncertainty)

I suggest that he *work* full time in the future. (suggestion)

The supervisor insists that the bookkeeper *prove* his report. (a demand)

It is imperative that the play *begin* at once. (a necessity)

The subjunctive is used in certain parliamentary expressions, such as the following:

I move that the nominations *be closed.*

He moved that the report of the committee *be accepted.*

She moved that the minutes *be adopted* as read.

I move that the meeting *be adjourned.*

The *two most important* uses of the subjunctive are the subjunctive expressing a wish and the subjunctive in a contrary to fact condition after *if, as if,* and *as though.*

## EXERCISE 6

Complete the following sentences by supplying the correct form for the *subjunctive* in the blank spaces. The verb to use in the sentence is enclosed in parentheses.

1. If the manager ............ here, I am sure he would agree with me. (to be)

2. I wish that I ............ able to help you in this emergency. (to be)

3. I suggest that he ............ the building himself. (manage)

4. He talks as if he ............ the president of the concern. (to be)

5. If they ............ here, I should tell them about the case. (to be)

6. I should not buy that television set if I ............ you. (to be)

7. I wish that the speaker ............ here so that we might start the program. (to be)

8. If Martha ............ in town, I should invite her to the opera. (to be)

9. He always acts as if he ............ sure of the results. (to be)

10. ............ he innocent, he would try to prove it. (to be)

11. It is essential that you ............ on guard. (to be)

12. We suggest that he ............ his promise to buy the car. (keep)

13. If the president ............ in his office, he would see me. (to be)

14. It is necessary that he ............ overtime for several months. (work)

15. I suggest that the paper ............ ready by tonight. (to be)

## SUMMARY OF GRAMMAR UNIT FIFTEEN

*Voice* is that property of a verb which indicates whether the subject is performing the action or is receiving the action. There are two voices: active voice and passive voice.

A verb is in the **active voice** when it represents the subject as *performing* the action.

A verb is in the **passive voice** when it represents the subject as *receiving* the action.

Only a verb that takes an object (transitive verb) can be changed into the passive voice.

The passive voice is formed by combining some form of the verb *to be* with the past participle of the verb that names the action: Examples: *am called, will be elected, have been promoted, was interviewed.*

*Mood* indicates the manner in which the action or the state of being is expressed. There are three moods in English: indicative mood, imperative mood, and the subjunctive mood.

The **indicative mood** is used to state a fact or ask a question.

The **imperative mood** is used to express a command or make a request.

The **subjunctive mood** is used to express a wish, doubt, uncertainty, or a condition that is contrary to fact.

Although the subjunctive is rapidly passing out of use in informal speaking and writing, certain uses of the subjunctive are still observed by careful speakers and writers.

The subjunctive expresses certain distinctions in meaning which cannot be expressed by the indicative. This is true of the subjunctive of *wish,* and the subjunctive in a *contrary to fact condition. If I was you* does not express the same idea as *If I were you.* You can never be the other person. The subjunctive indicates that fact.

## SELF-GRADING ASSIGNMENT 1

Directions: Underline the **verbs** in the following sentences. On the line to the right, indicate whether the verb is in the *active voice* or in the *passive voice*.

Example: The streets <u>will be sprinkled</u> every day.           *passive*
.................

1. The soldiers were entertained by a comedian.      1. .................

2. All orders will be executed by the captain.       2. .................

3. The writer developed an unusual plot.             3. .................

4. Our Drama League will entertain the actors.       4. .................

5. The problem will be solved by a group of experts. 5. .................

6. The people in the audience applauded the speaker. 6. .................

7. A newspaper truck carried a camera platform.      7. .................

8. The charge has been confirmed by the officer.     8. .................

9. The wires had been disconnected by vandals.       9. .................

10. Refreshments will be served at the dance.        10. .................

11. The boys have taken pictures of their camp.      11. .................

12. I have driven that car thousands of miles.       12. .................

13. The editor has accepted the manuscript.          13. .................

14. The manuscript has been rejected.                14. .................

15. Father wants a book on atomic energy.            15. .................

*Caution: Check your answers to each assignment with the answer key at the back of the booklet before proceeding with the next assignment.*

## SELF-GRADING ASSIGNMENT 2

Directions: Rewrite the following sentences. Change the verbs in the *active voice* to the *passive voice,* and the verbs in the *passive voice* to the *active voice.*

1. The boys have assembled a collection of scrap iron.

2. The thermometer was fastened to the door by James.

3. Elinor designed a new color scheme.

4. The copy editor has made the assignments.

5. Allen submitted a radio script to the studio.

6. Telephone service has been discontinued by the company.

7. Walter has been promoted twice by the manager.

8. Behind the house the excavators found an old well.

9. The articles were written by several distinguished authors.

10. Martha won the first prize in the modeling contest.

11. All the evidence has been examined by the judge.

12. The patient was sent to a specialist by the doctor.

13. The boxes were thrown on the ground by the driver.

14. A publishing firm occupies the building.

15. Have you inspected the factory?

## SELF-GRADING ASSIGNMENT 3

Directions: On the lines to the right indicate the **mood** of the under-lined verbs: *indicative mood, imperative mood,* or *subjunctive mood.*

1.  The men are repairing the walk.                1. .................

2.  Is he looking for a position in the bank?      2. .................

3.  Stop that car!                                 3. .................

4.  If everybody were here, the program would start.  4. .................

5.  Were he in my place, I wonder what he would do. 5. .................

6.  I wish I were a musician.                       6. .................

7.  If today were a holiday we might go to the lake.  7. .................

8.  Were you ill last week?                         8. .................

9.  The soldiers were marching across the bridge.  9. .................

10. What is your opinion of that broadcast?        10. .................

11. She acts as if she were the head of the department. 11. .................

12. I suggest that he begin the project tomorrow.  12. .................

13. Be careful, or you will fall.                  13. .................

14. I insist that he pay the bill promptly.        14. .................

15. We were seated promptly by the head usher.     15. .................

## PROGRESS TEST FIFTEEN

### A.

Directions: Change the verbs in the *passive voice* to the *active voice.* Change the verbs in the *active voice* to the *passive voice.* Rewrite the sentence to show the change. Follow the form given in the example. (*15 points*)

Example: A report <u>was submitted</u> by the chairman. (*passive voice*)

The chairman <u>submitted</u> a report. (*active voice*)

1. We ordered the goods from the factory.

2. The signatures on the letters have been checked by the judge.

3. Ted has sent in his application for the position.

4. Norman has written several letters to his congressman.

5. The president's resignation was accepted by the board of directors.

6. A committee was appointed by the chairman.

7. My uncle will accept the position of auditor.

8. He raised the question for several reasons.

9. A large sum of money has been received by the orphanage.

10. The women have arranged the tables for the dinner.

11. Some strange tales were told by the speaker.

12. The telephone operator called her during the night.

13. Your rent will be increased by the landlord next month.

14. The contract has been accepted by the firm.

15. The manager dictated the letter.

## PROGRESS TEST FIFTEEN (continued)

### B.

Directions: Underline the **verbs** that are in the *subjunctive mood.* On the line to the right, give the reason for the use of the subjunctive; that is, *contrary to fact, condition of uncertainty, wish, suggestion, necessity,* or *a demand.* (30 points.)

1. If this plan fail, we shall give up the project.     1. ....................

2. The law requires that he keep his walks clean.     2. ....................

3. It is imperative that he leave the office at five.     3. ....................

4. Were he honest, he would return the money.     4. ....................

5. If Fred were older, he would join the Marines.     5. ....................

6. If his talk prove interesting, I shall stay for the rest of the program.     6. ....................

7. If this were gold, it would be worth a fortune.     7. ....................

8. If I were you, I should not think of going to Mexico.     8. ....................

9. If that be true, I have no more to say.     9. ....................

10. I suggest that he buy a new car.     10. ....................

11. He acts as if he were the president of the firm.     11. ....................

12. I wish I were younger.     12. ....................

13. How wonderful it would be if this were only true!     13. ....................

14. She wishes she were taller.     14. ....................

15. If that child were mine, I should teach her to swim.     15. ....................

## ANSWER KEY

for

## EXERCISES, ASSIGNMENTS, AND PROGRESS TEST

### Grammar Unit Fifteen

---

## CORRECT ANSWERS TO EXERCISE 1

1. The hunter killed the deer.
   D.　　　　　R.

1. *active*

2. The deer was killed by the hunter.
   R.　　　　　　　　D.

2. *passive*

3. John struck James.
   D.　　　R.

3. *active*

4. James was struck by John.
   R.　　　　　　D.

4. *passive*

5. The car was repaired by the mechanic.
   R.　　　　　　　　D.

5. *passive*

6. We finished the test yesterday.
   D.　　　　　R.

6. *active*

7. John was sent to New York by the manager.
   R.　　　　　　　　　　　D.

7. *passive*

8. Her beautiful mink coat was stolen by the maid.
   R.　　　　　　　　　D.

8. *passive*

9. We found an apartment in a good neighborhood.
   D.　　　　R.

9. *active*

10. Coffee is raised in Brazil by the planters.
    R.　　　　　　　　　D.

10. *passive*

11. The officers searched the ship.
    D.　　　　　R.

11. *active*

12. The broken bone was set by the doctor.
    R.　　　　　　　D.

12. *passive*

13. The <u>doctor</u> set the broken <u>bone</u>.                        13. *active*
       D.                              R.

14. The <u>snow</u> covered the <u>trees</u> and the <u>bushes</u>.      14. *active*
       D.                      R.                    R.

15. The <u>lawn</u> was mowed by <u>John</u> and his <u>father</u>.      15. *passive*
       R.                          D.                    D.

## CORRECT ANSWERS TO EXERCISE 2

Verbs in the passive voice are printed in **heavy type.**

1. An article about our trip **was written** by Fred.

2. Your courtesy **is appreciated** by us.

3. The sentence **was pronounced** by the judge.

4. The position **will be accepted** by John.

5. The letter **has been written** by the stenographer.

6. His recommendations **were adopted** by us.

7. The broken arm **will be set** by the physician.

8. The package **has been placed** on the table by me.

9. The invitations **have been sent** out by the committee.

10. Dresses for actresses **are designed** by Marian.

11. Ten men **were** recently **employed** by the manager.

12. The plane **was inspected** by the pilot.

13. The necessary supplies **have been obtained** by the explorers.

14. The refreshments **were served** by the women.

15. A new bridge **has** just **been built** by the engineers.

## CORRECT ANSWERS TO EXERCISE 3

Verbs in active voice are printed in **heavy type**.

1. The diplomats **planned** a meeting.

2. The doctor **has given** the boy emergency treatment.

3. My sister **calls** me at six o'clock every morning.

4. The men **have raised** many objections to the plan.

5. The examiners **will audit** the books.

6. A scientist **discovered** oil on the land.

7. The players **consulted** the coach.

8. The manager **has arranged** a meeting.

9. A metal helmet **protected** the soldier.

10. The producer **gave** Mary an important part in the play.

11. The owner **will sell** the farm.

12. WGN **will broadcast** the results of the election.

13. The librarian **ordered** a number of books.

14. The Indians **wove** that beautiful rug.

15. The clerks **copied** the records.

## CORRECT ANSWERS TO EXERCISE 4

1. Mr. Jones bought his camera in New York.                1. *active*

2. The story was written by the news editor.               2. *passive*

3. Men of different races delivered speechs.               3. *active*

4. He <u>blazed</u> a new trail for the air mail.     4. *active*

5. Many interesting stories <u>were related</u> by the travelers.     5. *passive*

6. The actors <u>will be entertained</u> by the Drama League.     6. *passive*

7. The date of the meeting <u>was set</u> by the president.     7. *passive*

8. I <u>have not seen</u> him at the bank lately.     8. *active*

9. The radio script <u>was written</u> by Norman.     9. *passive*

10. Reunions <u>have been planned</u> by the alumni.     10. *passive*

11. The packages <u>were handled</u> with care by the driver.     11. *passive*

12. The letters <u>were examined</u> by the postal authorities.     12. *passive*

13. The agent <u>authorized</u> the use of the building.     13. *active*

14. Crowds <u>cheered</u> the soldiers.     14. *active*

15. A cover <u>had been placed</u> on the table.     15. *passive*

## CORRECT ANSWERS TO EXERCISE 5

1. The officers saw a number of planes flying overhead. *(better)*

2. A famous bone specialist set the broken arm. *(better)*

3. I knew that professor of physics at college. *(better)*

4. Men's hats are sold in this department. *(better)*

5. Someone has left an umbrella in the hall. *(better)*

6. The bookkeeper gave us our salary checks. *(better)*

7. The garage mechanic has repaired our car. *(better)*

8. Mr. Allerton was elected president by the members of the club. *(better)*
   (The emphasis should be placed on Mr. Allerton.)

9. The inspector examined the boiler carefully. *(better)*

10. Tractors are used on many of our modern farms. *(better)*

### CORRECT ANSWERS TO EXERCISE 6

Correct form of the subjunctive is printed in **heavy type**.

1. If the manager **were** here, I am sure he would agree with me.

2. I wish that I **were** able to help you in this emergency.

3. I suggest that he **manage** the building himself.

4. He talks as if he **were** the president of the concern.

5. If they **were** here, I should tell them about the case.

6. I should not buy that television set if I **were** you.

7. I wish that the speaker **were** here, so that we might start the program.

8. If Martha **were** in town, I should invite her to the opera.

9. He always acts as if he **were** sure of the results.

10. **Were** he innocent, he would try to prove it. (If he were . . .)

11. It is essential that you **be** on guard.

12. We suggest that he **keep** his promise to buy the car.

13. If the president **were** in his office, he would see me.

14. It is necessary that he **work** overtime for several months.

15. I suggest that the paper **be** ready by tonight.

## CORRECT ANSWERS TO ASSIGNMENT 1

1. The soldiers were entertained by a comedian.          1. *passive*

2. All orders will be executed by the captain.          2. *passive*

3. The writer developed an unusual plot.          3. *active*

4. Our Drama League will entertain the actors.          4. *active*

5. The problem will be solved by a group of experts.          5. *passive*

6. The people in the audience applauded the speaker.          6. *active*

7. A newspaper truck carried a camera platform.          7. *active*

8. The charge has been confirmed by the officer.          8. *passive*

9. The wires had been disconnected by vandals.          9. *passive*

10. Refreshments will be served at the dance.          10. *passive*

11. The boys have taken pictures of their camp.          11. *active*

12. I have driven that car thousands of miles.          12. *active*

13. The editor has accepted the manuscript.          13. *active*

14. The manuscript has been rejected.          14. *passive*

15. Father wants a book on atomic energy.          15. *active*

## CORRECT ANSWERS TO ASSIGNMENT 2

Verbs that have been changed from active to passive voice, or passive to active voice, are printed in **heavy type.**

1. A collection of scrap iron **has been assembled** by the boys.

2. James **fastened** the thermometer to the door.

3. A new color scheme **was designed** by Elinor.

4. The assignments **have been made** by the copy editor.

5. A radio script **was submitted** to the studio by Allen.

6 The company **has discontinued** telephone service.

7. The manager **has promoted** Walter twice.

8. An old well **was found** behind the house by the excavators.

9. Several distinguished authors **wrote** the articles.

10. The first prize in the modeling contest **was won** by Martha.

11. The judge **has examined** all the evidence.

12. The doctor **sent** the patient to a specialist.

13 The driver **threw** the boxes on the ground.

14. The building **is occupied** by a publishing firm.

15. **Has** the factory **been inspected** by you?

## CORRECT ANSWERS TO ASSIGNMENT 3

1. are repairing—*indicative*

2. Is looking—*indicative*

3. Stop—*imperative*

4. were—*subjunctive*

5. Were—*subjunctive*

6. were—*subjunctive*

7. were—*subjunctive*

8. Were—*indicative*

9. were marching—*indicative*

10. is—*indicative*

11. were—*subjunctive*

12. begin—*subjunctive*

13. Be—*imperative*

14. pay—*subjunctive*

15. were seated—*indicative*

## CORRECT ANSWERS TO PROGRESS TEST FIFTEEN

### A. *(15 points)*

Verbs that have been changed from active to passive voice, or passive to active voice, are printed in **heavy type.**

1. The goods **were ordered** from the factory by us. (passive voice)

2. The judge **has checked** the signatures on the letters. (active voice)

3. His application for the position **has been sent** in by Ted. (passive)

4. Several letters to his congressman **have been written** by Norman. (passive)

5. The board of directors **accepted** the president's resignation. (active)

6. The chairman **appointed** a committee. (active voice)

7. The position of auditor **will be accepted** by my uncle. (passive)

8. The question **was raised** by him for several reasons. (passive)
   or For several reasons the question **was raised** by him.

9. The orphanage **has received** a large sum of money. (active voice)

10. The tables for the dinner **have been arranged** by the women. (passive)

11. The speaker **told** some strange tales. (active voice)

12. She **was called** during the night by the telephone operator. (passive)
    or During the night she **was called** by the telephone operator.

13. The landlord **will increase** your rent next month. (active)
    or Next month the landlord **will increase** your rent.

14. The firm **has accepted** the contract. (active)

15. The letter **was dictated** by the manager. (passive)

**B.** *(30 points)*

Verbs in subjunctive mood are printed in **heavy type**.

| | |
|---|---|
| 1. If this plan **fail,** we shall give up the project. | 1. *condition of uncertainty* |
| 2. The law requires that he **keep** his walks clean. | 2. *demand—order* |
| 3. It is imperative that he **leave** the office at five. | 3. *necessity* |
| 4. **Were** he honest, he would have returned the money. | 4. *contrary to fact* |
| 5. If Fred **were** older, he would join the Marines. | 5. *contrary to fact* |
| 6. If his talk **prove** interesting, I shall stay for the rest of the program. | 6. *condition of uncertainty* |
| 7. If this **were** gold, it would be worth a fortune. | 7. *contrary to fact* |
| 8. If I **were** you, I should not think of going to Mexico. | 8. *contrary to fact* |
| 9. If that **be** true, I have no more to say. | 9. *condition of uncertainty* |
| 10. I suggest that he **buy** a new car. | 10. *suggestion* |
| 11. He acts as if he **were** the president of the firm. | 11. *contrary to fact* |
| 12. I wish I **were** younger. | 12. *wish* |
| 13. How wonderful it would be if this **were** only true! | 13. *contrary to fact* |
| 14. She wishes she **were** taller. | 14. *wish* |
| 15. If that child **were** mine, I should teach her to swim. | 15. *contrary to fact* |

## HOW TO OBTAIN YOUR SCORE

*The test totals 45 points. To obtain your score, divide the number of your correct answers by 45. The answer will be your score on this test. For example, if you have 40 points correct, your score is 40 divided by 45 which is 89 per cent. In other words, your score on this test is 89. You can obtain your score on any of the exercises or assignments by following the same procedure.*

**Practical English Grammar**

## OUTLINE OF UNIT SIXTEEN

# AGREEMENT OF SUBJECT AND VERB

Page

1. AGREEMENT IN PERSON AND NUMBER...................... 5

2. AGREEMENT OF VERB WITH COMPOUND SUBJECT.... 6

3. AGREEMENT OF VERB WITH COLLECTIVE NOUNS......10

4. INTERVENING PHRASES .................................... 12

5. AGREEMENT OF SUBJECT WITH CONTRACTIONS........ 14

6. AGREEMENT OF VERB WITH INDEFINITE PRONOUNS 16

7. SPECIAL CASES OF AGREEMENT......................... 19

8. SUMMARY OF GRAMMAR UNIT SIXTEEN..................... 22

*Self-Grading Assignments* ................................ 23

*Progress Test Sixteen* .................................... 27

*Key to Correct Answers* .................................. 29

# AGREEMENT OF SUBJECT AND VERB

ONE of the common errors made both in speaking and writing is the lack of agreement between the subject noun or pronoun and the predicate verb. In order to have harmonious relations between the parts of the sentence, you must have this agreement.

## AGREEMENT IN PERSON AND NUMBER

The grammatical principle upon which agreement of subject and verb depends is very simple: *The verb must agree with its subject in person and number.* If the subject of the sentence is singular, the verb must also be in the singular. If the subject is plural, the verb must also be plural. If the subject is in the first person, the verb must also be in the first person. If the subject is in the second or third persons, the verb must agree.

> *He doesn't* know the answer. (correct—subject and verb are in third person)
>
> *He don't* know the answer. (incorrect—lack of agreement)
>
> *You were invited* to the meeting. (correct—subject and verb are in second person)
>
> *You was invited* to the meeting. (incorrect—lack of agreement)

In the first sentence the subject and verb agree. The subject *He* is in the third person, singular. The verb *doesn't* is also in the third person, singular. In the second sentence, *He don't* is incorrect. The correct form for third person, singular is *doesn't* not *don't.*

Although the rule is very simple, there are a number of problems involved in agreement of subject and verb. These problems are responsible for the errors that are commonly made. Sometimes the speaker or writer does not know whether the subject should be regarded as singular or plural. Sometimes he is not sure about the form of the verb for the singular and for the plural. Sometimes he does not know which word is the real subject of the sentence.

In this unit you will consider some of the problems that are responsible for the errors that occur in making the subject and the verb agree. Your first problem will be the one that occurs when you have a sentence with a compound subject.

## AGREEMENT OF VERB WITH COMPOUND SUBJECT

The parts of a compound subject are usually connected by *and, or, nor, either-or,* and *neither-nor.* Usually, when two or more subjects are connected by *and,* the subject is plural and requires a plural verb. The following examples have compound subjects:

Mary and Jane are taking Spanish.
compound subject

The president and the vice-president speak at every meeting.
compound subject

In the first sentence, the two parts of the compound subject are connected by *and.* The subject is plural and takes a plural verb, *are.* In the second sentence, the two parts of the compound subject are also connected by *and.* The subject takes the plural form of the verb which is *speak.*

There is one exception to the "and" rule. Sometimes the two subjects connected by *and* form a unit. In this case, *the subject is regarded as singular and takes a singular verb.*

Bacon and eggs is a popular combination. *(Verb is singular.)*
singular

The Stars and Stripes flies overhead. *(Verb is singular.)*
singular

When two subjects connected by *and* refer to the same person or thing, the subject is *singular.*

His companion and friend is very devoted to him.
<br>
<small>same person</small>

The secretary and treasurer was present at the meeting.
<br>
<small>same person</small>

If the subjects in the preceding sentences referred to *two individuals*, the verbs would be plural. The sentences would read as follows:

His companion and his friend are very devoted to him.

The secretary and the treasurer were present at the meeting.

By placing the word *his* before friend and the word *the* before treasurer, you clearly indicate that there are two individuals.

## Subjects Connected by "Or" or "Nor"

When two singular subjects are connected by the word *or*, the subject is singular. The sentence means *either the one or the other*. It does not mean *both*. The same rule applies when *nor* is used to join two singular subjects. *Either-or* and *neither-nor* follow the same rule.

Mary or Jane is going to the fashion show. (*the one or the other*)
<br>
<small>singular</small>

Neither the man nor the boy was responsible. (*neither the one nor the other*)
<br>
<small>singular</small>

When one of the subjects connected by *or, nor, either-or, neither-nor* is singular and the other is plural, the verb agrees with the subject that is nearer to it. If both subjects are plural, the verb is also plural.

Neither the boy nor the men were responsible. (*Verb is plural.*)
<br>
<small>singular     plural</small>

Neither the men nor the boy was responsible. (*Verb is singular.*)
<br>
<small>plural     singular</small>

Neither the men nor the boys were responsible. (*Verb is plural.*)
plural        plural

In the first sentence, the plural subject is nearer to the verb. In the second sentence, the singular subject is nearer to the verb. In the third sentence, both subjects are plural. When one of the subjects is singular and the other is plural, you should put the plural subject nearer to the verb. It makes the verb plural and sounds better.

If the subjects connected by these words differ in *person*, the verb should agree with the subject nearer to it. Such sentences are often very awkward and should be avoided, if possible.

Either I or they are responsible for the small attendance.
first    third

This sentence would sound better if it were written as follows:

Either I am responsible for the small attendance, or they are.

## EXERCISE 1

Decide whether the subject is *singular* or *plural*. Cross out the verb in the parentheses that does not agree with the subject.

Example: Neither Dan nor Harry (~~sing~~, sings) well.

1. Fresh air and exercise (builds, build) a strong body.

2. The workman or the supervisor (is, are) responsible.

3. Neither John nor Fred (does, do) good work.

4. Clothing and food (was, were) sent to the refugees.

5. Either Mr. Allen or his assistant (is, are) in the office.

6. My friend and fellow worker (is, are) very capable.

7. Ben and George (is, are) eligible for training.

8. Where (is, are) the men and the boys?

9. Neither I nor my friend (was, were) there.

10. Neither the plot nor the acting (was, were) commendable.

11. Either the lawyer or the detectives (is, are) following the case.

12. Either the detectives or the lawyer (is, are) following the case.

13. Neither the clerk nor the secretary (has, have) appeared.

14. Our cook and housekeeper (is, are) ill.

15. Allen and May (was, were) interviewed yesterday.

*Note: The correct answers to exercises will be found at the back of this booklet. Correct your mistakes and, if necessary, re-read the text material before going on to the next section.*

## AGREEMENT OF VERB WITH COLLECTIVE NOUNS

A *collective noun* is a noun that represents a group or a collection of objects usually considered as a unit. Words like *crowd, troop, herd, people, flock,* and *jury* are collective nouns.

A collective noun that is singular in meaning requires a singular verb. A collective noun that is plural in meaning requires a plural verb.

If the collective noun in a particular sentence represents the individuals acting as a unit, the noun is singular. If the sentence indicates clearly that the individuals are acting separately, the noun is plural. The following examples will help you see this distinction:

The *committee is opposed* to the plan. (*acting as a unit*)

The *board of directors is* in session. (*as a unit*)

The *jury returned its* verdict. (*as a unit*)

The *jury have returned* to their homes. (*as individuals*)

The *family have given* their contributions. (*as individuals*)

In most cases where the individuals composing a group are acting separately, it is better to use such expressions as *the members of the jury, the members of the family,* etc. These expressions sound better and clearly indicate that the individuals are acting separately.

The members of the jury have returned to their homes.

The people in the audience waved their hands.

The members of the band wore their uniforms.

## EXERCISE 2

Decide whether the subject should be considered as a *unit,* or as *individuals*. Cross out the verb enclosed in parentheses that does not agree with the subject.

Example: The company (has, ~~have~~) improved working conditions.

1. The crowd (was, were) unmanageable.

2. The regiment (are, is) putting on their new uniforms.

3. The public (demands, demand) a decision.

4. Our group (is, are) concerned with social problems.

5. The jury (have, has) returned to their homes.

6. The office staff (have, has) not submitted their reports.

7. The band (was, were) tuning up their instruments.

8. The band (is, are) playing its fifth concert tonight.

9. The choir (was, were) told to bring their hymnals.

10. The committee (was, were) not able to agree.

11. A committee on public relations (was, were) appointed.

12. The class (has, have) been divided into sections.

13. The Board of Directors (is, are) meeting today.

14. The faculty (do, does) not approve of the new plan.

15. The office staff (is, are) now complete.

## INTERVENING PHRASES

Sometimes the subject is followed by prepositional phrases or such expressions as *accompanied by, in accordance with, together with, as well as, including,* etc. The subject of the sentence is not affected in any way by the introduction of such phrases. You will never find the subject of the sentence in a prepositional phrase or in any one of the expressions listed in the following sentences:

A *package* (of books) *was delivered* today.

*Materials* (for the building) *have been shipped.*

Important *papers,* as well as his will, *were found* in his desk.

The *checks,* including a statement, *were mailed* today.

In the first sentence, the subject is the word *package.* Since package is singular, the verb must be singular. In the second sentence, the subject is the word *Materials.* Since the subject is plural, the verb must be plural. The prepositional phrases, *of books,* and *for the building,* do not affect the number of the subject.

The subject of the third sentence is *papers,* which is plural. The verb must also be plural to agree with the subject. The group of words, *as well as his will,* does not affect the number of the subject. In the fourth sentence, the expression, *including a statement,* does not affect the number of the subject. The subject is *checks,* which is plural. The verb must also be plural, to agree with the subject.

## EXERCISE 3

Underline the *simple subject*. Draw two lines under the *predicate verb*. On the line to the right, indicate whether the subject is singular or plural.

Example: Our horse, as well as our chickens, was killed.      *singular*

1. The pictures from Vienna were inspiring.                1. ................

2. The precious jewel, as well as other heirlooms, was lost.      2. ................

3. One of the players was dismissed yesterday.             3. ................

4. The ships at the dock are ready for service.            4. ................

5. Two of the delegates came from the A. F. of L.          5. ................

6. The mother, as well as the children, dreads the trip.      6. ................

7. This book about animals is very popular.                7. ................

8. Opportunities for improvement are offered in adult classes.      8. ................

9. The letter, including the checks, was mailed today.      9. ................

10. A pension, together with his investments, guarantees a steady income.      10. ................

11. Ways of finding materials were outlined by the librarian.      11. ................

12. Books about the lives of successful men are always an inspiration.      12. ................

13. Both of the delegates look weary.                      13. ................

14. Members of the team were entertained by the Women's Club.      14. ................

15. The men in the factory were opposed to the plan.       15. ................

## AGREEMENT OF SUBJECT WITH CONTRACTIONS

Contractions are verbs that have been shortened by the omission of one or more letters. The omission of the letters is indicated by the use of an apostrophe. Many persons make mistakes in agreement of subject and verb when they use contractions. The use of the contractions *don't* and *ain't* are responsible for a great many of these errors.

*Ain't* is always incorrect and is never used by persons with any degree of education or cultural background. However, since some adults continue to use *ain't*, the following caution should be kept in mind:

Do not use *ain't* for *am not, are not*, or *isn't*. The contraction *aren't* should be used for *are not*. There is no contraction for the words *am not*.

I *am not* interested in the position. (not *ain't*)

We *are not* going to the theater. (not *ain't*)

We *aren't* going to the meeting. (not *ain't*)

*Isn't* this a beautiful day! (not *ain't*)


Another error commonly made is the use of **don't** for **doesn't**. **Don't** is a contraction for *do not*. It should not be used in the third person, singular. The expressions, *it don't, he don't* and *she don't* are incorrect. Do not misuse them for *it doesn't, he doesn't*, and *she doesn't*.


It *don't* make any difference. (incorrect)

It *doesn't* make any difference. (correct)


He *don't* belong to our union. (incorrect)

He *doesn't* belong to our union. (correct)


She *don't* want the position. (incorrect)

She *doesn't* want the position. (correct)

**EXERCISE 4**

Correct the errors in the use of **contractions** in the following sentences. Cross out the incorrect form and write the correct form above it.

                      doesn't
Example: If George ~~don't~~ hurry, he'll miss the plane.

1. I heard that you wasn't pleased with the election.

2. He ain't going to buy a new car.

3. The men wasn't interested in that report.

4. The plan don't look right to me.

5. Why wasn't you at the meeting last night?

6. That man don't need our help.

7. There ain't any room for doubt.

8. Don't he want an appointment?

9. Harvey ain't pleased with the new appointments.

10. She don't know any better.

11. We wasn't ready for the debate.

12. Wasn't your friends coming this evening?

13. The manager don't want to employ that man.

14. Wasn't Fred and Harry at the stadium?

15. This door don't seem to have a lock.

## AGREEMENT OF VERB WITH INDEFINITE PRONOUNS

The indefinite pronouns *one, no one, anyone, everyone, someone, anybody, nobody, everybody, somebody, each, either,* and *neither* are always singular. Since these pronouns are singular, they take a singular verb.

Only *one* of the candidates is eligible. (*singular verb*)

*Each* of these bags has been examined. (*singular verb*)

*Neither* has lost his ticket. (*singular verb*)

*Somebody* is responsible for the accident. (*singular verb*)

*Anyone* has the right to offer criticism. (*singular verb*)

*Nobody* has access to the vault. (*singular verb*)

When *many a, each,* and *every* are used to introduce a sentence and function as adjectives, the *subject* is singular.

Many a *man* wishes that he had gone to college.

Each *window* and *door* was locked securely.

Every *man, woman,* and *child* is expected to report.

The indefinite pronouns *several, few, both* and *many* are always plural.

*Several* were called to the platform. (*plural verb*)

A *few* were opposed to the bill. (*plural verb*)

*Both* were anxious to receive the award. (*plural verb*)

*Many* in the audience objected to his speech. (*plural verb*)

The indefinite pronouns *some, none, any,* and *all* are singular or plural according to the meaning of the sentence. When these words refer to a *quantity* or a *mass* taken as a whole, they are generally considered as singular. When they refer to a *number,* they are regarded as plural in meaning.

*Some are* going by plane. (*more than one*—plural)

*Some* of the ice cream *is* left. (*mass or quantity*—singular)

*Are any* of the men going by plane? (*more than one*—plural)

*Is* there *any* gasoline in the tank? (*mass or quantity*—singular)

*None* of these apples *are* ripe. (*more than one*—plural)

We needed a ball but *none was* available. (*not one*—singular)

*All* of the gasoline *has been sold.* (*mass or quantity*—singular)

*All* of the women *have brought* gifts. (*more than one*—plural)

Some nouns are plural in form, but singular in meaning. Examples of nouns that take a singular verb are *mumps, measles, news, summons, physics, mathematics.*

Physics is a very interesting subject. (*Verb is singular.*)

The news this week is startling. (*Verb is singular.*)

Measles is a contagious disease. (*Verb is singular.*)

The summons was served by the bailiff. (*Verb is singular.*)

Mathematics was his favorite study. (*Verb is singular.*)

## EXERCISE 5

Select the form of the **verb** that agrees with the *subject*. Determine the meaning of the sentence before you make your decision. Cross out the incorrect form of the verb in parentheses.

Example: Every man, woman, and child (was, ~~were~~) examined.

1. Some of the guests (has, have) left.

2. Many a town (has, have) been in danger of floods.

3. All of the members (was, were) present last night.

4. None of the money (was, were) spent without his knowledge.

5. All of the oil (has been, have been) spilled.

6. (Is, Are) any of the men working overtime?

7. Some of the work (is, are) not finished.

8. Each of the designs (has, have) its merits.

9. Neither of the men (has, have) paid his dues this year.

10. Several (has, have) already registered for the tournament.

11. Only one of the candidates (is, are) eligible.

12. Both of my cousins (is, are) going to South America.

13. Many (is, are) in favor of the bill against gambling.

14. Anyone (has, have) the right to offer suggestions.

15. None of these pears (is, are) fit to eat.

## SPECIAL CASES OF AGREEMENT

1. Words like *pants, trousers, pliers, scissors, shears,* and *tongs* are plural and take a plural verb. When the word *pair* is used as the subject, the subject is regarded as singular and takes a singular verb.

The *scissors* are very sharp. (*plural*)

A *pair* of scissors was left on the desk. (*singular*)

2. A plural noun which shows *weight, extent,* or *quantity* is singular, and takes a singular verb.

Ten miles is a long distance to walk. (*singular*)

Five dollars is the price of the hat. (*singular*)

Twelve inches is the proper length. (*singular*)

3. The words *half* and *part* are singular or plural according to the meaning of the sentence. When these words refer to a *mass* or a *section,* they are singular. When they refer to a *number* of individuals or things, they are plural.

Half of the boys are in camp. (*number*—plural)

Half of the pie is left. (*mass or section*—singular)

Part of the roof was destroyed. (*mass or section*—singular)

Part of the guests have arrived. (*number*—plural)

4. When the word *number* is preceded by the article *a,* it takes a plural verb. When it is immediately preceded by the article *the,* it takes a singular verb.

A *number* of men *were working* on the project. (*plural*)

The *number* of men present *was* small. (*singular*)

5. The name of a firm is often regarded as singular even when there

is a plural form in the title. If the entire name carries a plural idea, the name is regarded as plural.

*Mandel Brothers* are having a sale on furs. (*plural*)

*The Macmillan Company* publishes books. (*singular*)

*General Motors Company* has declared a dividend. (*singular*)

6.   Sometimes a sentence begins with the word *there* or *here*. Neither of these words could be the subject of the sentence. The word *there* is used either as an expletive or as an adverb. The word *here* is an adverb. When a sentence begins with *here* or *there*, you should transpose it so that the true subject will appear at the beginning of the sentence. Then it will be possible for you to determine whether the subject is singular or plural.

*There* are six men on the committee.

Six men are on the committee. (*plural subject—plural verb*)

*Here* comes the general with his staff.

The general comes here with his staff. (*singular subject and verb*)

Sometimes a sentence beginning with the introductory *there* or *here* has a *compound subject*, which requires a plural verb. Mistakes in the number of the verb are frequently made because the speaker or the writer does not realize that the subject is *compound*. When the sentence is transposed, it is easy to determine whether the subject is simple or compound. The following sentences have compound subjects:

*There* goes the boy and his mother. (incorrect)

*There* go the boy and his mother. (correct)

The boy and his mother go there. (*compound subject—plural verb*)

*Here* comes John and Mary. (incorrect)

*Here* come John and Mary. (correct)

John and Mary come here. (*compound subject—plural verb*)

## EXERCISE 6

In the blank space, write the *form of the verb* that should be used in the sentence. Select the form from the verbs enclosed in parentheses.

Example: There ............ a man and a boy in the waiting room. (is, are)

There *are* a man and a boy in the waiting room.

1. These scissors ............ not large enough for our purpose. (is, are)

2. Fifty dollars ............ the amount enclosed. (is, are)

3. A large number of people ............ present. (was, were)

4. A pair of pliers ............ left on the ground. (was, were)

5. The number of candidates for the office ............ small. (is, are)

6. Five hundred miles ............ a long distance to drive. (is, are)

7. Greene and Company ............ advertised for a manager. (have, has)

8. Half of the melon ............ left. (is, are)

9. Here ............ found many evidences of civilization. (was, were)

10. Here ............ the general and his staff. (comes, come)

11. Part of the audience ............... not union members. (was, were)

12. Part of the building ............ wrecked. (was, were)

13. Half of the letters ............ filed in the cabinet. (was, were)

14. A number of soldiers ............ returned. (have, has)

15. The number of enlistments ............ increased. (have, has)

## SUMMARY OF GRAMMAR UNIT SIXTEEN

A verb must agree with its subject in **person** and **number**. If the subject is singular, the verb must be singular. If the subject is plural, the verb must be plural.

If the subject is in the first person, the verb must be in the first person. If the subject is in the second person, the verb must be in the second person. If the subject is in the third person, the verb must be in the third person.

A **compound subject** connected by *and* is usually plural and takes a plural verb. If the parts of the compound subject refer to a *unit* or to *one person*, the subject is singular and takes a singular verb.

**Singular subjects** connected by *or, nor, either-or, neither-nor*, take a singular verb. If both of the subjects are plural, the verb is plural. If one of the subjects is singular and the other is plural, the verb agrees with the subject that is *nearer* to it.

A **collective noun** that is *singular in meaning* takes a singular verb. A collective noun that is *plural in meaning* takes a plural verb. If the collective noun represents the individuals acting as a unit, the verb is singular. If the collective noun represents the individuals acting separately, the verb is plural. The meaning of the sentence will determine whether a collective noun should be regarded as singular or plural.

The subject of a sentence *is not affected* in any way by the introduction of phrases or other expressions that come between the subject and the verb. The subject of a sentence *is never found* in a prepositional phrase.

Some of the **indefinite pronouns** are always singular. Some are always plural. The indefinite pronouns *some, none, any*, and *all* are singular or plural according to the meaning of the sentence.

### SELF-GRADING ASSIGNMENT 1

Directions: Cross out the **verb** that is used incorrectly and write the correct form above it. If there is no error in the sentence, write *correct* after the sentence. Two sentences are correct.

*is*
Example: Neither of these machines ~~are~~ in working order.

1. A typewriter and a desk is always available.

2. Either Mr. Ames or his secretary are responsible for the error.

3. Neither Harold nor Frank have a car.

4. The vice-president and treasurer have made several recommendations.

5. The ebb and flow of the sea attract a tourist.

6. Neither of the trunks look large enough.

7. Were either of the girls present at the conference?

8. Either the maid or the housekeeper was in the room.

9. The committee are opposed to the plan.

10. The staff were selected by the president.

11. The group is ready to take action.

12. Her companion and secretary are very capable.

13. Neither are the correct answer.

14. Either of the secretaries are available.

15. The house and the grounds is beautiful.

*Caution:* *Check your answers to each assignment with the answer key at the back of the booklet before proceeding with the next assignment.*

### SELF-GRADING ASSIGNMENT 2

Directions: Underline the **subject** in each sentence. Fill in the blank with the correct form of the *verb* found in the parentheses.

Example: One of the delegates ............ leaving. (is, are)

One of the delegates *is* leaving.

1. The president, with his advisers, ............ arrived. (has, have)

2. The value of these books ............ in the illustrations. (lie, lies)

3. The use of these new devices ............ reduced our expenses. (has, have)

4. Jack, no less than his brother, ............ assistance. (needs, need)

5. The children, as well as the widow, ............ an allotment. (receives, receive)

6. The barn, as well as the farmhouse, ............ burned to the ground. (was, were)

7. This department, with the aid of experts, ............ made some outstanding improvements. (has, have)

8. Several copies of his book ............ placed in the library. (have been, has been)

9. The automobile industries in this country ............ developed rapidly. (has, have)

10. New methods of filing ............ introduced. (have been, has been)

11. The meaning of the marked passages ............ not quite clear. (is, are)

12. Neither of the men ............ the operation of the machine. (understand, understands)

## SELF-GRADING ASSIGNMENT 3

Directions: Read the sentence carefully and decide whether the subject is singular or plural. Cross out the *incorrect verb* enclosed in parentheses.

Example: All (was, were) present at the meeting.

1. None of the money (was, were) spent.

2. Some of the pencils (is; are) sharp.

3. All of the tires (is, are) new.

4. None of the employees (was, were) late.

5. (Is, Are) either of the salesmen going to the New York office?

6. Somebody always (pay, pays) the price in the end.

7. (Have, Has) any of the men reported?

8. Every boy and girl (expect, expects) a gift.

9. Not one of the books (belong, belongs) to her.

10. Neither of the girls (has, have) improved her typing speed.

11. The merger of the companies (wasn't, weren't) completed.

12. Every one of the clerks (was, were) given an increase in salary.

13. Many a man and boy (enjoys, enjoy) fishing.

14. One or the other of these statements (is, are) false.

15. Both of our typists (take, takes) dictation.

## SELF-GRADING ASSIGNMENT 4

Directions: Rewrite the following sentences making any corrections that are necessary to make the verb agree with the subject. Underline the *subject*, and draw two lines under the *verb* in the corrected sentence.

Example:  It don't make any difference to me.

It does(n't) make any difference to me.

1. I ain't going with you Saturday.

2. Wasn't you pleased with our play?

3. There is twenty students in our class in composition.

4. The number of errors I make in English have decreased recently.

5. Here comes some officers from Fort Knox.

6. We was expecting a call from you.

7. Was you happy about your promotion?

8. Mary don't speak Spanish very well.

9. The tongs is near the fireplace.

10. There is several books on atomic energy in the library.

11. Each of us prepare his own breakfast.

12. Nobody were lost in the flood.

13. Both swimmers was awarded a prize.

14. The jury include three doctors.

15. There is many opportunities in the field of television.

## PROGRESS TEST SIXTEEN

This progress test should not be taken until a day or two after you have completed the assignments. The score you make on the test will then more clearly reflect your understanding of the material in the unit.

Directions: Make any necessary changes in the verbs in the following sentences to make them agree with the subject. Two sentences are correct. (*35 points*)

1. Half of the cookies is left.

2. The class have been dismissed.

3. All of the officers was present today.

4. Many a town and village have been destroyed by earthquakes.

5. My cousin, with her children, have sailed for France.

6. There was no errors in his report.

7. The jury are casting their ballots.

8. A large number of refugees is leaving the village.

9. Where is the carbon copies?

10. Some of the copies has disappeared.

11. Has the results of the election been posted?

12. There is magazines on the table in the library.

13. That set of instruments are very expensive.

14. There goes James and his friend.

15. My brother, together with his wife and sons, live here.

16. Each of the players was making every effort to win.

17. The number of applicants are not large.

18. Has any of you failed to register?

19. Either John or Harry are under suspicion.

20. A box of books were shipped to you yesterday.

21. The supervisor, as well as the clerks, deserve a raise.

22. Neither of these typewriters are in good condition.

23. Was you interested in the proposition?

24. Mother, accompanied by several friends, are going to a luncheon.

25. Mathematics, as well as physics, are difficult for Alice.

26. Both methods of preparing the report is correct.

27. The number of complaints have decreased recently.

28. Neither the producer nor the actors likes the play.

29. The reason for his failures are not known.

30. The radio don't disturb me.

31. The corporation have decided to declare a dividend.

32. The detective don't believe that story.

33. His collection of pictures are worth a fortune.

34. One hundred dollars are the cost of the operation.

35. Ten miles are the shortest distance to the next town.

## ANSWER KEY

for

## EXERCISES, ASSIGNMENTS, AND PROGRESS TEST

### Grammar Unit Sixteen

---

## CORRECT ANSWERS TO EXERCISE 1

Correct verbs are printed in **heavy type.**

1. Fresh air and exercise **build** a strong body.

2. The workman or the supervisor **is** responsible.

3. Neither John nor Fred **does** good work.

4. Clothing and food **were** sent to the refugees.

5. Either Mr. Allen or his assistant **is** in the office.

6. My friend and fellow worker **is** very capable.

7. Ben and George **are** eligible for training.

8. Where **are** the men and the boys?

9. Neither I nor my friend **was** there.

10. Neither the plot nor the acting **was** commendable.

11. Either the lawyer or the detectives **are** following the case.

12. Either the detectives or the lawyer **is** following the case.

13. Neither the clerk nor the secretary **has** appeared.

14. Our cook and housekeeper **is** ill.

15. Allen and May **were** interviewed yesterday.

## CORRECT ANSWERS TO EXERCISE 2

Correct verbs are printed in **heavy type**.

1. The crowd **was** unmanageable.

2. The regiment **are** putting on their new uniforms.

3. The public **demands** a decision.

4. Our group **is** concerned with social problems.

5. The jury **have** returned to their homes.

6. The office staff **have** not submitted their reports.

7. The band **were** tuning up their instruments.

8. The band **is** playing its fifth concert tonight.

9. The choir **were** told to bring their hymnals.

10. The committee **were** not able to agree.

11. A committee on public relations **was** appointed.

12. The class **has** been divided into sections.

13. The Board of Directors **is** meeting today.

14. The faculty **does** not approve of the new plan.

15. The office staff **is** now complete.

## CORRECT ANSWERS TO EXERCISE 3

1. The pictures from Vienna were inspiring.                    1. plural

2. The precious jewel, as well as other heirlooms, was lost.   2. singular

3. One of the players was dismissed yesterday.                 3. singular

4. The ships at the dock are ready for service.     **4. plural**

5. Two of the delegates came from the A. F. of L.     **5. plural**

6. The mother, as well as the children, dreads the **trip**.     **6. singular**

7. This book about animals is very popular.     **7. singular**

8. Opportunities for improvement are offered in adult classes.     **8. plural**

9. The letter, including the checks, was mailed today.     **9. singular**

10. A pension, together with his investments, guarantees a steady income.     **10. singular**

11. Ways of finding materials were outlined by the librarian.     **11. plural**

12. Books about the lives of successful men are always an inspiration.     **12. plural**

13. Both of the delegates look weary.     **13. plural**

14. Members of the team were entertained by the Women's Club.     **14. plural**

15. The men in the factory were opposed to the plan.     **15. plural**

## CORRECT ANSWERS TO EXERCISE 4

Correct verbs are printed in *heavy type*.

1. I heard that you *weren't* pleased with the election.

2. He *isn't* going to buy a new car.

3. The men *weren't* interested in that report.

4. The plan *doesn't* look right to me.

5. Why **weren't** you at the meeting last night?

6. That man **doesn't** need our help.

7. There **isn't** any room for doubt.

8. **Doesn't** he want an appointment?

9. Harvey **isn't** pleased with the new appointments.

10. She **doesn't** know any better.

11. We **weren't** ready for the debate.

12. **Weren't** your friends coming this evening?

13. The manager **doesn't** want to employ that man.

14. **Weren't** Fred and Harry at the stadium?

15. This door **doesn't** seem to have a lock.

## CORRECT ANSWERS TO EXERCISE 5

Correct verbs are printed in **heavy type.**

1. Some of the guests **have** left.

2. Many a town **has** been in danger of floods.

3. All of the members **were** present last night.

4. None of the money **was** spent without his knowledge.

5. All of the oil **has been** spilled.

6. **Are** any of the men working overtime?

7. Some of the work **is** not finished.

8. Each of the designs **has** its merits.

9. Neither of the men **has** paid his dues this year.

10. Several *have* already registered for the tournament.

11. Only one of the candidates *is* eligible.

12. Both of my cousins *are* going to South America.

13. Many *are* in favor of the bill against gambling.

14. Anyone *has* the right to offer suggestions.

15. None of these pears *are* fit to eat.

## CORRECT ANSWERS TO EXERCISE 6

Correct verbs are printed in *heavy type.*

1. These scissors *are* not large enough for our purpose.

2. Fifty dollars *is* the amount enclosed.

3. A large number of people *were* present.

4. A pair of pliers *was left* on the ground.

5. The number of candidates for the office *is* small.

6. Five hundred miles *is* a long distance to drive.

7. Greene and Company *has advertised* for a manager.

8. Half of the melon *is* left.

9. Here *were* found many evidences of civilization.

10. Here *come* the general and his staff.

11. Part of the audience *were* not union members.

12. Part of the building *was wrecked.*

13. Half the letters *were filed* in the cabinet.

14. A number of soldiers *have returned.*

15. The number of enlistments *has increased.*

## CORRECT ANSWERS TO ASSIGNMENT 1

Correct verbs are printed in **heavy type.**

1. A typewriter and a desk **are** always available.

2. Either Mr. Ames or his secretary **is** responsible for the error.

3. Neither Harold nor Frank **has** a car.

4. The vice-president and treasurer **has** made several recommendations.

5. The ebb and flow of the sea **attracts** a tourist.

6. Neither of the trunks **looks** large enough.

7. **Was** either of the girls present at the conference?

8. Either the maid or the housekeeper was in the room. (correct**)**

9. The committee **is** opposed to the plan.

10. The staff **was** selected by the president.

11. The group is ready to take action. (correct)

12. Her companion and secretary **is** very capable.

13. Neither **is** the correct answer.

14. Either of the secretaries **is** available.

15. The house and the grounds **are** beautiful.

## CORRECT ANSWERS TO ASSIGNMENT 2

The subject and verb are printed in **heavy type.**

1. The **president,** with his advisers, **has arrived.**

2. The **value** of these books **lies** in the illustrations.

3. The **use** of these new devices **has reduced** our expenses.

4. **Jack,** no less than his brother, **needs** assistance.

5. The **children,** as well as the widow, **receive** an allotment.

6. The **barn,** as well as the farmhouse, **was burned** to the ground.

7. This **department,** with the aid of experts, **has made** some outstanding improvements.

8. Several **copies** of his book **have been placed** in the library.

9. The automobile **industries** in this country **have developed** rapidly.

10. New **methods** of filing **have been introduced.**

11. The **meaning** of the marked passages **is** not quite clear.

12. **Neither** of the men **understands** the operation of the machine.

## CORRECT ANSWERS TO ASSIGNMENT 3

Correct verbs are printed in **heavy type.**

1. None of the money **was** spent.

2. Some of the pencils **are** sharp.

3. All of the tires **are** new.

4. None of the employees **were** late.

5. **Is** either of the salesmen going to the New York office?

6. Somebody always **pays** the price in the end.

7. **Have** any of the men reported?

8. Every boy and girl **expects** a gift.

9. Not one of the books **belongs** to her.

10. Neither of the girls **has** improved her typing speed.

11. The merger of the companies **wasn't** completed.

12. Every one of the clerks **was** given an increase in salary.

13. Many a man and boy **enjoys** fishing.

14. One or the other of these statements **is** false.

15. Both of our typists **take** dictation.

## CORRECT ANSWERS TO ASSIGNMENT 4

1. I am not going with you Saturday.

2. Were(n't) you pleased with our play?

3. There are twenty students in our class in composition.

4. The number of errors I make in English has decreased recently.

5. Here come some officers from Fort Knox.

6. We were expecting a call from you.

7. Were you happy about your promotion?

8. Mary does(n't) speak Spanish very well.

9. The tongs are near the fireplace.

10. There are several books on atomic energy in the library.

11. Each of us prepares his own breakfast.

12. Nobody was lost in the flood.

13. Both swimmers were awarded a prize.

14. The jury includes three doctors.

15. There are many opportunities in the field of television.

## CORRECT ANSWERS TO PROGRESS TEST SIXTEEN

Correct verbs are printed in **heavy type.**

1. Half of the cookies **are** left.

2. The class **has** been dismissed.

3. All of the officers **were** present today.

4. Many a town and village **has** been destroyed by earthquakes.

5. My cousin, with her children, **has** sailed for France.

6. There **were** no errors in his report.

7. The jury are casting their ballots. *(correct)*

8. A large number of refugees **are** leaving the village.

9. Where **are** the carbon copies?

10. Some of the copies **have** disappeared.

11. **Have** the results of the election been posted?

12. There **are** magazines on the table in the library.

13. That set of instruments **is** very expensive.

14. There **go** James and his friend.

15. My brother, together with his wife and sons, **lives** here.

16. Each of the players was making every effort to win. *(correct)*

17. The number of applicants **is** not large.

18. **Have** any of you failed to register?

19. Either John or Harry **is** under suspicion.

20. A box of books **was** shipped to you yesterday.

21. The supervisor, as well as the clerks, **deserves** a raise.

22. Neither of these typewriters **is** in good condition.

23. **Were** you interested in the proposition?

24. Mother, accompanied by several friends, **is** going to a luncheon.

25. Mathematics, as well as physics, **is** difficult for Alice.

26. Both methods of preparing the report **are** correct.

27. The number of complaints **has** decreased recently.

28. Neither the producer nor the actors **like** the play.

29. The reason for his failures **is** not known.

30. The radio **doesn't** disturb me.

31. The corporation **has** decided to declare a dividend.

32. The detective **doesn't** believe that story.

33. His collection of pictures **is** worth a fortune.

34. One hundred dollars **is** the cost of the operation.

35. Ten miles **is** the shortest distance to the next town.

## HOW TO OBTAIN YOUR SCORE

The test totals 35 points. To obtain your score, divide the number of your correct answers by 35. The answer will be your score on this test. For example, if you have 30 points correct, your score is 30 divided by 35 which is 86 per cent. In other words, your score on this test is 86. You can obtain your score on any of the exercises or assignments by following the same procedure.

## Practical English Grammar

## OUTLINE OF UNIT SEVENTEEN

# PREPOSITIONAL PHRASES

Page

1. ADJECTIVE PHRASES........................................................ 6

2. COMMONLY USED PREPOSITIONS............................... 7

3. ADVERBIAL PHRASES ................................................... 9

4. COMPOUND OR PHRASAL PREPOSITIONS.................... 11

5. PRONOUNS USED AS OBJECTS OF PREPOSITIONS...... 13

6. DIAGRAMMING THE PREPOSITIONAL PHRASE.......... 15

7. THE CORRECT USE OF PREPOSITIONS........................... 18

8. POSITION OF THE PREPOSITION................................... 21

9. SUMMARY OF GRAMMAR UNIT SEVENTEEN............. 23

Self-Grading Assignments................................................. 24

Progress Test Seventeen .................................................. 29

Key to Correct Answers.................................................... 31

# PREPOSITIONAL PHRASES

IN GRAMMAR UNIT TWO you learned that a preposition is a word that shows the relation between its object and some other word in the sentence. In this unit you will study the function of the phrase which the preposition introduces.

*A prepositional phrase consists of the preposition and its object.* Sometimes the noun which serves as the object of the preposition has modifiers, but the important words in the phrase are the two words—the *preposition* and the *object.*

I walked <u>down</u> the winding <u>street</u>.
      preposition             object

The girl <u>with</u> red <u>hair</u> is an artist.
      preposition   object

In the first sentence, the preposition is the word *down.* The object is *street.* The entire phrase is *down the winding street.* The two important words in the phrase are the preposition *down* and the object *street.*

In the second sentence, the preposition is *with* and the object is *hair.* The prepositional phrase is the group of words, *with red hair.*

In grammar, a **phrase** is a group of words, *without a subject and predicate,* that functions as *a single part of speech.* A prepositional phrase is a phrase that functions as an *adjective* or an *adverb.* Since adjectives and adverbs are modifiers, the prepositional phrase is also a modifier.

## ADJECTIVE PHRASES

An *adjective phrase* is a prepositional phrase that modifies a *noun* or a *pronoun*. An adjective phrase is often the equivalent of an adjective, as you will readily see from the following illustrations:

The man at the gate sold us the tickets.
　　　　　adjective phrase

We followed the path near the river.
　　　　　　　adjective phrase

In the first sentence, the prepositional phrase is *at the gate.* It is an adjective phrase because it modifies the noun *man.* The phrase, *at the gate,* is the equivalent of an adjective because it means the *gate* man.

In the second sentence, the prepositional phrase is *near the river.* This is also an adjective phrase because it modifies the noun *path.* The sentence means that we followed the *river* path. The phrase *near the river* is the equivalent of an adjective.

Like the adjective, the adjective phrase *describes* or *limits* the noun or pronoun which it modifies.

She wore a hat *with blue trimming.* (describes the hat)

He lives in the house *to your right.* (limited to a particular house)

An adjective phrase may follow the noun which it modifies, or it may be used in the predicate after a linking verb.

The accident *on the bridge* was not serious. (follows the noun)

The injured man seemed *in a daze.* (follows a linking verb)

You will not acquire skill in recognizing prepositional phrases unless you become familiar with the words that are commonly used as prepositions. This list appeared in Grammar Unit Two, and it is repeated here for reference. When you are working with the exercises and assignments, you should refer to this list until you are able to identify the prepositions that are in common use.

### Commonly Used Prepositions

| | | | | |
|---|---|---|---|---|
| above | at | by | into | toward |
| about | before | down | like | through |
| across | behind | during | near | under |
| after | below | except | of | until |
| against | beneath | for | off | up |
| along | beside | from | on | upon |
| among | between | in | since | with |
| around | but (except) | inside | to | within |

The fact that a word appears in this list does not mean that it is always used as a preposition. Many of the words that are commonly used as prepositions are also used as adverbs.

Planes were flying <u>above the city</u>. (*Above* is a preposition.)
prepositional phrase

Planes were flying <u>above</u>. (*Above* is an adverb.)
adverb

## EXERCISE 1

Enclose the **adjective phrases** in parentheses. Draw one line under the *preposition* and two lines under the *object*. On the line to the right, indicate the word that the prepositional phrase modifies.

**Modifies**

Example: James opened the door (of the car).     door
..................

1. A course in cooking was offered.     1. ............

2. The chair behind the screen is broken.     2. ............

3. The man with the highest rating was promoted.     3. ............

4. The buildings along the wharf are vacant.     4. ............

5. Did you see the messenger from the bank?     5. ............

6. The people below us looked very small.     6. ............

7. Give us a list of fifty names.     7. ............

8. The boy from Idaho won the contest.     8. ............

9. The company wanted a salesman with experience.     9. ............

10. Do you know the extent of his injuries?     10. ............

11. The notes in his diary were translated.     11. ............

12. Magazines for adults were listed separately.     12. ............

13. The ambassador from Brazil presented his credentials. 13. ............

14. Have you read the book on atomic energy?     14. ............

15. The concern needed a man with money.     15. ............

*Note: The correct answers to exercises will be found at the back of this booklet. Correct your mistakes and, if necessary, re-read the text material before going on to the next section.*

## ADVERBIAL PHRASES

An *adverbial phrase* is a prepositional phrase that modifies a *verb,* an *adjective,* or an *adverb.* Like the adverb, the adverbial phrase answers the questions: *when? where? how?* and *to what extent?* Adverbial phrases express *time, place, manner,* and *degree.*

I shall return at noon. (Phrase expresses *time.*)
<u>adverbial phrase</u>

The sailor was working <u>on the deck.</u> (Phrase expresses *place.*)
adverbial phrase

Tell the story <u>in your own words.</u> (Phrase expresses *manner.*)
adverbial phrase

In the first sentence, the adverbial phrase is *at noon.* The phrase tells *when* or at what time I shall return. It modifies the verb *shall return.* The adverbial phrase in the second sentence is *on the deck.* This phrase tells *where* or *at what place* the sailor was working. It modifies the verb *was working.* The adverbial phrase in the third sentence is *in your own words.* It tells *how* or *in what manner* you should tell the story. The phrase modifies the verb *tell.*

Adverbial phrases that modify verbs are very easy to identify. Those that modify adjectives and adverbs are not always easy to identify. The adverbial phrase that modifies an adjective usually follows that adjective. Study the following illustration carefully:

The child seemed afraid <u>of the noise.</u> (modifies *afraid*)
adverbial phrase

In this sentence, the adverbial phrase *of the noise* modifies the predicate adjective *afraid.* Adverbial phrases that modify adjectives usually follow this pattern.

## EXERCISE 2

Enclose the **adverbial phrases** in parentheses. Draw one line under the *preposition* and two lines under the *object*. On the line to the right, indicate the word the adverbial phrase modifies.

**Modifies**

Example: We arrived (at the airport) early.      arrived
...........................

1. The woman opened the telegram with trembling fingers.      1. ...................

2. During the summer we played golf.      2. ...................

3. A blackbird hopped over the grass.      3. ...................

4. The unskilled work was done by natives.      4. ...................

5. What have you in your hand?      5. ...................

6. What could you see through the telescope?      6. ...................

7. The invalid raised himself on his elbow.      7. ...................

8. We spend several hours in the library every day. 8. ...................

9. The dress was too small in the shoulders.      9. ...................

10. From her window she could see the passing ships. 10. ...................

11. In what magazines are the books reviewed?      11. ...................

12. A footfall was heard among the leaves.      12. ...................

13. The farmer planted the seeds before sunrise.      13. ...................

14. The fleeing refugee jumped into the stream.      14. ...................

15. The officers traveled by the aerial route.      15. ...................

## COMPOUND OR PHRASAL PREPOSITIONS

A preposition is not always a single word. There are a number of prepositions in common use that are made up of a group of two or more words. Such prepositions are called **compound prepositions** or **phrasal prepositions**.

Although the *compound preposition* consists of two or more words, it is regarded as a unit, or as a single preposition. The following list includes the compound prepositions that are in common use:

| | | |
|---|---|---|
| according to | for the sake of | in respect to |
| along side of | in addition to | in spite of |
| along with | in accordance with | instead of |
| because of | in case of | on account of |
| by means of | in consideration of | out of |
| by reason of | in apposition with | with reference to |
| by way of | in front of | with regard to |
| contrary to | in regard to | with respect to |

### Compound Prepositions in Sentences

In compliance with his request, we closed the account.
<u>compound preposition</u>
        prepositional phrase

According to our schedule, the job will be completed tomorrow.
compound preposition
        prepositional phrase

The president resigned on account of illness.
        compound preposition
          prepositional phrase

## EXERCISE 3

Underline the **compound prepositions** and the **objects** of the prepositions. Write **c.p.** under the compound preposition and **o.** under the object.

Example: We arranged the meeting <u>in accordance with</u> his <u>plan.</u>
                                        c.p.                o.

1. The speaker arrived on time in spite of an accident.

2. Henry met his father in front of the University Club.

3. The treasurer resigned on account of illness.

4. The judge made his decision according to the law.

5. The fish escaped in spite of my efforts.

6. The firm paid the bill in accordance with our agreement.

7. He granted my request for the sake of the family honor.

8. Contrary to our usual custom, we sold him the goods on credit.

9. A figure clothed in white came out of the old mansion.

10. From among her keepsakes, she gave me a diamond brooch.

11. We left the city on account of Mother's health.

12. We settled the boundary by way of a compromise.

13. Instead of reading, we listened to the radio.

14. The manager interviewed me in regard to the position.

15. In accordance with their custom, the parents danced first.

## PRONOUNS USED AS OBJECTS OF PREPOSITIONS

You have already learned that the object of a preposition is always in the **objective case.** When nouns are used as objects of prepositions, they do not present a problem because nouns do not have different forms for the objective case.

Pronouns do present a problem in case because some of the *personal pronouns* and the pronoun *who* have one form for the nominative case and another form for the objective case. When a pronoun is used as the object of a preposition, the form for the objective case must be used.

It is incorrect to use the forms *I, he, she, wc, they,* or *who* as objects of prepositions. They are **nominative case** forms. The correct forms to use are *me, him, her, us, them,* and *whom.* In the following sentences, all the pronouns that are used as objects of prepositions are in the **objective case:**

The speaker spoke to **me** after the meeting. (*me*—objective case)

I went to the Art Institute with **her.** (*her*—objective case)

We looked at **him** while he was dancing. (*him*—objective case)

The women prepared a dinner for **them.** (*them*—objective case)

The librarian found the books for **us.** (*us*—objective case)

For **whom** are you working now? (*whom*—objective case)

Watch the two words, *but* and *like,* carefully when they are followed by pronouns. The word *but* is a preposition when it means *except.* When the word *but* is used as a preposition, it must be followed by the objective case. The word *like* is always a preposition. It is never used as a conjunction. The word *like* must be followed by the objective case of the pronoun.

No one knew the answer **but** me. (*but*—preposition)

His son looks **like** him. (*like*—preposition)

In the first sentence, the word *but* is a preposition meaning *except.*

It is followed by the objective case of the pronoun, which is *me*. In the second sentence, the word *like* is a preposition. It is followed by the objective case of the pronoun, which is *him*.

### EXERCISE 4

Cross out the incorrect form of the pronoun enclosed in parentheses.

Example: She called for Mary and (me, ~~I~~).

1. The argument was between Mary and (me, I).

2. Please keep behind Allen and (we, us).

3. The book was written by his brother and (he, him).

4. We are going to the conference with Dan and (she, her).

5. No one stayed for the reception but (we, us).

6. He gave the part in the play to a blonde girl like (I, me).

7. To (who, whom) did you give the message?

8. I secured the tickets from (her, she).

9. Reservations were made for (we, us) by the agent.

10. The bill was paid by Jack and (they, them).

11. The child looks like you and (he, him).

12. Nobody came but (her, she) and (he, him).

13. Were you talking about (they, them) and (he, him)?

14. Everyone was frightened but (she, her).

15. Send the books to (us, we).

## DIAGRAMMING THE PREPOSITIONAL PHRASE

The following is the method generally used in diagramming a prepositional phrase:

Place the *preposition* on a slanted line which is joined to the word which the phrase modifies. Place the *object* of the preposition on a horizontal line which is joined to the slanted line. Place the *modifiers* of the object on slanted lines which are joined to the line on which the object is placed.

*Sentence:* His face was turned toward the speaker.
<u>adverbial phrase</u>

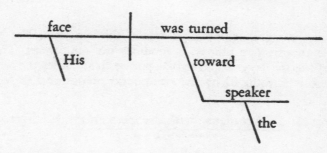

In this sentence, *toward the speaker* is an adverbial phrase modifying the verb *was turned. Toward* is the preposition, and *speaker* is the object of the preposition. *Speaker* is modified by the definite article *the.*

*Sentence:* The house at the corner was struck by lightning.
<u>adjective phrase</u>       <u>adverbial phrase</u>

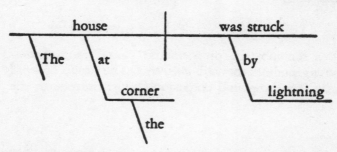

In this sentence there are two prepositional phrases. The phrase *at the corner* is an adjective phrase. It modifies the noun *house.* The phrase *by lightning* is an adverbial phrase. It modifies the verb *was struck*. Adjective and adverbial phrases are prepositional phrases.

*Sentence*:  A man in uniform stood in front of the library.
adjective phrase                 adverbial phrase

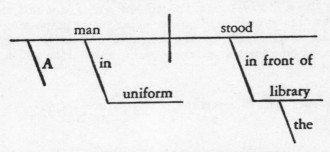

There are two prepositional phrases in this sentence. The phrase *in uniform* is an adjective phrase. It modifies the noun *man*. The phrase *in front of the library* is an adverbial phrase. It modifies the verb *stood*. This phrase is introduced by the compound preposition *in front of*.

*Sentence*:  In accordance with my instructions, I delivered the car.
prepositional phrase

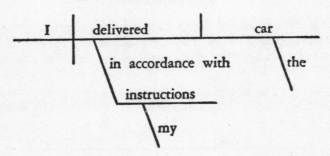

In this sentence the prepositional phrase *in accordance with my instructions* modifies the verb *delivered*. The group of words *in accordance with* is a compound preposition which introduces the phrase.

## EXERCISE 5

Diagram the following sentences. Follow the methods of diagramming that have been presented in this unit.

1. The firing of the guns caused a panic.

2. The directors met the president at the bank.

3. We went to the theater with our guests.

4. In spite of his illness, he attended the meeting.

## THE CORRECT USE OF PREPOSITIONS

Many of the common prepositions are often used incorrectly. Since a preposition expresses a relationship between the object and some other word in the sentence, the preposition that you use must be selected with care. Very often the speaker or writer is not aware of the distinctions in meaning that careful writers and speakers observe in using prepositions.

The following are some of the prepositions that you should use with discrimination. As a student of language, you should be aware of the distinctions in meaning that are indicated here. Success in writing and speaking depends to a great extent upon the choice of words. For that reason, care should be exercised in choosing words that convey the exact meaning intended.

### Differences in Meaning

1. **Around, about.** *Around* means encircling. *About* often means approximately. Do not use *around* when you mean approximately.

The fish weighed *around* three pounds. (incorrect)

The fish weighed *about* two pounds. (correct)

She tied a ribbon *about* her head. (incorrect)

She tied a ribbon *around* her head. (correct)

2. **Agree to, agree with.** One *agrees to* a proposal, but *agrees with* a person.

The members *agreed with* the president. (correct—*person*)

I *agree to* your plan for saving money. (correct—*proposal*)

3. **Beside, besides.** *Beside* means by the side of. *Besides* means in addition to.

Margaret sat *beside* her father. (*by the side of*)

There were three *besides* Jerry in the boat. (*in addition to*)

4. **Between, among.** *Between* is used when referring to two. *Among* is used when referring to more than two.

Frank and Harry divided the money *between* them. (*two persons*)

The money was divided *among* the five heirs. (*more than two*)

5. **Differ with, differ from.** One differs *with a person* in the matter of opinion. A person or thing *differs from* another in certain respects; that is, it is *unlike* another in certain respects.

I *differ with* you about his qualifications. (*matter of opinion*)

Maine *differs from* Florida in many ways. (*in certain respects*)

6. **Different from, different than.** *Different from* is correct. Do not use *different than*, which is incorrect.

The motion picture is *different from* the book. (correct)

The motion picture is *different than* the book. (incorrect)

7. **In, into.** The preposition *in* indicates location or motion within a place. *Into* indicates motion *toward the inside* of a place from the outside.

The tea was held *in* the garden. (*within a place*)

The swimmer jumped *into* the pool. (*from the outside*)

He swam *in* the pool. (*motion within a place*)

8. **In back of, behind.** *In back of* should never be used for *behind*.

> The car is *in back of* the house. (incorrect)

> The car is *behind* the house. (correct)

9. **Over, more than.** *Over* expresses the idea of *place*. *More than* expresses the idea of *quantity*.

> The actress has *over* a hundred dresses. (incorrect)

> The actress has *more than* a hundred dresses. (correct)

> She wore a cape *over* her shoulders. (correct—*place*)

10. **Outside of, except.** Do not use *outside of* when you mean *except*.

> No one went *outside of* James. (incorrect)

> No one went *except* James. (correct)

11. **To, too.** The preposition *to* should not be confused with the adverb *too*.

> I am going *to* the Dunes. (preposition *to*)

> Will you go, *too*? (adverb, meaning *also*)

12. **Within, inside of.** Do not use *inside of* to express time. Use *within*.

> He will leave *inside of* a week. (incorrect)

> He will leave *within* a week. (correct)

13. **In regard to, with regard to.** Do not say *in regards to* or *with regards to*. The correct expressions are *in regard to* and *with regard to*.

> *In regards to* your order (incorrect)

> *In regard to* your order (correct)

14. **Unnecessary prepositions.** Do not use *off of* for *off*. The *of* should not be added. Always omit the unnecessary prepositions in sentences like the following:

He jumped *off of* the pier. (*of* is superfluous)

He jumped *off* the pier. (correct)

Where is he *at?* (incorrect)

Where is he? (correct)

Where is he going *to?* (incorrect)

Where is he going? (correct)

Is the rain over *with?* (incorrect)

Is the rain over? (correct)

## POSITION OF THE PREPOSITION

Many students believe that it is incorrect to end a sentence with a preposition. Very often it is more natural and more emphatic to place the preposition at the end of the sentence. In many questions, the preposition comes naturally at the end. But a preposition should not be used at the end of a sentence if it sounds awkward or changes the meaning of the sentence. The following sentences end with a preposition. The prepositions fall naturally and correctly at the end.

Whom are you looking *for?*

What kind of plane is he traveling *in?*

They sold the car you were looking *at.*

Ordinarily, the preposition should not be placed at the end of the sentence. However, many of our best writers and speakers occasionally end sentences in this way.

## EXERCISE 6

Rewrite the following sentences making any corrections that are necessary.

1. Where did you go to?

2. The temperature is around zero.

3. My skates are different than yours.

4. This picture is worth over ten dollars.

5. The building was completed inside of seven months.

6. Over three thousand people crowded into the hall.

7. Chicago differs with New York in many respects.

8. A well-known actor sat in back of me.

9. The vegetables rolled off of the cart.

10. The nurse sat besides the patient.

11. Among you and me there can be no ill will.

12. We received a letter in regards to our order.

13. The diver jumped in the water from the pier.

14. He opened the door and walked in the church.

15. There are many problems beside yours to consider.

## SUMMARY OF GRAMMAR UNIT SEVENTEEN

A **preposition** is a word that shows the relation between its object and some other word in the sentence.

A *phrase* is a group of words, *without a subject and a predicate,* that functions as a single part of speech. A **prepositional phrase** is a phrase that functions as an *adjective* or an *adverb.*

Like the adjective and the adverb, an **adjective phrase** or an **adverbial phrase** is a modifier. An adjective phrase modifies a noun or a pronoun. An adverbial phrase modifies a verb, an adjective, or another adverb.

A **compound preposition** is a preposition that consists of two or more words. A compound preposition functions as a unit or as one word.

The *object* of a preposition is always in the **objective case**. The correct form of the pronoun for the objective case should always be used as the object of a preposition. The forms *me, him, her, us, them,* and *whom* are the correct forms to use as objects of prepositions.

The word *like* is always a preposition. The word *but* is a preposition when it means *except.* When *like* and *but* are used in prepositional phrases, they should be followed by the objective case.

Ordinarily, a preposition should not be placed at the end of a sentence. Many writers and speakers occasionally place the preposition in this position. This is done for emphasis. In many questions, the preposition comes naturally at the end of the sentence.

## SELF-GRADING ASSIGNMENT 1

Directions: Draw a line under the **prepositional phrases**. On the line to the right, indicate whether the phrase is *adjective* or *adverbial*.

**Kind of Phrase**

Example: Jack studied <u>until midnight</u>.     *adverbial*

.........................

1. He made an entry in his assignment book.    1. ..................

2. The bill was paid by Martha and me.    2. ..................

3. People of strong opinions opposed the bill.    3. ..................

4. I prefer the hat with the blue trimming.    4. ..................

5. The officer sat beside the injured soldier.    5. ..................

6. Delegates from several countries met in Paris.    6. ..................

7. Did you get the announcement of her wedding?    7. ..................

8. The accident occurred near the river.    8. ..................

9. Dresses for women were displayed at the convention.    9. ..................

10. We walked through the house with the agent.    10. ..................

11. The men with superior records were interviewed.    11. ..................

12. The book is arranged by chapters.    12. ..................

13. The unusual sound came from the bird's wings.    13. ..................

14. We heard the sound of marching feet.    14. ..................

15. One should read books about other countries.    15. ..................

*Caution: Check your answers to each assignment with the answer key at the back of the booklet before proceeding with the next assignment.*

## SELF-GRADING ASSIGNMENT 2

Directions: On the line to the right, indicate the *form of the pronoun* enclosed in parentheses that should be used in the sentence.

**Correct Form of Pronoun**

Example: I sat near (they, them).                      them
........................

1. Bicycles were given to William and (he, him).      1. ...................

2. I should like to go to Mexico with (they, them).   2. ...................

3. I stood behind (her, she) and (he, him).           3. ...................

4. Did you get the books for (we, us)?                4. ...................

5. I received a message from Grace and (her, she).    5. ...................

6. Some of (us, we) girls are going to a camp.        6. ...................

7. Everyone was frightened but (her, she).            7. ...................

8. The office manager spoke well of Alfred and
   (he, him).                                         8. ...................

9. Behind (who, whom) did you sit?                    9. ...................

10. The clerk brought a message to (we, us).          10. ...................

11. To (who, whom) am I indebted for this favor?      11. ...................

12. Does Janice look like (me, I)?                    12. ...................

13. With (who, whom) did you drive to the lake?       13. ...................

14. There is a close friendship between Alfred and
    (I, me).                                          14. ...................

15. We went to the theater with Tom and (her,
    she).                                             15. ...................

## SELF-GRADING ASSIGNMENT 3

Directions: On the line to the right, write the word *correct* after the sentence in which the preposition is used correctly. Write *incorrect* after the sentence in which the preposition is used incorrectly.

1. We had six blankets **besides** mine at the camp.     1. ................
   We had six blankets **beside** mine at the camp.     ................

2. Pamphlets were thrown **between** the crowd.     2. ................
   Pamphlets were thrown **among** the crowd.     ................

3. **About** sixty pounds of paper was delivered.     3. ................
   **Around** sixty pounds of paper was delivered.     ................

4. Robert dived **into** the water from the pier.     4. ................
   Robert dived **in** the water from the pier.     ................

5. The committee **differed from** me in regard to our future plans.     5. ................
   The committee **differed with** me in regard to our future plans.     ................

6. The messenger stepped **in** the room.     6. ................
   The messenger stepped **into** the room.     ................

7. The factory will be ready **inside of** two weeks.     7. ................
   The factory will be ready **within** two weeks.     ................

8. Where are you living **at** now?     8. ................
   Where are you living now?     ................

9. Louis stepped **off** the train at four o'clock.　　9. ..................

　　Louis stepped **off of** the train at four o'clock.　　..................

10. It was **around** seven when the director appeared.　10. ..................

　　It was **about** seven when the director appeared.　　..................

11. There is peace **between** the two nations.　　11. ..................

　　There is peace **among** the two nations.　　..................

12. We sat **besides** the fire until midnight.　　12. ..................

　　We sat **beside** the fire until midnight.　　..................

13. My standards of living are **different from** yours.　13. ..................

　　My standards of living are **different than** yours.　　..................

14. Is the storm over **with**?　　14. ..................
　　Is the storm over?　　..................

15. The manager has **agreed to** my proposition.　　15. ..................

　　The manager has **agreed with** my proposition.　　..................

16. The general sat **in back of** me.　　16. ..................

　　The general sat **behind** me.　　..................

17. Mary's costume is **different than** mine.　　17. ..................

　　Mary's costume is **different from** mine.　　..................

18. He interviewed Fred **in regards to** a position.　18. ..................

　　He interviewed Fred **in regard to** a position.　　..................

## SELF-GRADING ASSIGNMENT 4

Directions: Diagram the following sentences. Use the methods of diagramming that have been presented in this unit:

1. The pilot stood at the head of the runway.

2. The author wrote a story about his travels.

3. Turn the boat toward the south.

## PROGRESS TEST SEVENTEEN

This progress test should not be taken until a day or two after you have completed the assignments. The score you make on the test will then more clearly reflect your understanding of the material in the unit.

Directions: Rewrite the following sentences, making any corrections that are necessary. (*32 points*)

1. The engineer needed over a hundred men.

2. The officer was speaking to Bob and I.

3. Were you sending the books to us and to they?

4. The speaker will be here around eight o'clock.

5. Your television set is different than mine.

6. None were invited outside of the family.

7. The argument was between Harry and I.

8. The boy fell off of the fence.

9. Father has agreed with my plan for saving money.

10. I found the will in back of the mantel.

11. Who did you give the letter to?

12. There were only two players beside Frank.

13. No one stayed for the program but he.

14. Where is the inspector at?

15. Divide the candy among Carol and Eugene.

16. My sister looks very much like I.

17. Gerald completed the course inside of three years.

18. For who was that typewriter purchased?

19. I differ from you in regard to the value of the plan.

20. We have several musical organizations beside the band.

21. I shall meet you outside of the theater.

22. I heard them talking about he and I.

23. No one stayed but the chairman and she.

24. Did you receive an invitation from we girls?

25. Your Buick car is different than mine.

26. With who are you planning to go to Europe?

27. The four men divided the money between themselves.

28. This soil is different than that found on the plains.

29. Jim fell in the pool and was almost drowned into it.

30. To who are you sending the books?

## ANSWER KEY

### for

### EXERCISES, ASSIGNMENTS, AND PROGRESS TEST
#### *Grammar Unit Seventeen*

---

### CORRECT ANSWERS TO EXERCISE 1

1. A course (in cooking) was offered.                          1. course
2. The chair (behind the screen) is broken.                    2. chair
3. The man (with the highest rating) was promoted.             3. man
4. The buildings (along the wharf) are vacant.                 4. buildings
5. Did you see the messenger (from the bank)?                  5. messenger
6. The people (below us) looked very small.                    6. people
7. Give us a list (of fifty names).                            7. list
8. The boy (from Idaho) won the contest.                       8. boy
9. The company wanted a salesman (with experience).            9. salesman
10. Do you know the extent (of his injuries)?                   10. extent
11. The notes (in his diary) were translated.                  11. notes
12. Magazines (for adults) were listed separately.             12. magazines
13. The ambassador (from Brazil) presented his credentials.    13. ambassador
14. Have you read the book (on atomic energy)?                  14. book
15. The concern needed a man (with money).                      15. man

### CORRECT ANSWERS TO EXERCISE 2

1. The woman opened the telegram (with trembling
   fingers).                                                    1. opened
2. (During the summer) we played golf.                          2. played

3. A blackbird hopped (over the grass).                3. hopped

4. The unskilled work was done (by natives).           4. was done

5. What have you (in your hand)?                        5. have

6. What could you see (through the telescope)?          6. could see

7. The invalid raised himself (on his elbow).          7. raised

8. We spend several hours (in the library) every day.  8. spend

9. The dress was too small (in the shoulders).         9. small

10. (From her window) she could see the passing ships. 10. could see

11. (In what magazines) are the books reviewed?        11. are reviewed

12. A footfall was heard (among the leaves).           12. was heard

13. The farmer planted the seeds (before sunrise).     13. planted

14. The fleeing refugee jumped (into the stream).      14. jumped

15. The officers traveled (by the aerial route).       15. traveled

## CORRECT ANSWERS TO EXERCISE 3

1. The speaker arrived on time in spite of an accident.
   c.p.              o.

2. Henry met his father in front of the University Club.
   c.p.                o.

3. The treasurer resigned on account of illness.
   c.p.        o.

4. The judge made his decision according to the law.
   c.p.        o.

5. The fish escaped in spite of my efforts.
   c.p.        o.

6. The firm paid the bill in accordance with our agreement.
   c.p.              o.

7. He granted my request for the sake of the family honor.
   c.p.              o.

8. Contrary to our usual custom, we sold him the goods on credit.
   <u>c.p.</u>                <u>o.</u>

9. A figure clothed in white came out of the old mansion.
                             <u>c.p.</u>         <u>o.</u>

10. From among her keepsakes, she gave me a diamond brooch.
    <u>c.p.</u>         <u>o.</u>

11. We left the city on account of Mother's health.
                    <u>c.p.</u>         <u>o.</u>

12. We settled the boundary by way of a compromise.
                             <u>c.p.</u>      <u>o.</u>

13. Instead of reading, we listened to the radio.
    <u>c.p.</u>   <u>o.</u>

14. The manager interviewed me in regard to the position.
                               <u>c.p.</u>      <u>o.</u>

15. In accordance with their custom, the parents danced first.
    <u>c.p.</u>            <u>o.</u>

## CORRECT ANSWERS TO EXERCISE 4

Correct pronouns are printed in *heavy type.*

1. The argument was between Mary and **me.**
2. Please keep behind Allen and **us.**
3. The book was written by his brother and **him.**
4. We are going to the conference with Dan and **her.**
5. No one stayed for the reception but **us.**
6. He gave the part in the play to a blonde girl like **me.**
7. To **whom** did you give the message?
8. I secured the tickets from **her.**
9. Reservations were made for **us** by the agent.
10. The bill was paid by Jack and **them.**
11. The child looks like you and **him.**
12. Nobody came but **her** and **him.**
13. Were you talking about **them** and **him?**
14. Everyone was frightened but **her.**
15. Send the books to **us.**

## CORRECT ANSWERS TO EXERCISE 5

1. *Sentence:* **The firing of the guns caused a panic.**

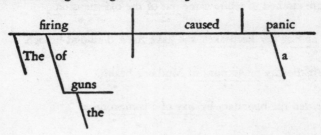

2. *Sentence:* **The directors met the president at the bank.**

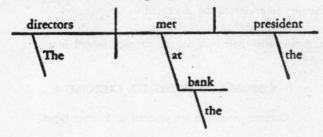

3. *Sentence:* **We went to the theater with our guests.**

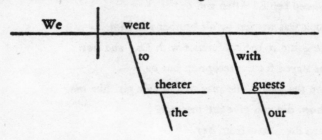

4. *Sentence:* **In spite of his illness, he attended the meeting.**

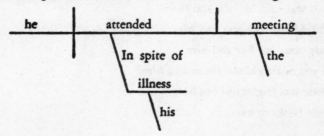

## CORRECT ANSWERS TO EXERCISE 6

1. Where did you go? (Omit *to*.)
2. The temperature is **about** zero.
3. My skates are **different from** yours.
4. This picture is worth **more than** ten dollars.
5. The building was completed **within** seven months.
6. **More than** three thousand people crowded into the **hall.**
7. Chicago **differs from** New York in many respects.
8. A well-known actor sat **behind** me.
9. The vegetables rolled **off** the cart. (Omit *of*.)
10. The nurse sat **beside** the patient.
11. **Between** you and me there can be no ill will.
12. We received a letter **in regard to** our order.
13. The diver jumped **into** the water from the pier.
14. He opened the door and walked **into** the church.
15. There are many problems **besides** yours to consider.

## CORRECT ANSWERS TO ASSIGNMENT 1

| Phrase | Kind |
|---|---|
| 1. in his assignment book | 1. *adverbial* |
| 2. by Martha and me | 2. *adverbial* |
| 3. of strong opinions | 3. *adjective* |
| 4. with the blue trimming | 4. *adjective* |
| 5. beside the injured soldier | 5. *adverbial* |
| 6. from several countries in Paris | 6. *adjective* *adverbial* |
| 7. of her wedding | 7. *adjective* |
| 8. near the river | 8. *adverbial* |
| 9. for women at the convention | 9. *adjective* *adverbial* |

| | |
|---|---|
| 10. with the agent<br>through the house | 10. *adverbial*<br>*adverbial* |
| 11. with superior records | 11. *adjective* |
| 12. by chapters | 12. *adverbial* |
| 13. from the bird's wings | 13. *adverbial* |
| 14. of marching feet | 14. *adjective* |
| 15. about other countries | 15. *adjective* |

## CORRECT ANSWERS TO ASSIGNMENT 2

| | | |
|---|---|---|
| 1. him | 6. us | 11. whom |
| 2. them | 7. her | 12. me |
| 3. her—him | 8. him | 13. whom |
| 4. us | 9. whom | 14. me |
| 5. her | 10. us | 15. her |

## CORRECT ANSWERS TO ASSIGNMENT 3

| | | |
|---|---|---|
| 1. correct<br>incorrect | 7. incorrect<br>correct | 13. correct<br>incorrect |
| 2. incorrect<br>correct | 8. incorrect<br>correct | 14. incorrect<br>correct |
| 3. correct<br>incorrect | 9. correct<br>incorrect | 15. correct<br>incorrect |
| 4. correct<br>incorrect | 10. incorrect<br>correct | 16. incorrect<br>correct |
| 5. incorrect<br>correct | 11. correct<br>incorrect | 17. incorrect<br>correct |
| 6. incorrect<br>correct | 12. incorrect<br>correct | 18. incorrect<br>correct |

## CORRECT ANSWERS TO ASSIGNMENT 4

1. The pilot stood at the head of the runway.

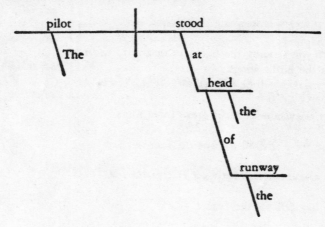

2. The author wrote a story about his travels.

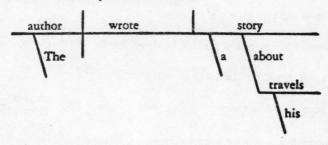

3. Turn the boat toward the south.

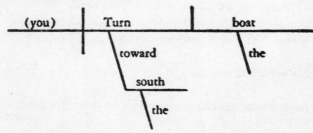

## CORRECT ANSWERS TO PROGRESS TEST SEVENTEEN

1. The engineer needed *more than* a hundred men.

2. The officer was speaking to Bob and *me*.

3. Were you sending the books to us and to *them?*

4. The speaker will be here *about* eight o'clock.

5. Your television set is *different from* mine.

6. None were invited *except* the family.

7. The argument was between Harry and *me*.

8. The boy fell *off* the fence.

9. Father has *agreed to* my plan for saving money.

10. I found the will *behind* the mantel.

11. *Whom* did you give the letter to?

12. There were only two players *besides* Frank.

13. No one stayed for the program but *him*.

14. Where is the inspector? (Omit *at*.)

15. Divide the candy *between* Carol and Eugene.

16. My sister looks very much like *me*.

17. Gerald completed the course *within* three years.

18. For *whom* was that typewriter purchased?

19. I *differ with* you in regard to the value of the plan.

20. We have several musical organizations *besides* the band.

21. I shall meet you **outside** the theater.

22. I heard them talking about **him** and **me.**

23. No one stayed but the chairman and **her.**

24. Did you receive an invitation from **us** girls?

25. Your Buick car is **different from** mine.

26. With **whom** are you planning to go to Europe?

27. The four men divided the money **among** themselves.

28. This soil is **different from** that found on the plains.

29. Jim fell **into** the pool and was drowned **in** it.

30. To **whom** are you sending the books?

## HOW TO OBTAIN YOUR SCORE

*The test totals 32 points. To obtain your score, divide the number of your correct answers by 32. The answer will be your score on this test. For example, if you have 29 points correct, your score is 29 divided by 32 which is 90 per cent. In other words, your score on this test is 90. You can obtain your score on any of the exercises or assignments by following the same procedure.*

**Practical English Grammar**

## OUTLINE OF UNIT EIGHTEEN

# THE COMPOUND SENTENCE

Page

1. KINDS OF CLAUSES............................................................ 5

2. THE SIMPLE SENTENCE .................................................. 7

3. THE COMPOUND SENTENCE.......................................... 9

4. CO-ORDINATE CONJUNCTIONS ................................... 10

5. USE OF THE SEMICOLON IN THE COMPOUND SENTENCE ................................................. 13

6. THE COMMA FAULT...................................................... 13

7. THE RUN-ON SENTENCE .............................................. 15

8. TRANSITIONAL WORDS................................................. 18

9. DIAGRAMMING THE COMPOUND SENTENCE............ 21

10. SUMMARY OF GRAMMAR UNIT EIGHTEEN.............. 23

*Self-Grading Assignments*.................................................. 25

*Progress Test Eighteen*....................................................... 29

*Key to Correct Answers*...................................................... 31

# THE COMPOUND SENTENCE

U P TO this point in your study of grammar, you have been working with four types of sentences: *declarative, interrogative, imperative,* and *exclamatory sentences.* You have learned that a particular sentence falls into one of these groups according to the purpose which it serves.

When you make a statement, you use a declarative sentence, but when you ask a question, you use an interrogative sentence. If your purpose is to issue a command or make a request, you use the imperative sentence. When you want to express strong feeling or sudden emotion, you use an exclamatory sentence.

## KINDS OF CLAUSES

There is still another way of classifying sentences. This classification is based upon the internal structure of the sentence or the way in which it is built up. Thus far, we have been dealing with the sentence that has the simplest form of internal structure—the *simple sentence.* We have been dealing with the simple sentence because our chief problem has been the relationships that words have to each other.

In this unit you will begin a study of the more complicated sentence patterns. You will learn how to build up sentences in a number of different ways. This knowledge will enable you to express your ideas in a variety of ways and will give you more power over language.

The type of classification of sentences which you will study is based upon the *number* and *kinds* of **clauses** which a sentence contains. According to this classification, sentences are divided into four groups: *simple, compound, complex,* and *compound-complex.* In this unit we shall limit our study to the simple sentence and the compound sentence.

Before you can understand the difference between a simple sentence and a compound sentence, you must have a very clear idea of what is meant by a clause in grammar.

A **clause** is a group of words that has a *subject* and a *predicate.* There are two kinds of clauses: *independent* or *main* clauses and *dependent* or *subordinate* clauses.

## INDEPENDENT CLAUSES

An **independent clause** is a group of words that has a subject and a predicate. An independent clause does not depend upon anything else for its meaning. It expresses a complete thought. An independent clause is a simple sentence when it stands alone.

The officer blew his whistle and the cars stopped.
     independent clause             independent clause

In this sentence, there are two independent clauses. The first independent clause is *The officer blew his whistle.* The second independent clause is *the cars stopped.* These clauses could be written as two simple sentences by omitting the conjunction *and.* The conjunction *and* does not belong to either of the independent clauses. It simply brings the two independent clauses together in one sentence.

The officer blew his whistle.    The cars stopped.
     simple sentence            simple sentence

## SUBORDINATE CLAUSES

A **subordinate clause** is a group of words that has a subject and a predicate, *but the clause cannot stand alone.* A subordinate clause does not express a complete thought. It depends upon the main clause for its meaning. The connective, or the word that introduces the subordinate clause, plays an important part in making it a dependent clause. An illustration will make this clear:

The cars stopped when the officer blew his whistle.
     main clause             subordinate clause

In this sentence, the group of words, *when the officer blew his whistle,* is a subordinate clause. It cannot stand alone although it has both a subject and a predicate. The word *when,* which introduces the clause, makes the words which follow it dependent upon the main clause for the meaning. That is the reason why the clause, *when the officer blew his whistle,* is called a dependent or a subordinate clause.

The group of words, *the cars stopped,* is an independent clause. It could stand alone. It is the main clause in the sentence because it states the main idea in the sentence.

## THE SIMPLE SENTENCE

A **simple sentence** is a sentence having *one* subject and *one* predicate, either or both of which may be *compound*. A simple sentence consists of one and only one independent clause. All of the following sentences are simple sentences, but some have compound subjects or predicates. The last sentence has both a compound subject and a compound predicate.

John joined the Navy.

John and Fred joined the Marines.
compound subject

Mary sang and played at the concert.
compound predicate

Mary and Jane sang and played at the concert.
compound subject     compound predicate

Note that a compound subject does not mean two subjects. It means that *one* subject is made up of two or more nouns or pronouns. A *compound predicate* does not mean two predicates. It means that *one* predicate is made up of two or more verbs or verb phrases.

### EXERCISE 1

Draw one line under the subject *nouns* or *pronouns*. Draw two lines under the predicate *verbs* or *verb phrases*. On the line to the right, indicate whether the subject or the predicate is compound.

Example:  Mary and Don did the proofreading.          *subject*
........................

1.  The boys swept the walks and mowed the lawn.    1.  ................

2.  Harry and Jim built a canoe.                    2.  ................

3.  The stenographer wrote the letters and mailed
    them.                                           3.  ................

4. The president and the manager interviewed the candidates for the position.

4. ................

5. Paper, pencils, and erasers were piled on the top of the desk.

5. ................

6. Snow and ice covered the ground and made driving difficult.

6. ................

7. Either Charles or Henry will conduct the meeting.

7. ................

8. The money and the bonds were taken out of the safe.

8. ................

9. I sold my old car and purchased another.

9. ................

10. Both the men and the women worked overtime.

10. ................

11. Neither the employees nor the officers are satisfied with the working conditions.

11. ................

12. The editor read the manuscript and revised it.

12. ................

13. The letters and the bills have lain on his desk for a week.

13. ................

14. The typewriters have been cleaned and have been repaired.

14. ................

15. The officers left Friday and returned today.

15. ................

*Note: The correct answers to exercises will be found at the back of this booklet. Correct your mistakes and, if necessary, re-read the text material before going on to the next section.*

## THE COMPOUND SENTENCE

A **compound sentence** is a sentence that *contains two or more independent clauses.* The independent clauses of a compound sentence must be joined in some way to indicate that the independent clauses form one sentence.

When you put two independent clauses or two simple sentences together to form one longer sentence, you have a compound sentence:

John joined the Navy. (simple sentence)

Harry joined the Marines. (simple sentence)

If you join these two simple sentences in order to make a compound sentence, you have the problem of punctuation and the problem of using a conjunction. The following sentences show the ways in which two simple sentences might be joined to form one compound sentence:

John joined the Navy, **but** Harry joined the Marines. *(comma* and *conjunction)*

John joined the Navy; Harry joined the Marines. *(semicolon)*

John joined the Navy **but** Harry joined the Marines. *(conjunction only)*

From these illustrations you can see that the independent clauses of of a compound sentence may be connected in one of three ways:

1. By using a comma before a conjunction

2. By using a semicolon without a conjunction

3. By using a conjunction without a comma

All three methods of writing a compound sentence are correct. However, you will use the first method, a comma before a conjunction, much more frequently than the other two methods. You will learn more about each method of punctuation as you progress in this unit.

## IDENTIFYING THE COMPOUND SENTENCE

Some students have difficulty in distinguishing between a simple sentence with a compound subject or predicate, and a compound sentence. The point to keep in mind is that the compound sentence must be the equivalent of at least *two complete simple sentences.* Examine the following illustration carefully:

The Indian squaw cooks, sews, and builds the wigwam.

This is not a compound sentence. It is a simple sentence with a compound predicate. You could not possibly make two independent clauses out of the sentence as it is written. In order to turn it into a compound sentence, you would have to supply another subject and write the sentence as two independent clauses:

The Indian squaw cooks and sews, **and** she builds the wigwam.
<u>independent clause</u>                    <u>independent clause</u>

# CO-ORDINATE CONJUNCTIONS

The independent clauses of a compound sentence are often connected by a co-ordinate conjunction. **Co-ordinate** means of the *same rank* or of *equal rank.* **Co-ordinate conjunctions** are used *to connect words, phrases, and clauses of equal rank.* The independent clauses of a compound sentence are of the same rank; therefore, we use a co-ordinate conjunction to connect them. The co-ordinate conjunctions that are commonly used for this purpose are *for, and, but, or, nor,* and *while* when it means the same as *but.*

### Use of the Comma and Co-ordinate Conjunction

When a co-ordinate conjunction is used in a compound sentence, it is usually preceded by a comma. The comma should not be omitted unless the independent clauses are very short and the thought is closely connected. Observe the use of the comma and the co-ordinate conjunction in each of the following compound sentences:

Arthur washed our new car, **and** Ned polished it.
<u>independent clause</u>      <u>independent clause</u>

I may consider your plan, **or** I may disregard it.
<u>independent clause</u>      <u>independent clause</u>

I did not seek the position, **nor** do I want it.
<u>independent clause</u>      <u>independent clause</u>

Michael likes tennis, **but** he prefers to play golf.
<u>independent clause</u>      <u>independent clause</u>

Their team was untrained, **while** ours was highly trained.
<u>independent clause</u>      <u>independent clause</u>

Jack went to bed early, **for** he was very tired.
<u>independent clause</u>      <u>independent clause</u>

In modern writing, the comma is often omitted before the conjunctions *and* and *or*. Careful writers, however, usually place a comma before the conjunctions *but* and *for*. If a comma is not placed before the word *for* when it is used as a co-ordinate conjunction, it might be mistaken for a preposition.

## EXERCISE 2

On the line to the right, indicate whether the sentence is a *simple sentence* or a *compound sentence*. Underline the *independent clauses* in the compound sentences.

1. Jack and Ned built the garage and painted it.    1. .................

2. We located the cabin, but the owner was not there.    2. .................

3. The architect made the plans, and the contractor carried them out.

3. ..................

4. Both the man and the boy were honored for bravery.

4. ..................

5. Eat nourishing food, or you may become anemic.

5. ..................

6. Neither the speaker nor the soloist has arrived.

6. ..................

7. The wind blew, and the rain fell in torrents.

7. ..................

8. We must finish the job, or we must give up the contract.

8. ..................

9. We found the manuscript, but it was not complete.

9. ..................

10. Obey the traffic lights, or the officer will give you a ticket.

10. ..................

11. Philip receives a commission, but I work on a salary basis.

11. ..................

12. We met the general in Italy, and we met him again in New York.

12. ..................

## USE OF THE SEMICOLON IN THE COMPOUND SENTENCE

You have learned that a comma and a co-ordinate conjunction are often used to separate the clauses of a compound sentence. Sometimes the ideas combined in a compound sentence are so closely related that it is not necessary to use a conjunction. In that case, a semicolon is used to separate the two clauses. The following are two important uses of the semicolon in the compound sentence:

1. A semicolon should be used between the independent clauses of a compound sentence *when they are not joined by a co-ordinate conjunction.* In the following sentence, there is no conjunction between the two independent clauses; therefore, a semicolon is used.

The doctor came in late; he did not stop to read the telegram.

2. When the independent clauses of a compound sentence are very long, or have *internal punctuation,* a semicolon is generally used before the co-ordinate conjunction. **Internal punctuation** means that there are commas within one or both of the independent clauses.

Shakespeare, a great dramatist, wrote a great many plays; and he also wrote a number of sonnets.

Temperamental and lazy, John managed to get along without working; but he was never contented or happy.

Both of these sentences have one or more commas in the first independent clause; that is, the first clause has *internal punctuation.* A semicolon is used between the two independent clauses even though a co-ordinate conjunction is used.


## THE "COMMA FAULT"

You have just learned that two independent clauses may be joined by a semicolon when no conjunction is used. You have also learned that two independent clauses are often joined by a co-ordinate conjunction and a comma. The point to keep in mind is that two independent clauses should not be joined by a comma unless a co-ordinate conjunction is used. When a writer uses a comma between the independent clauses of a compound sentence, he makes an error known as the "comma fault." The following sentence illustrates the "comma fault."

> The author wrote many stories for children, she also wrote a number of historical novels. *(comma fault)*

In this sentence, two independent clauses are joined by means of a comma. This is known as the *"comma fault"* because the comma is the sole connection between two independent clauses. This error may be eliminated by punctuating the sentence in any one of the three ways that have been given in this unit:

1. Use a co-ordinate conjunction after the comma:

   The author wrote many stories for children, and she also wrote a number of historical novels. *(correct)*

2. Use a semicolon between the two independent clauses:

   The author wrote many stories for children; she also wrote a number of historical novels. *(correct)*

3. Punctuate the two independent clauses as two simple sentences:

   The author wrote many stories for children. She also wrote a number of historical novels. *(correct)*

A skillful writer sometimes puts commas between the independent clauses of a compound sentence. This is done deliberately for the purpose of producing a certain effect. The clauses are usually very short and similar in length and structure. The following sentence is a famous example:

> "I came, I saw, I conquered."

## THE RUN-ON SENTENCE

The **run-on sentence error** is very similar to the *"comma fault."* The only difference is that the run-on sentence consists of two or more independent statements that are run together without any mark of punctuation, or without any connecting word. The following sentence is an illustration of the run-on sentence:

> Money provided by stockholders has helped the company purchase equipment and supplies it has also enabled the company to expand its production.

In this sentence, two independent statements have been run together without any punctuation or without any connecting word or words. The sentence might be correctly written by following any of the suggestions given for removing the *"comma fault."*

Since the run-on sentence error is commonly made, you should check your writing carefully. Be sure that you do not run sentences together without punctuation or proper connectives.

### EXERCISE 3

Rewrite the following sentences. Show two ways of punctuating them without using a conjunction. On the line to the right, indicate whether the original sentence is a run-on sentence, or whether it contains the "comma fault."

1. Ted earned money during the summer, during the winter, he went to college.

   1. ...................

2. People by the hundreds were flocking to the scene some brought their cameras with them.

   2. ...................

3. I didn't lose that money in business, I lost it in
   speculation.                                          3. ....................

4. The members of the committee will meet on
   Friday they will discuss plans for a new building.   4. ....................

5. I shall arrive on the noon train Donald will
   meet me at the station.                               5. ....................

6. The fifteenth of March is the income tax deadline
   many people send in their returns on that date.      6. ....................

7. Please call at the office at ten o'clock on Saturday
   morning, I should like to show you our new
   models.                                               7. ....................

8. A man was seriously hurt today his car skidded on
   the wet pavement.                                     8. ....................

## EXERCISE 4

Insert the necessary punctuation in the following sentences. Do not add any words. Draw a line under the independent clauses. All the sentences are compound.

1. We went to the lake but it was too cold for a swim.

2. I shall not go nor do I want you to go.

3. The office was light, airy, and cheerful we enjoyed working there.

4. The great English ship arrived at the port and the distinguished visitors came ashore.

5. My brother volunteered for military service and I followed his example.

6. I must leave now I promised to be at the club at six.

7. Mr. Adams, our manager, called for me at the office but I had gone to the bank.

8. On Tuesday, March 15, the Board will hold its regular meeting but the representative from Chicago will not be present.

9. John's sales were the highest this month Bill's sales were the lowest.

10. Dale had experienced many failures but he still held the hope of becoming a successful business man.

11. Give me the money now I shall need it to buy the new equipment.

12. I enjoy bowling but my sister's favorite pastime is reading.

13. Everything was wrong that day nothing seemed to turn out right.

14. Alice walked to the library on the way she met an old friend.

## TRANSITIONAL WORDS

There is another type of connecting word that you may use between the independent clauses of a compound sentence. The words that belong in this group are not co-ordinate conjunctions. They are sometimes called **transitional words** because they are not pure conjunctions.

Some of these words have a slight connecting force. Others have some adverbial force. But they all belong to the independent clause which they introduce or in which they are found. Connectives that belong to this group *are always preceded by a semicolon.*

Since many of these words are regarded as independent elements, they are usually set off by commas. Words like *moreover, however, therefore,* and *nevertheless* are usually set off. Words like *then, still, yet,* and *so* are seldom set off by commas when they retain their adverbial force.

Sometimes the connection is made by a group of words. Expressions like the following are transitional words and are regarded as a single connecting word: *in fact, on the other hand, that is,* etc. Study the following illustrations carefully:

The road was unpaved; **nevertheless,** we drove on in the rain.

I missed the first boat; **however,** I arrived on time.

The president introduced the speaker; **then** he sat down.

Ethel was sick; **in fact,** she had one of her usual colds.

We arrived early; **as a result,** we had time to visit with our friends.

We cannot get materials; **consequently,** we cannot finish the job.

I became tired of doing his work; **moreover,** I had my own work to do.

I did not dislike the play; **on the contrary,** I enjoyed it immensely.

## Commonly Used Transitional Words

| | | |
|---|---|---|
| accordingly | indeed | as a result |
| afterwards | likewise | at last |
| again | meanwhile | at the same time |
| anyhow | moreover | for example |
| besides | namely | for instance |
| consequently | nevertheless | for this reason |
| doubtless | next | in any case |
| eventually | otherwise | in fact |
| evidently | perhaps | in like manner |
| finally | possibly | in short |
| furthermore | still | on the contrary |
| hence | then | on the other hand |
| however | therefore | that is |
| yet | thus | in addition |

## EXERCISE 5

Underline the *transitional* or **connecting words** in the following sentences. Insert the necessary punctuation.

1. The factory is closed however your order will be delivered.

2. You have had the training therefore you should have the position.

3. I used the right key yet the door would not open.

4. We had an unusual teacher hence we mastered the subject.

5. The job was difficult nevertheless we enjoyed working on it.

6. Our stock is low consequently we cannot fill your order.

7. The injured man was in pain still he uttered no sound.

8. The janitor is not taking care of the building furthermore he is not giving us sufficient heat.

9. We worked far into the night finally we closed the office.

10. The play was wonderful indeed it surpassed my expectations.

11. I do not believe in the plan nevertheless I shall adopt it.

12. Alex waited for me for an hour then he went home.

13. Employees must follow instructions otherwise there will be considerable waste of material.

14. I can do it however I want to give you this opportunity.

15. He was pleased with our performance in fact he was very complimentary.

## DIAGRAMMING THE COMPOUND SENTENCE

In diagramming a compound sentence, the *independent clauses* are diagrammed in exactly the same way as a simple sentence. The important point in the diagram is to show the co-ordinate conjunction, the transitional word or words, or the semicolon, if no conjunction is used.

**1. Diagram Showing the Use of the Co-ordinate Conjunction.**

*Sentence*: I used the right key, but the door would not open.

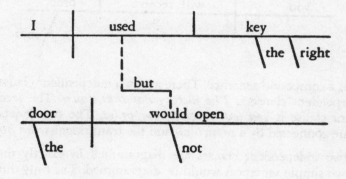

**2. Diagram Showing the Use of the Semicolon.**

*Sentence*: Some came late; others came early.

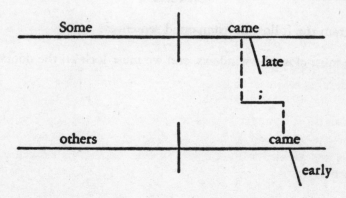

### 3. Diagram Showing the Use of the Transitional Word.

*Sentence*: The factory has shut down; however, you will receive your order.

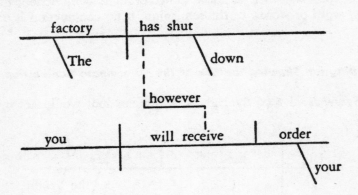

This is a compound sentence. There are two independent clauses. The first independent clause is *The factory has shut down.* The second independent clause is *you will receive your order.* The two independent clauses are connected by a *semicolon* and the transitional word *however.*

The two independent clauses are diagrammed in exactly the same way as two simple sentences would be diagrammed. The only difference is that the connection between the two clauses is shown in the diagram. The *semicolon* and the connecting word, *however,* serve to join the two independent clauses.

### EXERCISE 6

Diagram the following compound sentences:

1. We must close the windows, and we must lock all the doors.

2. The president prepared a speech, but he did not deliver it.

3. Howard is the office manager; William is the personnel director.

## SUMMARY OF GRAMMAR UNIT EIGHTEEN

According to the way in which they are constructed, sentences are classified into four groups: *simple, compound, complex,* and *compound-complex.* The structure of a particular sentence is determined by the number and kinds of clauses which it contains.

1. A **clause** is a group of words that has a *subject* and a *predicate.* There are two kinds of clauses—*independent* clauses and *dependent* or *subordinate* clauses.

2. An **independent clause** is a group of words that has a subject and a predicate. It expresses a complete thought. An independent clause is the equivalent of a simple sentence.

3. A dependent or **subordinate clause** is a group of words that has a subject and a predicate, but does not express a complete thought. It depends upon the main clause for its meaning.

4. A **simple sentence** is a sentence that has one subject and one predicate, either or both of which may be compound.

5. A **compound sentence** is a sentence that contains two or more independent clauses. The independent clauses of a compound sentence must be connected in some way. They are often connected by a comma used with a co-ordinate conjunction.

6. A **co-ordinate conjunction** is a conjunction that connects words, phrases, and clauses of *equal rank*.

7. The two independent clauses of a compound sentence are often connected by transitional words. **Transitional words** are words that are used to show the relation between two independent clauses. Many of these transitional words have some adverbial force; that is, they modify the verb in the independent clause of which they are a part. Transitional words are always preceded by a semicolon. They are usually followed by a comma.

8. A **run-on sentence** is a sentence in which two independent clauses are written as a single sentence without a co-ordinate conjunction or any mark of punctuation between them.

9. The **"comma fault"** is the use of a comma as the sole connection between two independent statements. If the comma is used for this purpose, a co-ordinate conjunction should also be used.

## SELF-GRADING ASSIGNMENT 1

Directions: On the line to the right, indicate whether the sentence is *simple* or *compound*. Underline the **independent clauses** in the compound sentences.

1. John, Ted, and Anthony attended the meeting.   1. ................

2. The papers were delivered and were sold immediately.   2. ................

3. Mary likes swimming, but Jane prefers dancing.   3. ................

4. The general called in the officers and gave them their instructions.   4. ................

5. You may go home, or you may stay with Alice.   5. ................

6. I read the article, but I did not understand it.   6. ................

7. He opened the door and looked out into the darkness.   7. ................

8. We could not see the speaker, but we could hear him.   8. ................

9. The carpenters and the painters received an increase in salary last week.   9. ................

10. You stay here; I will go to the meeting for you.   10. ................

11. I will not sign the contract; moreover, I do not want you to sign it.   11. ................

12. We visited Boston, but we did not see the harbor.   12. ................

*Caution:* Check your answers to each assignment with the answer key at the back of the booklet before proceeding with the next assignment.

## SELF-GRADING ASSIGNMENT 2

Directions: Supply the necessary *punctuation* in the following compound sentences, but do not add any words. Underline **co-ordinate conjunctions,** but *do not* underline transitional words.

Example: The child screamed but nobody heard him.

The child screamed, **but** nobody heard him.

1. The lecturer will come or he will send a substitute.

2. I like to read however I have very little time at my disposal.

3. The parade passed by and the bystanders cheered loudly.

4. The actress arrived early as a result she had time for an interview.

5. You have your orders pay close attention to every detail.

6. The clerk telephoned the office then she went home.

7. I cannot afford a new car besides I have an old Ford.

8. Nothing was left in the town the bombs had destroyed everything.

9. His work was not satisfactory nevertheless they kept him in the firm.

10. The players were well trained however they lost the game.

11. I will not accept the position nor do I want you to take it.

12. You must relax or you will become ill.

13. The returns of the election were tabulated but they were not published.

14. I studied in France but my brother was educated in Italy.

15. Sylvia sang for us and Bob played the violin.

## SELF-GRADING ASSIGNMENT 3

Directions: *Punctuate* the following sentences correctly. Draw a line under the **transitional words** that are used to connect the two clauses.

1. It is raining today in fact it has been raining all week.

2. Thomas has a large vocabulary as a result he passed the English test.

3. I refused the assignment at the same time I wanted it.

4. Skiing is an exciting sport on the other hand golf is less strenuous.

5. The chairman introduced the speaker then he left the hall.

6. I had to discipline Ned still I wished there had been another way.

7. He has no money in short he is penniless.

8. The piano was too large besides the price was too high.

9. The rainfall has been heavy consequently we expect a flood.

10. There wasn't a scratch on the body of the car in fact it looked like new.

11. Norman was lazy furthermore he was destitute.

12. Climbing the hill was strenuous however everyone enjoyed it.

13. The director did not criticize the play on the contrary he was enthusiastic about it.

14. Carl spent his inheritance consequently he had to find a job.

15. All of the men favored the plan as a result we adopted it.

## SELF-GRADING ASSIGNMENT 4

Directions: Diagram the following compound sentences:

1. The guides warned us; however, we began the climb up the mountain.

2. John had the necessary experience; nevertheless, he refused the position.

3. The directors favored the plan; in fact, they adopted it.

### PROGRESS TEST EIGHTEEN

This progress test should not be taken until a day or two after you have completed the assignments. The score you make on the test will then more clearly reflect your understanding of the material in the unit.

Directions: Supply the necessary *punctuation* in the following compound sentences. Do not add any words. Underline the **co-ordinate conjunctions** and the **transitional words**. (*60 points*)

1. Roger will take the course however it will not prepare him for the state examination.

2. Mr. Atkins would not renew the contract moreover he refused to buy any more merchandise.

3. George is an excellent swimmer but he cannot match David's record.

4. Marian is becoming very thrifty she even refuses to buy new clothes.

5. Jerry was late this morning in fact he is late almost every morning.

6. Our first plan failed however we were not discouraged.

7. The weather was cold and rainy for this reason we remained at home.

8. You may pay for the furniture now or you may charge it on your account.

9. The sea was rough and the sky looked threatening.

10. There are two motion picture theaters in the town one is on Main Street.

11. During the winter, Harold worked at the bank during the summer, he traveled.

12. There was nothing left in the entire area the fire had destroyed all the buildings.

13. Everybody applauded consequently we waited for an encore.

14. Fred played tennis all summer but he never won a game.

15. The postman hurried down the street then he stopped suddenly.

16. It was a beautiful scene but the rider did not notice it he looked straight ahead.

17. Many came to the city to see the Fair a few remained overnight.

18. Jane is very ill however her physician promises a permanent recovery.

19. Alice belongs to the club therefore she has special privileges.

20. Jean is too young for the position on the other hand she is the only one trained to do the work.

21. Edward refused to save his money consequently he could not go to the mountains with us.

22. We do not like to sign a lease now on the other hand we cannot afford to lose this opportunity.

23. We wanted to feature Ellen in the play but she became very ill consequently we trained Martha.

24. We could not find a suitable hall hence there will not be a meeting on Thursday.

25. I paid all the outstanding bills today as a result I cannot loan you the money.

**ANSWER KEY**

for

EXERCISES, ASSIGNMENTS, AND PROGRESS TEST

*Grammar Unit Eighteen*

---

## CORRECT ANSWERS TO EXERCISE 1

**Compound**

1. The boys swept the walks and mowed the lawn.

    1. *predicate*

2. Harry and Jim built a canoe.

    2. *subject*

3. The stenographer wrote the letters and mailed them.

    3. *predicate*

4. The president and the manager interviewed the candidates for the position.

    4. *subject*

5. Paper, pencils, and erasers were piled on the top of the desk.

    5. *subject*

6. Snow and ice covered the ground and made driving difficult.

    6. *subject* *predicate*

7. Either Charles or Henry will conduct the meeting.

    7. *subject*

8. The money and the bonds were taken out of the safe.

    8. *subject*

9. I sold my old car and purchased another.

    9. *predicate*

10. Both the men and the women worked overtime.

    10. *subject*

11. Neither the employees nor the officers are satisfied with the working conditions.

    11. *subject*

12. The editor read the manuscript and revised it.

    12. *predicate*

13. The letters and the bills have lain on his desk for a week.

    13. *subject*

14. The typewriters have been cleaned and have been repaired.

    14. *predicate*

15. The officers left Friday and returned today.

    15. *predicate*

## CORRECT ANSWERS TO EXERCISE 2

1. Jack and Ned built the garage and painted it.    1. *simple*
2. We located the cabin, but the owner was not there.    2. *compound*
3. The architect made the plans, and the contractor carried them out.    3. *compound*
4. Both the man and the boy were honored for bravery.    4. *simple*
5. Eat nourishing food, or you may become anemic.    5. *compound*
6. Neither the speaker nor the soloist has arrived.    6. *simple*
7. The wind blew, and the rain fell in torrents.    7. *compound*
8. We must finish the job, or we must give up the contract.    8. *compound*
9. We found the manuscript, but it was not complete.    9. *compound*
10. Obey the traffic lights, or the officer will give you a ticket.    10. *compound*
11. Philip receives a commission, but I work on a salary basis.    11. *compound*
12. We met the general in Italy, and we met him again in New York.    12. *compound*

## CORRECT ANSWERS TO EXERCISE 3

1. Ted earned money during the summer; during the winter, he went to college.    1. comma fault

    Ted earned money during the summer. During the winter, he went to college.

2. People by the hundreds were flocking to the scene; some brought their cameras with them.    2. run-on sentence

    People by the hundreds were flocking to the scene. Some brought their cameras with them.

3. I didn't lose that money in business; I lost it by speculation.    3. comma fault

    I didn't lose that money in business. I lost it by speculation.

4. The members of the committee will meet on Friday; they will discuss plans for a new building.    4. run-on sentence

The members of the committee will meet on Friday.
They will discuss plans for a new building.

5. I shall arrive on the noon train; Donald will meet me     5. **run-on sentence**
at the station.

I shall arrive on the noon train. Donald will meet me
at the station.

6. The fifteenth of March is the income tax deadline;     6. **run-on sentence**
many people send in their returns on that date.

The fifteenth of March is the income tax deadline.
Many people send in their returns on that date.

7. Please call at the office at ten o'clock on Saturday     7. **comma fault**
morning; I should like to show you our new models.

Please call at the office at ten o'clock on Saturday
morning. I should like to show you our new models.

8. A man was seriously hurt today; his car skidded on     8. **run-on sentence**
the wet pavement.

A man was seriously hurt today. His car skidded on
the wet pavement.

## CORRECT ANSWERS TO EXERCISE 4

1. We went to the lake, but it was too cold for a swim.

2. I shall not go, nor do I want you to go.

3. The office was light, airy, and cheerful; we enjoyed working there.

4. The great English ship arrived at the port, and the distinguished visitors came ashore.

5. My brother volunteered for military service, and I followed his example.

6. I must leave now; I promised to be at the club at six.

7. Mr. Adams, our manager, called for me at the office; but I had gone to the bank.

8. On Tuesday, March 15, the Board will hold its regular meeting; but the representative from Chicago will not be present.

9. John's sales were the highest this month; Bill's sales were the lowest.

10. Dale had experienced many failures, but he still held the hope of becoming a successful business man.

11. Give me the money now; I shall need it to buy the new equipment.

12. I enjoy bowling, but my sister's favorite pastime is reading.

13. Everything was wrong that day; nothing seemed to turn out right.

14. Alice walked to the library; on the way, she met an old friend.

## CORRECT ANSWERS TO EXERCISE 5

Transitional words are printed in **heavy type**.

1. The factory is closed; **however,** your order will be delivered.

2. You have had the training; **therefore,** you should have the position.

3. I used the right key; **yet** the door would not open.

4. We had an unusal teacher; **hence** we mastered the subject.

5. The job was difficult; **nevertheless,** we enjoyed working on it.

6. Our stock is low; **consequently,** we cannot fill your order.

7. The injured man was in pain; **still** he uttered no sound.

8. The janitor is not taking care of the building; **furthermore,** he is not giving us sufficient heat.

9. We worked far into the night; **finally** we closed the office.

10. The play was wonderful; **indeed,** it surpassed my expectations.

11. I do not believe in the plan; **nevertheless,** I shall adopt it.

12. Alex waited for me for an hour; **then** he went home.

13. Employees must follow instructions; **otherwise,** there will be considerable waste of material.

14. I can do it; **however,** I want to give you this opportunity.

15. He was pleased with our performance; **in fact,** he was very complimentary.

*Note: The comma may be omitted in sentences 2, 5, 11, and 13.*

## CORRECT ANSWERS TO EXERCISE 6

**1.** We must close the windows, and we must lock all the doors.

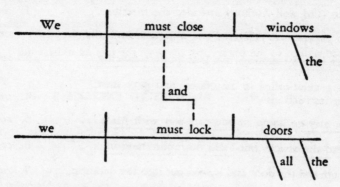

**2.** The president prepared a speech, but he did not deliver it.

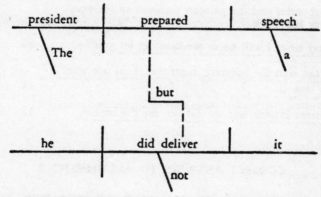

**3.** Howard is the office manager; William is the personnel director.

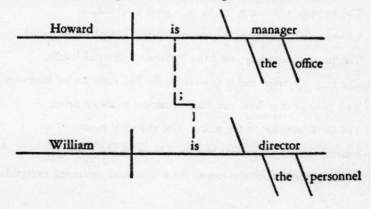

## CORRECT ANSWERS TO ASSIGNMENT 1

**Kind of Sentence**

1. John, Ted, and Anthony attended the meeting.    1. *simple*

2. The papers were delivered and were sold immediately.    2. *simple*

3. Mary likes swimming, but Jane prefers dancing.    3. *compound*

4. The general called in the officers and gave them their instructions.    4. *simple*

5. You may go home, or you may stay with Alice.    5. *compound*

6. I read the article, but I did not understand it.    6. *compound*

7. He opened the door and looked out into the darkness.    7. *simple*

8. We could not see the speaker, but we could hear him.    8. *compound*

9. The carpenters and the painters received an increase in salary last week.    9. *simple*

10. You stay here; I will go to the meeting for you.    10. *compound*

11. I will not sign the contract; moreover, I do not want you to sign it.    11. *compound*

12. We visited Boston, but we did not see the harbor.    12. *compound*

## CORRECT ANSWERS TO ASSIGNMENT 2

Co-ordinate conjunctions are printed in **heavy type.**

1. The lecturer will come, **or** he will send a substitute.

2. I like to read; however, I have very little time at my disposal.

3. The parade passed by, **and** the bystanders cheered loudly.

4. The actress arrived early; as a result, she had time for an interview.

5. You have your orders; pay close attention to every detail.

6. The clerk telephoned the office; then she went home.

7. I cannot afford a new car; besides, I have an old Ford.

8. Nothing was left in the town; the bombs had destroyed everything.

9. His work was not satisfactory; nevertheless, they kept him in the firm.

10. The players were well trained; however, they lost the game.

11. I will not accept the position, **nor** do I want you to take it.

12. You must relax, **or** you will become ill.

13. The returns of the election were tabulated, **but** they were not published.

14. I studied in France, **but** my brother was educated in Italy.

15. Sylvia sang for us **and** Bob played the violin. (Since this sentence is short, no comma is needed before *and*.)

## CORRECT ANSWERS TO ASSIGNMENT 3

Transitional words are printed in **heavy type.**

1. It is raining today; **in fact,** it has been raining all week.

2. Thomas has a large vocabulary; **as a result,** he passed the English test.

3. I refused the assignment; **at the same time,** I wanted it.

4. Skiing is an exciting sport; **on the other hand,** golf is less strenuous.

5. The chairman introduced the speaker; **then** he left the hall.

6. I had to discipline Ned; **still I** wished there had been another way.

7. He has no money; **in short,** he is penniless.

8. The piano was too large; **besides,** the price was too high.

9. The rainfall has been heavy; **consequently,** we expect a flood.

10. There wasn't a scratch on the body of the car; **in fact,** it looked like new.

11. Norman was lazy; **furthermore,** he was destitute.

12. Climbing the hill was strenuous; **however,** everyone enjoyed it.

13. The director did not criticize the play; **on the contrary,** he was enthusiastic about it.

14. Carl spent his inheritance; **consequently,** he had to find a job.

15. All of the men favored the plan; **as a result,** we adopted it.

*Note*: *The comma may be omitted in sentences 11 and 12.*

## CORRECT ANSWERS TO ASSIGNMENT 4

1. The guides warned us; however, we began the climb up the mountain.

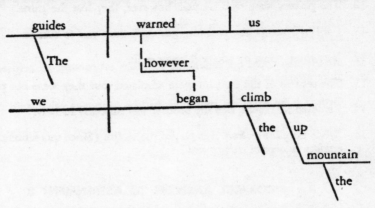

2. John had the necessary experience; nevertheless, he refused the position.

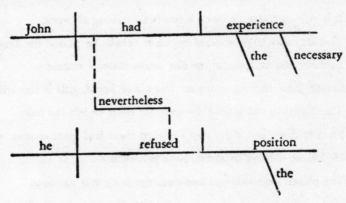

3. The directors favored the plan; in fact, they adopted it.

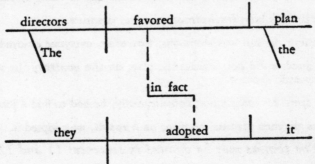

## CORRECT ANSWERS TO PROGRESS TEST EIGHTEEN

Co-ordinate conjunctions and transitional words are printed in **heavy type.**

1. Roger will take the course; **however,** it will not prepare him for the state examination.

2. Mr. Atkins would not renew the contract; **moreover,** he refused to buy any more merchandise.

3. George is an excellent swimmer, **but** he cannot match David's record.

4. Marian is becoming very thrifty; she even refuses to buy new clothes.

5. Jerry was late this morning; **in fact,** he is late almost every morning.

6. Our first plan failed; **however,** we were not discouraged.

7. The weather was cold and rainy; **for this reason,** we remained at home.

8. You may pay for the furniture now, **or** you may charge it on your account.

9. The sea was rough, **and** the sky looked threatening.

10. There are two motion picture theaters in the town; one is on Main Street.

11. During the winter, Harold worked at the bank; during the summer, he traveled.

12. There was nothing left in the entire area; the fire had destroyed all the buildings.

13. Everybody applauded; **consequently,** we waited for an encore.

14. Fred played tennis all summer, **but** he never won a game.

15. The postman hurried down the street; **then** he stopped suddenly.

16. It was a beautiful scene, **but** the rider did not notice it; he looked straight ahead.

17. Many came to the city to see the Fair; a few remained overnight.

18. Jane is very ill; **however,** her physician promises a permanent recovery.

19. Alice belongs to the club; **therefore,** she has special privileges.

20. Jean is too young for the position; **on the other hand,** she is the only one trained to do the work.

21. Edward refused to save his money; **consequently,** he could not go to the mountains with us.

22. We do not like to sign a lease now; **on the other hand,** we cannot afford to lose this opportunity.

23. We wanted to feature Ellen in the play, **but** she became very ill; **consequently,** we trained Martha.

24. We could not find a suitable hall; **hence** there will not be a meeting on Thursday.

25. I paid all the outstanding bills today; **as a result,** I cannot loan you the money.

## HOW TO OBTAIN YOUR SCORE

*The test totals 61 points. To obtain your score, divide the number of your correct answers by 61. The answer will be your score on this test. For example, if you have 55 points correct, your score is 55 divided by 61 which is 90 per cent. In other words, your score on this test is 90. You can obtain your score on any of the exercises or assignments by following the same procedure.*

**Practical English Grammar**

## OUTLINE OF UNIT NINETEEN

# THE COMPLEX SENTENCE

## ADJECTIVE CLAUSES

Page

1. THE COMPLEX SENTENCE.................................................. 5

2. KINDS OF SUBORDINATE CLAUSES................................. 6

3. ADJECTIVE CLAUSES ..................................................... 7

4. ADJECTIVE CLAUSES INTRODUCED BY
   RELATIVE ADVERBS.................................................... 10

5. "WHO" AND "WHOM" IN SUBORDINATE CLAUSES...... 12

6. RESTRICTIVE AND NON-RESTRICTIVE CLAUSES.......... 14

7. DIAGRAMMING THE COMPLEX SENTENCE.................... 17

8. SUMMARY OF GRAMMAR UNIT NINETEEN.................... 21

*Self-Grading Assignments* ................................................ 22

*Progress Test Nineteen* .................................................... 26

*Key to Correct Answers*.................................................... 28

# THE COMPLEX SENTENCE

IN GRAMMAR UNIT EIGHTEEN you learned how to form a compound sentence by combining two or more simple sentences into one longer sentence. You also learned how to punctuate the compound sentence when a co-ordinate conjunction is used, when transitional words are used, and when no conjunction is used.

The compound sentence is an important type of sentence because it enables us to combine two or more related ideas. However, it is just as ineffective to use a number of compound sentences strung along with *ands* and *buts* as it is to use a number of short, choppy sentences.

In this unit you will learn how to use a type of sentence that will enable you to put less important ideas in subordinate positions in the sentence. This type of sentence is called the *complex sentence.*

A **complex sentence** is a sentence that consists of *one independent clause* and *one or more subordinate clauses. Subordinate* means lower in rank, power, or importance. A subordinate clause is less important than an independent clause because it depends upon the main clause for its meaning.

A **subordinate clause** is a group of words that has a subject and a predicate, but *cannot stand alone.* A subordinate clause does not express a complete thought. It should never be punctuated as if it were a complete sentence.

A subordinate clause is usually introduced by some type of *subordinate conjunction* or by a *relative pronoun.* These connecting words make it clear that the clause expresses an idea that is subordinate to the main clause. They also join the subordinate clause to some word in the independent clause.

### Complex Sentences

I shall be at the station when you arrive.
<u>independent clause</u>    <u>subordinate clause</u>

I shall not go to the park if it rains.
<u>independent clause</u>    <u>subordinate clause</u>

She wore a beautiful dress which her grandmother had worn.
<u>independent clause</u>    <u>subordinate clause</u>

In the first sentence, the subordinate clause is *when you arrive.* The clause is introduced by the **subordinate conjunction** *when.* The group of words, *when you arrive,* has a subject and a predicate, but it cannot stand alone. That is the reason why the clause is called a *subordinate clause.* It depends upon the main clause for its meaning.

The subordinate clause in the second sentence is *if it rains.* This group of words cannot stand alone. The clause is introduced by the subordinate conjunction *if.* This conjunction helps the subordinate clause express the idea that there is a condition upon which *my going* depends.

The subordinate clause in the third sentence is *which her grandmother had worn.* This clause is introduced by the relative pronoun *which.* The word *which* refers to the word *dress* in the independent clause. It also introduces the subordinate clause. A **relative pronoun** always joins a clause to the *antecedent* of the pronoun. In this sentence, the antecedent of the relative pronoun is *dress. Dress* is the word to which the pronoun refers.

The relative pronoun also has an important function in the subordinate clause. It might be the subject of the clause, the object of the verb in the clause, the object of a preposition, or a predicate pronoun after a linking verb.

## KINDS OF SUBORDINATE CLAUSES

There are three kinds of subordinate clauses: *adverbial clauses, adjective clauses,* and *noun clauses.* Each of these different types is used as a part of speech. That is why subordinate clauses are called adverbial clauses, adjective clauses, and noun clauses.

The **adverbial clause** functions as an adverb. The **adjective clause** functions as an adjective, and the **noun clause** functions as a noun.

Adverbs modify verbs, adjectives, and other adverbs. Adverbial clauses also modify verbs, adjectives, and adverbs. Adjectives modify nouns and pronouns. Adjective clauses also modify nouns and pronouns. Nouns are used as subjects of sentences, as objects of verbs, and as objects of prepositions. Noun clauses are used in the same ways.

### Subordinate Clauses

The man who received the medal was my uncle.
adjective clause

We always stop working when the bell rings.
adverbial clause

I believe that the bookkeeper is honest.
noun clause

In the first sentence, the subordinate clause is the group of words, *who received the medal.* The subordinate clause is an **adjective clause** and modifies the word *man.* In the second sentence, the subordinate clause is *when the bell rings.* It is an **adverbial clause** and modifies the verb *stop.* This clause expresses *time* just as an adverb expresses *time.* The subordinate clause in the third sentence is the group of words, *that the bookkeeper is honest.* This subordinate clause is a **noun clause** and is used as the object of the verb *believe.*

## ADJECTIVE CLAUSES

An **adjective clause** *is a subordinate clause that functions as an adjective.* Adjectives are used to describe or limit nouns or pronouns. An adjective clause is also used to describe or limit a noun or a pronoun.

An adjective clause is usually introduced by a relative pronoun. A **relative pronoun** *is a pronoun that joins an adjective clause to some word in the independent or main clause.* The word to which it joins the clause is the *antecedent* of the relative pronoun. The relative pronouns used in this way are *who* (*whom*), *which,* and *that.*

### Adjective Clauses Introduced by Relative Pronouns

John brought the books that you ordered. (*that* — relative
adjective clause
pronoun)

I favored the plan which the senator proposed. (*which*—relative
adjective clause
pronoun)

Men who are thinkers look for facts. (*who*—relative pronoun)
adjective clause

I saw the salesman whom I met at the office. (*whom*—relative
adjective clause
pronoun)

The subordinate clause in the first sentence is *that you ordered*. It is an adjective clause and modifies the noun *books*. This clause is introduced by the relative pronoun *that*. The antecedent of the relative pronoun *that* is the word *books*. The pronoun *that* joins its clause to the word *books* in the main clause.

The subordinate clause in the second sentence is *which the senator proposed*. It is an adjective clause and modifies the noun *plan*. The antecedent of the relative pronoun *which* is the word *plan*. The adjective clause limits the meaning to the *plan which the senator proposed*.

The subordinate clause in the third sentence is *who are thinkers*. The main clause is *Men look for facts*. In this sentence the subordinate clause comes between the subject and the predicate of the main clause. The subordinate clause is introduced by the relative pronoun *who*. The antecedent of *who* is *men*.

The adjective clause in the fourth sentence is *whom I met at the office*. This clause is introduced by the relative pronoun *whom*. The antecedent of the pronoun is the word *salesman*. *Whom* is in the objective case because it is the object of the verb *met* in the subordinate clause.

### Relative Adjectives

Sometimes an adjective clause is introduced by the word *whose*, which is the possessive form of the pronoun *who*. In such cases the word *whose* modifies a noun which follows it. When the word *whose* is used in an adjective clause, it is called a **relative adjective**. The word *relative* is used to show that the word *whose* refers to its antecedent in the main clause.

That is the *man* **whose** car was stolen. (*man*—antecedent)

In this sentence the word *whose* is a relative adjective, modifying the word *car*. The antecedent of *whose* is the word *man* in the main clause. The word *whose* connects the clause *whose car was stolen* to the word *man*.

## EXERCISE 1

Underline the **adjective clauses** in the following sentences. On the line to the right, indicate the *word* the adjective clause modifies.

Example: I received the message which you sent.          *message*
...................

1. The road that leads to the house is steep.          1. ...................

2. The witness who was called last solved the mystery.          2. ...................

3. He presented a plan which they will endorse.          3. ...................

4. The girl who operates the switchboard is efficient.          4. ...................

5. Some of the men who work overtime receive double pay.          5. ...................

6. The ring which you bought is pure gold.          6. ...................

7. The book that he wrote recently will be published.          7. ...................

8. Mother invited several friends whom she met in London.          8. ...................

9. The one who wins the prize will receive a watch.          9. ...................

10. The letter which I received altered my plans.          10. ...................

11. He is the man whose factory I purchased.          11. ...................

12. I saw a play in New York that you would enjoy.          12. ...................

13. The artist whose picture won the award is my uncle.          13. ...................

14. The model whom I selected did not appear at the fashion show.          14. ...................

15. The house which was bombed was a frame building.          15. ...................

## ADJECTIVE CLAUSES INTRODUCED BY RELATIVE ADVERBS

Adjective clauses are often introduced by the relative adverbs *where,* *when,* and *why.* When these adverbs introduce adjective clauses they relate to some word in the main clause in much the same way as a relative pronoun does. A relative adverb always has an antecedent and joins its clause to that antecedent. In addition, a relative adverb performs the function of an adverb in its own clause. It is called a *relative adverb* because it relates to an antecedent.

I found the house where the poet lived. (*where*—relative adverb)
adjective clause

The doctor selected a time when I was not working. (*when*— relative adverb)
adjective clause

I discovered the reason why he is leaving. (*why*—relative adverb)
adjective clause

In the first sentence, the relative adverb is *where.* It introduces the clause, *where the poet lived.* It also refers to its antecedent, *house.* As an adverb, it modifies the verb *lived* in the subordinate clause.

The relative adverb in the second sentence is *when.* Its antecedent is *time.* The relative adverb *when* joins the clause, *when I was not working,* to its antecedent *time.* It also functions as an adverb, modifying the verb *was working.*

The relative adverb in the third sentence is *why.* Its antecedent is *reason.* It modifies the verb *is leaving* in its own clause.

The only difference between a relative adverb and a simple adverb is the fact that the relative adverb is found in an adjective clause and refers to its antecedent in the main clause. Both relative adverbs and simple adverbs modify verbs.

## EXERCISE 2

Underline the **adjective clauses** in the following sentences. On the line to the right, indicate the *relative adverb* which introduces the clause.

Example: This is the place <u>where he worked.</u>

**Relative Adverb**
where
.................

1. This is the hour when strange things may happen.

    1. .................

2. This is the spot where Harold left the car.

    2. .................

3. He lived in a time when prosperity prevailed.

    3. .................

4. I visited the place where Lincoln was born.

    4. .................

5. That was the day when I won a thousand dollars.

    5. .................

6. This is the studio where Jean studied music.

    6. .................

7. Is this the school where you were educated?

    7. .................

8. The men gathered in the coffee houses where they discussed the latest books.

    8. .................

9. He did not know the reason why he was dismissed.

    9. .................

10. We specified the time when we could play golf.

    10. .................

11. This is the corner of the lobby where we usually sit.

    11. .................

12. I should like to know the name of the place where you dine in the evening.

    12. .................

13. This is a time when there are differences of opinion regarding public policies.

    13. .................

14. April 15 is the date when income tax returns must be sent to the Collector of Internal Revenue.

    14. .................

15. This is the year when our sales will reach the highest point.

    15. .................

## "WHO" AND "WHOM" IN SUBORDINATE CLAUSES

It is often difficult to determine whether to use "who" or "whom" when one of these words is used to introduce a subordinate clause. Always keep in mind that *who* is the correct form for the nominative case, and *whom* is the correct form for the objective case.

When a relative pronoun introduces a clause, it has a double function. It joins the clause to its antecedent which is in the main clause, and in addition it performs one of the following three functions in the subordinate clause:

1. The pronoun may be the *subject* of the subordinate clause.

2. The pronoun may be used as a *predicate pronoun* after a linking verb.

3. The pronoun may be used as the *object* of the verb or a preposition.

In order to determine how the pronoun is used, it is often necessary to put the subordinate clause in grammatical order, or to transpose it.

Allen was the one *who published the report.* (*who*—subject)

In this sentence, it is clear that *who* is the subject of the subordinate clause. The form *who* is correct because the subject is in the nominative case.

The president is a man *whom everyone admires.* (*whom*—direct object)

In this sentence, the word *whom* is the direct object of the verb *admires.* By transposing the clause, you will be able to see this clearly: *everyone admires whom.* The subject of the clause is *everyone,* not *whom.*

Jack is the boy *to whom they gave the camera.* (*whom*—object of preposition)

In this sentence, the pronoun *whom* is the object of the preposition *to.* When the subordinate clause is transposed, the use of *whom* becomes clear: *they gave the camera to whom. They* is the subject of the clause, not *whom.*

## EXERCISE 3

Fill in the blank space with the form *who* or *whom*. On the line to the right, indicate the reason for your choice: *subject, direct object,* or *object* of a preposition.

1. She did not know the man to..............they were speaking.

    1. ...................

2. I suddenly saw the woman with ................ I traveled in Spain.

    2. ...................

3. The men ................ wrote our constitution had clear vision.

    3. ...................

4. There is only one writer ................ I know well.     4. ...................

5. The man................discovered oil on his farm is very wealthy.

    5. ...................

6. Mary is the one for ................ you made the coat.

    6. ...................

7. Mr. Ellis, the reporter ................ I met in New York, is very ambitious.

    7. ...................

8. The candidate ................ is well prepared should pass the test.

    8. ...................

9. Alice is the stenographer ................ the president prefers.

    9. ...................

10. Many men..............are physically handicapped will be given positions.

    10. ...................

11. Who was the agent to ................ you were speaking?

    11. ...................

12. We all enjoyed the guest ................ Mother invited.

    12. ...................

13. The man for ................ I work is an engineer.   12. ...................

14. The committee included two men ................ were opposed to the project.

    14. ...................

## RESTRICTIVE AND NON-RESTRICTIVE CLAUSES

Adjective clauses present a problem in meaning and in punctuation. Sometimes the adjective clause is set off by commas. Sometimes the adjective clause is not set off by commas. The following sentences are illustrations of adjective clauses that are *not* set off by commas:

I spoke to the woman *who was giving the demonstration.*

This is the man *who discovered the leak in the pipe.*

I dislike driving in a town *where there are no stop signals.*

In the first sentence, the adjective clause is *who was giving the demonstration.* If you leave the clause out, the meaning of the sentence is changed. The sentence now gives no indication of *who* the woman was. Since the clause indentifies that woman, it is essential to the meaning of the sentence.

In the second sentence, the clause is *who discovered the leak in the pipe.* This clause identifies the man and is essential to the meaning of the sentence. The clause restricts the meaning of the sentence to the man *who discovered the leak in the pipe.* Therefore, it is essential to the meaning of the sentence.

The third sentence does not mean that *I dislike driving in a town.* The meaning is restricted to driving in a certain type of town; that is, in a town *where there are no stop signals.*

Clauses that are necessary to the meaning of the sentence are called *restrictive clauses.* A restrictive clause is not set off by commas. A **restrictive clause** identifies the word it modifies.

Some adjective clauses are not essential to the meaning of the sentence. They give added information, but the essential meaning of the sentence would not be changed if such clauses were omitted. Study the following sentences carefully:

Mr. Miller, *who lived next door,* moved to Canada.

Will James, *who was once a cowboy,* wrote many stories.

Father, *who was working in the garden,* missed the broadcast.

The speaker, *who was accompanied by his wife,* left early.

In the first sentence, the clause, *who lived next door,* gives additional information about Mr. Miller, but the meaning of the sentence is not changed if you leave the clause out. The clause does not place any restrictions on the meaning. Therefore it is called a *non-restrictive clause.* Non-restrictive clauses are set off by commas.

A **non-restrictive clause** is a clause that is *not* essential to the meaning of the sentence. All the clauses in the preceding illustrations are non-restrictive clauses. They are set off by commas. They are not needed in the sentence to identify the person who is mentioned in the main clause.

A non-restrictive clause is a subordinate clause which is not essential to the meaning of the sentence. A non-restrictive clause functions more like an appositive or a parenthetical expression. You might call it a thrown-in remark. That is the reason why the non-restrictive clause is set off by commas.

### EXERCISE 4

Underline the **adjective clauses** in the following sentences. On the line to the right, indicate whether the clause is *restrictive* or *non-restrictive.* Supply any necessary punctuation.

Example: Don who is a pilot wrote the article.
Don, who is a pilot, wrote the article.     *non-restrictive*
........................

1. We visited Quebec which is a very old city.      1. ..................

2. The man who captured the bandit was rewarded.    2. ..................

3. Here is the spot where the pirates buried their treasure.                                          3. ..................

4. John Harvey who sat near me gave the signal.     4. ..................

5.  We are interested in advertisements that bring
    results.                                              5.  ..................

6.  The man who just knocked on the door is the
    plumber.                                              6.  ..................

7.  The road that we should have taken was not
    paved.                                                7.  ..................

8.  He receives a very large salary which he does not
    deserve.                                              8.  ..................

9.  "Treasure Island" which was written by Steven-
    son is a very popular book.                           9.  ..................

10. The play which I saw yesterday was written
    by Shaw.                                             10.  ..................

11. Our canoe which was very light bobbed up and
    down in the water.                                   11.  ..................

12. My uncle who lives near us has a new Buick.         12.  ..................

13. The winner is the man who is sitting in the
    front row of the theater.                           13.  ..................

14. The town where our business is located is in
    Pennsylvania.                                        14.  ..................

## DIAGRAMMING THE COMPLEX SENTENCE

A complex sentence consists of one independent clause and one or more subordinate clauses. The independent clause is diagrammed in exactly the same way as a simple sentence is diagrammed. Adjective and adverbial clauses are diagrammed to show that they are modifiers.

### Diagramming the Adjective Clause

*Sentence:* Jane is the girl who won the beauty contest.
                  main clause                   adjective clause

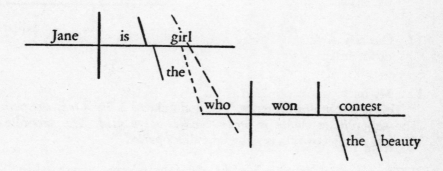

The sentence that was diagrammed is a complex sentence. The main clause is *Jane is the girl.* The subordinate clause is *who won the beauty contest.* The subordinate clause is an adjective clause. It modifies the noun *girl* in the main clause. The pronoun *who* is the subject of the subordinate clause. *Who* is in the nominative case.

The broken line in the diagram connecting *girl* and *who* is used to show that the antecedent of *who* is the noun *girl.*

### Diagramming the Adjective Clause
### (continued)

*Sentence*: That was the period when candles were used.
main clause    adjective clause

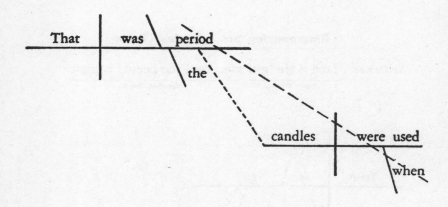

This is a complex sentence. The main clause is *That was the period*. The subordinate clause is *when candles were used*. The subordinate clause is an adjective clause which modifies *period*.

The adjective clause is introduced by the relative adverb *when*. The antecedent of the relative adverb is the noun *period* in the main clause. The adverb *when* also modifies the verb *were used* in the subordinate clause.

The broken line in the diagram connecting *period* and *when* is used to show that the antecedent of *when* is the noun *period*. The subordinate clause is diagrammed to show that it modifies *period*.

## Diagramming the Adjective Clause
### (continued)

*Sentence*: The delegates <u>whose terms had expired</u> left yesterday.
adjective clause

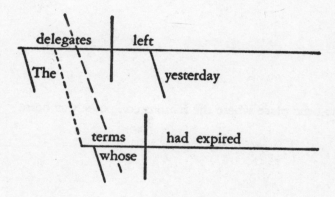

This is a complex sentence. The main clause is *The delegates left yesterday.* The subordinate clause is *whose terms had expired.* The subordinate clause is introduced by the relative adjective *whose.*

The antecedent of the pronoun *whose* is the noun *delegates.* The pronoun *whose* has a special function in the subordinate clause. It is used as a relative adjective, modifying *terms.*

The broken line in the diagram connecting *delegates* and *whose* shows that the antecedent of *whose* is *delegates.* The subordinate clause is diagrammed to show that it modifies the noun *delegates.*

### EXERCISE 5

Diagram the following **complex** sentences:

1. The actress wore a dress which she purchased in Paris.

2. I visited the place where the famous composer was born.

3. People who have large incomes must pay heavy taxes.

## SUMMARY OF GRAMMAR UNIT NINETEEN

A **complex sentence** is a sentence that consists of one independent clause and one or more subordinate clauses.

A **subordinate clause** is a group of words that has a subject and a predicate, but cannot stand alone. A subordinate clause depends upon the main clause for its meaning.

There are three kinds of subordinate clauses: *adjective clauses, adverbial clauses,* and *noun clauses.*

An **adjective clause** is a subordinate clause that functions as an adjective. An adjective clause may be introduced by a *relative pronoun,* a *relative adverb,* or a *relative adjective.*

A **relative adverb** is an adverb that refers to an antecedent in the main clause and functions as an adverb in the subordinate clause. *When, where,* and *why* are commonly used as relative adverbs.

A **relative pronoun** is a pronoun that joins the subordinate clause to its own antecedent in the main clause. A relative pronoun also has an important function in the subordinate clause.

A **relative adjective** is a relative pronoun that is used as an adjective. It refers to its antecedent in the main clause and modifies a noun in the subordinate clause. *Whose* is commonly used in this way.

A **restrictive adjective clause** is a clause that is essential to the meaning of the sentence. A restrictive clause explains or identifies the word in the main clause to which it refers. A restrictive clause is *not* set off by commas. A **non-restrictive adjective clause** is *not* essential to the meaning of the sentence. A non-restrictive clause *is* set off by commas.

### SELF-GRADING ASSIGNMENT 1

Directions: Underline the **adjective clauses** in the following sentences. On the line to the right, indicate whether the word that introduces the clause is a *relative pronoun,* a *relative adverb,* or a *relative adjective.*

1.  The man who sold the house is my cousin.     1. ................

2.  The book that you sent me is very interesting.     2. ................

3.  Some employees give services which are not required.     3. ................

4.  I visited the inn where Susan and I met.     4. ................

5.  He did not know the reason that I left the hall.     5. ................

6.  She was absent at a time when we needed her most.     6. ................

7.  There was no way by which we could reach him.     7. ................

8.  This is the pebble that caused her fall.     8. ................

9.  The house where I stayed was beautifully furnished.     9. ................

10.  Lola was the one who gave the information.     10. ................

11.  The men whose records were excellent were given an increase in salary.     11. ................

12.  There were many who refused aid.     12. ................

13.  The books which Churchill writes sell rapidly.     13. ................

14.  Everett is the artist whose picture won the award.     14. ................

15.  He inherited the land from an old man whom he had befriended.     15. ................

*Caution*: *Check your answers to each assignment with the answer key at the back of the booklet before proceeding with the next assignment.*

## SELF-GRADING ASSIGNMENT 2

Directions: Fill in the blank space with the form *who* or *whom*. On the line to the right, indicate why you chose that form: *subject, direct object,* or *object* of a *preposition*.

1. I gave him the name of the agent to ............... he could apply for aid.

     1. ...................

2. Constance is the girl ............... I invited to the dance.

     2. ....... .........

3. The man ............... the lawyer is defending is a famous physician.

     3. ...................

4. She is a person ............... I have always admired.

     4. ...................

5. Two of the men ............... were chosen as delegates could not go to the conference.

     5. ...................

6. Do you know anyone ............... has a car for sale?

     6. ...................

7. In the service I met several officers ............... were educated at West Point.

     7. ...................

8. The friends ............... I visit often are those ...............like to discuss the latest books.

     8. ...................

9. It was my father to ............... you sold the car.

     9. ...................

10. He is the one ............... will become the champion.

     10. ...................

11. The manager interviewed the men ............... applied for the position.

     11. ...................

12. She is the actress of ............... I spoke.

     12. ...................

## SELF-GRADING ASSIGNMENT 3

Directions: Underline the **adjective clauses** in the following sentences. On the line to the right, indicate whether the clause is *restrictive* or *non-restrictive*. Supply any necessary punctuation.

1. My employer's son who attended Harvard plans to be a musician.
   1. .................

2. The contractor will not start building until April when the ground is soft.
   2. .................

3. Oranges which are a citrus fruit are very healthful.
   3. .................

4. The leading role which many wanted was given to Jane.
   4. .................

5. My friend attended the concert which I recommended.
   5. .................

6. Curtain material that matches the office furnishings is very expensive.
   6. .................

7. Julia who is a college graduate wants a position in New York.
   7. .................

8. A word that names a person, place, or thing is called a noun.
   8. .................

9. I sent for the book which the speaker recommended.
   9. .................

10. The men who work in our factory have hospital insurance.
    10. .................

11. The boats which belong to the members of the club are anchored in Belmont Harbor.
    11. .................

12. The flowers that you have in your hand are dahlias.
    12. .................

## SELF-GRADING ASSIGNMENT 4

Directions: Diagram the following **complex sentences,** containing *adjective clauses.*

1. He invented a machine which does the work of many men.

2. This is the place where the army surrendered.

3. The football players whom we saw were professionals.

## PROGRESS TEST NINETEEN

This progress test should not be taken until a day or two after you have completed the assignments. The score you make on the test will then more clearly reflect your understanding of the material in the unit.

Directions: Underline the **adjective clauses** in the following sentences. On the line to the right, indicate the *word* the adjective clause modifies. *(50 points)*

**Modifies**

1. This is the car that we bought last year.     1. ................

2. I have called on the customers whose names are on your list.     2. ................

3. The man who presented the speaker is a famous scientist.     3. ................

4. We recommended the hotel where I stayed in London.     4. ................

5. This is a time when we should analyze the news carefully.     5. ................

6. He told the manager the reason why he wanted to leave.     6. ................

7. Is this the diamond that you gave to Marian?     7. ................

8. New York is the city to which I referred.     8. ................

9. She is the author about whom I spoke yesterday.     9. ................

10. The books which were written by the monks were illuminated.     10. ................

11. The suits which he purchased in London were very expensive.     11. ................

## PROGRESS TEST NINETEEN (continued)

12. The girl who understands our system of
    bookkeeping will be employed.                12. ..................

13. The furniture that she treasures most belonged to
    her grandmother.                            13. ..................

14. Those who have served as officers in our club
    still retain their membership.              14. ..................

15. I remember the day when John met Frances.   15. ..................

16. There is the colonel whom I met at the club.  16. ..................

17. The girl whom you met at the station is
    my sister.                                  17. ..................

18. Here is a man who will qualify for the position.  18. ..................

19. That is the hotel where I live in the summer.  19. ..................

20. This is the hour when we listen to the radio.  20. ..................

21. They gave the prize to the one who answered all
    the questions.                              21. ..................

22. The girl who won the award is a commercial
    artist.                                     22. ..................

23. The reporter found a place where he could watch
    the game.                                   23. ..................

24. We shall send bills to those who have not paid
    their July accounts.                        24. ..................

25. The university will not accept students who have
    low scholastic averages.                    25. ..................

## ANSWER KEY

for

## EXERCISES, ASSIGNMENTS, AND PROGRESS TEST

### *Grammar Unit Nineteen*

---

## CORRECT ANSWERS TO EXERCISE 1

Adjective clauses are printed in *heavy type*.

| | |
|---|---|
| 1. The road *that leads to the house* is steep. | 1. road |
| 2. The witness *who was called last* solved the mystery. | 2. witness |
| 3. He presented a plan *which they will endorse.* | 3. plan |
| 4. The girl *who operates the switchboard* is efficient. | 4. girl |
| 5. Some of the men *who work overtime* receive double pay. | 5. men |
| 6. The ring *which you bought* is pure gold. | 6. ring |
| 7. The book *that he wrote recently* will be published. | 7. book |
| 8. Mother invited several friends *whom she met in London.* | 8. friends |
| 9. The one *who wins the prize* will receive a watch. | 9. one |
| 10. The letter *which I received* altered my plans. | 10. letter |
| 11. He is the man *whose factory I purchased.* | 11. man |
| 12. I saw a play in New York *that you would enjoy.* | 12. play |
| 13. The artist *whose picture won the award* is my uncle. | 13. artist |
| 14. The model *whom I selected* did not appear at the fashion show. | 14. model |
| 15. The house *which was bombed* was a frame building. | 15. house |

## CORRECT ANSWERS TO EXERCISE 2

Adjective clauses are printed in *heavy type.*

| | |
|---|---|
| 1. This is the hour *when strange things may happen.* | 1. when |
| 2. This is the spot *where Harold left the car.* | 2. where |

3. He lived in a time **when prosperity prevailed.**

3. when

4. I visited the place **where Lincoln was born.**

4. where

5. That was the day **when I won a thousand dollars.**

5. when

6. This is the studio **where Jean studied music.**

6. where

7. Is this the school **where you were educated?**

7. where

8. The men gathered in the coffee houses **where they discussed the latest books.**

8. where

9. He did not know the reason **why he was dismissed.**

9. why

10. We specified the time **when we could play golf.**

10. when

11. This is the corner of the lobby **where we usually sit.**

11. where

12. I should like to know the name of the place **where you dine in the evening.**

12. where

13. This is a time **when there are differences of opinion regarding public policies.**

13. when

14. April 15 is the date **when income tax returns must be sent to the Collector of Internal Revenue.**

14. when

15. This is the year **when our sales will reach the highest point.**

15. when

## CORRECT ANSWERS TO EXERCISE 3

1. She did not know the man to **whom** they were speaking.

1. object of preposition

2. I suddenly saw the woman with **whom** I traveled in Spain.

2. object of preposition

3. The men **who** wrote our constitution had clear vision.

3. subject

4. There is only one writer **whom** I know well.

4. object of *know*

5. The man **who** discovered oil on his farm is very wealthy.

5. subject

6. Mary is the one for **whom** you made the coat.

6. object of preposition

7. Mr. Ellis, the reporter **whom** I met in New York, is very ambitious.

7. object of *met*

8. The candidate **who** is well prepared should pass the test.

8. subject

9. Alice is the stenographer **whom** the president prefers.

9. object of *prefers*

10. Many men *who* are physically handicapped will be given positions.

    10. subject

11. Who was the agent to *whom* you were speaking?

    11. object of preposition

12. We all enjoyed the guest *whom* Mother invited.

    12. object of *invited*

13. The man for *whom* I work is an engineer.

    13. object of preposition

14. The committee included two men *who* were opposed to the project.

    14. subject

## CORRECT ANSWERS TO EXERCISE 4

Adjective clauses are printed in **heavy type.**

1. We visited Quebec, **which is a very old city.**

    1. *non-restrictive*

2. The man **who captured the bandit** was rewarded.

    2. *restrictive*

3. Here is the spot **where the pirates buried their treasure.**

    3. *restrictive*

4. John Harvey, **who sat near me,** gave the signal.

    4. *non-restrictive*

5. We are interested in advertisements **that bring results.**

    5. *restrictive*

6. The man **who just knocked on the door** is the plumber.

    6. *restrictive*

7. The road **that we should have taken** was not paved.

    7. *restrictive*

8. He receives a very large salary, **which he does not deserve.**

    8. *non-restrictive*

9. "Treasure Island," **which was written by Stevenson,** is a very popular book.

    9. *non-restrictive*

10. The play **which I saw yesterday** was written by Shaw.

    10. *restrictive*

11. Our canoe, **which was very light,** bobbed up and down in the water.

    11. *non-restrictive*

12. My uncle, **who lives near us,** has a new Buick.

    12. *non-restrictive*

13. The winner is the man **who is sitting in the front row of the theater.**

    13. *restrictive*

14. The town **where our business is located** is in Pennsylvania.

    14. *restrictive*

## CORRECT ANSWERS TO EXERCISE 5

1. The actress wore a dress which she purchased in Paris.

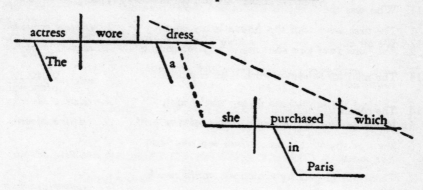

2. I visited the place where the famous composer was born.

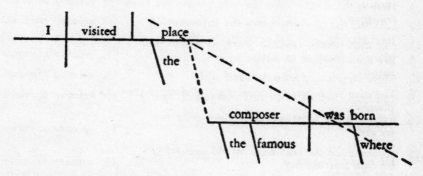

3. People who have large incomes must pay heavy taxes.

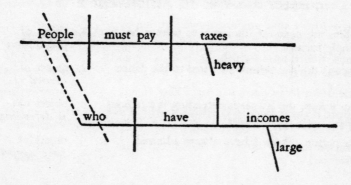

## CORRECT ANSWERS TO ASSIGNMENT 1

Adjective clauses are printed in **heavy type.**

1. The man **who sold the house** is my cousin.
   1. *relative pronoun*

2. The book **that you sent me** is very interesting.
   2. *relative pronoun*

3. Some employees give services **which are not required.**
   3. *relative pronoun*

4. I visited the inn **where Susan and I met.**
   4. *relative adverb*

5. He did not know the reason **why I left the hall.**
   5. *relative adverb*

6. She was absent at a time **when we needed her most.**
   6. *relative adverb*

7. There was no way **by which we could reach him.**
   7. *relative pronoun*

8. This is the pebble **that caused her fall.**
   8. *relative pronoun*

9. The house **where I stayed** was beautifully furnished.
   9. *relative adverb*

10. Lola was the one **who gave the information.**
    10. *relative pronoun*

11. The men **whose records were excellent** were given an increase in salary.
    11. *relative adjective*

12. There were many **who refused aid.**
    12. *relative pronoun*

13. The books **which Churchill writes** sell rapidly.
    13. *relative pronoun*

14. Everett is the artist **whose picture won the award.**
    14. *relative adjective*

15. He inherited the land from an old man **whom he had befriended.**
    15. *relative pronoun*

## CORRECT ANSWERS TO ASSIGNMENT 2

1. I gave him the name of the agent to **whom** he could apply for aid.
   1. object of preposition

2. Constance is the girl **whom** I invited to the dance.
   2. object of *invited*

3. The man **whom** the lawyer is defending is a famous physician.
   3. object of *is defending*

4. She is a person **whom** I have always admired.
   4. object of *have admired*

5. Two of the men **who** were chosen as delegates could not go to the conference.

    5. subject

6. Do you know anyone **who** has a car for sale?

    6. subject

7. In the service I met several officers **who** were educated at West Point.

    7. subject

8. The friends **whom** I visit often are those **who** like to discuss the latest books.

    8. object of *visit* subject of *like*

9. It was my father to **whom** you sold the car.

    9. object of preposition

10. He is the one **who** will become the champion.

    10. subject

11. The manager interviewed the men **who** applied for the position.

    11. subject

12. She is the actress of **whom** I spoke.

    12. object of preposition

## CORRECT ANSWERS TO ASSIGNMENT 3

Adjective clauses are printed in **heavy type.**

1. My employer's son, **who attended Harvard,** plans to be a musician.

    1. *non-restrictive*

2. The contractor will not start building until April, **when the ground is soft.**

    2. *non-restrictive*

3. Oranges, **which are a citrus fruit,** are very healthful.

    3. *non-restrictive*

4. The leading role, **which many wanted,** was given to Jane.

    4. *non-restrictive*

5. My friend attended the concert **which I recommended.**

    5. *restrictive*

6. Curtain material **that matches the office furnishings** is very expensive.

    6. *restrictive*

7. Julia, **who is a college grauate,** wants a position in New York.

    7. *non-restrictive*

8. A word **that names a person, place, or thing** is called a noun.

    8. *restrictive*

9. I sent for the book **which the speaker recommended.**

    9. *restrictive*

10. The men **who work in our factory** have hospital insurance.

           10. *restrictive*

11. The boats **which belong to the members of the club** are anchored in Belmont Harbor.

           11. *restrictive*

12. The flowers **that you have in your hand** are dahlias.

           12. *restrictive*

## SELF-GRADING ASSIGNMENT 4

1. He invented a machine which does the work of many men.

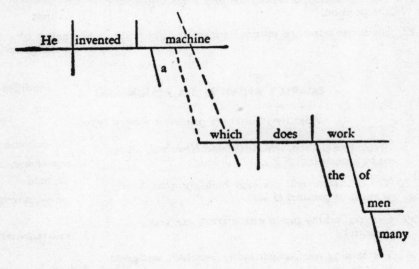

2. This is the place where the army surrendered.

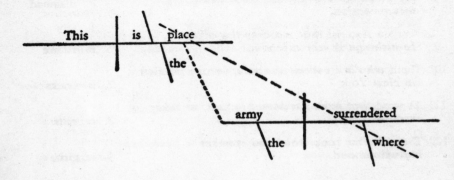

3. The football players whom we saw were professionals.

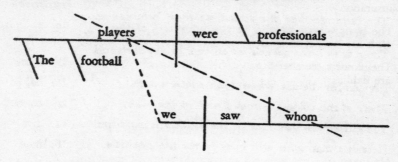

## CORRECT ANSWERS TO PROGRESS TEST NINETEEN

Adjective clauses are printed in **heavy type.**

**Modifies**

1. This is the car **that we bought last year.**
       1. car

2. I have called on the customers **whose names are on your list.**
       2. customers

3. The man **who presented the speaker** is a famous scientist.
       3. man

4. We recommended the hotel **where I stayed in London.**
       4. hotel

5. This is a time **when we should analyze the news carefully.**
       5. time

6. He told the manager the reason **why he wanted to leave.**
       6. reason

7. Is this the diamond **that you gave to Marian?**
       7. diamond

8. New York is the city **to which I referred.**
       8. city

9. She is the author **about whom I spoke yesterday.**
       9. author

10. The books **which were written by the monks** were illuminated.
       10. books

11. The suits **which he purchased in London** were very expensive.
       11. suits

12. The girl **who understands our system of bookkeeping** will be employed.
       12. girl

## ANSWERS TO PROGRESS TEST NINETEEN (continued)

13. The furniture *that she treasures most* belonged to her grandmother.     13. furniture

14. Those *who have served as officers in our club* still retain their membership.     14. those

15. I remember the day *when John met Frances*.     15. day

16. There is the colonel *whom I met at the club*.     16. colonel

17. The girl *whom you met at the station* is my sister.     17. girl

18. Here is a man *who will qualify for the position*.     18. man

19. That is the hotel *where I live in the summer*.     19. hotel

20. This is the hour *when we listen to the radio*.     20. hour

21. They gave the prize to the one *who answered all the questions*.     21. one

22. The girl *who won the award* is a commercial artist.     22. girl

23. The reporter found a place *where he could watch the game*.     23. place

24. We shall send bills to those *who have not paid their July accounts*.     24. those

25. The university will not accept students *who have low scholastic averages*.     25. students

## HOW TO OBTAIN YOUR SCORE

*The test totals 50 points. To obtain your score, divide the number of your correct answers by 50. The answer will be your score on this test. For example, if you have 45 points correct, your score is 45 divided by 50 which is 90 per cent. In other words, your score on this test is 90. You can obtain your score on any of the exercises or assignments by following the same procedure.*

**Practical English Grammar**

## OUTLINE OF UNIT TWENTY

# ADVERBIAL CLAUSES

Page

1. SUBORDINATE CONJUNCTIONS ........................................ 5

2. WORDS USED AS SUBORDINATE CONJUNCTIONS.... 6

3. KINDS OF ADVERBIAL CLAUSES.................................... 8

4. CLAUSES OF DEGREE ............................................. 9

5. POSITION OF THE ADVERBIAL CLAUSE........................ 10

6. CLAUSES OF COMPARISON ..................................... 13

7. "AS—AS" AND "NOT SO—AS" IN COMPARISONS........ 14

8. INCORRECT USE OF "LIKE" IN CLAUSES....................... 15

9. DIAGRAMMING THE ADVERBIAL CLAUSE.................. 20

10. SUMMARY OF GRAMMAR UNIT TWENTY.................. 22

*Self-Grading Assignments* ............................................... 23

*Progress Test Twenty* ................................................... 27

*Key to Correct Answers* ................................................ 29

# ADVERBIAL CLAUSES

IN GRAMMAR UNIT NINETEEN you learned that an adjective clause functions in the same way as an adjective functions. Adjectives modify nouns and pronouns. Adjective clauses also modify nouns and pronouns.

An *adverbial clause* functions in the same way as an adverb functions. Adverbs tell *how, when, where,* and *to what extent* the action is performed. Adverbial clauses answer the same questions and, in addition, express several other ideas which the simple adverb does not express.

Adverbs modify verbs, adjectives, and other adverbs. Adverbial clauses also modify verbs, adjectives, and adverbs. The adverbial clause modifies a verb more often than it modifies an adjective or an adverb.

## SUBORDINATE CONJUNCTIONS

An adverbial clause is usually introduced by a *subordinate conjunction.* This connecting word is called a subordinate conjunction because it makes the idea expressed by its clause *subordinate to the main idea in the sentence.* The subordinate conjunction also shows the relation between the subordinate clause and the word in the main clause which the subordinate clause modifies.

The **subordinate conjunction** is used to show that the clause which it introduces is a subordinate clause, and not a main clause. The subordinate conjunction also indicates the exact type of relationship that the subordinate clause has to the main clause.

The following illustrations will make clear the function of the *subordinate conjunction* in a subordinate clause:

We <u>listened</u> to the radio <u>because we wanted to hear the news.</u>
   verb                             adverbial clause—modifies listened

She <u>will find</u> the telegram on her desk <u>when she returns.</u>
  verb phrase                          adverbial clause—modifies will find

In the first sentence, the subordinate clause is *because we wanted to hear the news*. It is an adverbial clause and modifies the verb *listened* in the main clause. The subordinate conjunction is the word *because*.

If you leave out the word *because*, the words that follow no longer express a subordinate idea. They express a complete thought. It is the word *because* that makes the group of words, *we wanted to hear the news*, subordinate to the main clause. The **subordinate conjunction** is the key to the adverbial clause.

You should become familiar with the subordinate conjunctions that are commonly used to introduce *adverbial clauses*. The subordinate conjunction will help you identify the adverbial clause. It will also help you determine the **kind** of adverbial clause which it introduces.

## WORDS USED AS SUBORDINATE CONJUNCTIONS

| | | | |
|---|---|---|---|
| after | because | provided that | unless |
| although | before | since | until |
| as | even if | so—as | when |
| as—as | even though | so that | whenever |
| as if | except | than | where |
| as long as | if | that | wherever |
| as soon as | in order that | till | whether |
| as though | provided | though | while |

## EXERCISE 1

Underline the **adverbial clauses.** On the line to the right, indicate the *subordinate conjunction* which introduces the clause.

1. Ned will show you his paintings while you are
   waiting for the doctor.                          1. ...................

2. I opened the door when I heard his footsteps.    2. ...................

3. Fred's health has improved since I saw him
   in June.                                          3. ...................

4. David accepted the position although the salary
   was inadequate.                                   4. ...................

5. The men work overtime whenever it is
   necessary.                                        5. ...................

6. We didn't take the trip because we couldn't
   afford it.                                        6. ...................

7. Alex is a much better worker than I am.          7. ...................

8. Listen carefully so that you will not miss any
   of the details.                                   8. ...................

9. Mrs. Brown sold her home after the estate
   was settled.                                      9. ...................

10. We purchased the book before we heard the
    professor's review of it.                       10. ...................

11. Your account will be cancelled unless you pay
    your bills more promptly.                       11. ...................

12. You will be able to keep your appointment
    if you hurry.                                   12. ...................

13. I would not accept the position even if they
    offered me a bonus.                             13. ...................

*Note: The correct answers to exercises will be found at the back of
this booklet. Correct your mistakes and, if necessary, re-read
the text material before going on to the next section.*

## KINDS OF ADVERBIAL CLAUSES

Adverbial clauses are used to express a number of different ideas. The following are the ten important ideas which are expressed by adverbial clauses: *time, place, manner, degree, comparison, purpose, result, condition, concession, cause* (*reason*).

Since the subordinate conjunction helps the adverbial clause express the idea intended, you should become familiar with the conjunctions that are used to express certain ideas, such as *time, place,* etc. The following is a list of the subordinate conjunctions commonly used in adverbial clauses of the various types:

**Time:** after, before, when, whenever, since, until, as soon as, while

**Place:** where, wherever

**Manner:** as, as if, as though

**Degree:** that, as—as, not so—as, than

**Comparison:** as, than, so—as, as—as

**Purpose:** that, so that, in order that

**Result:** that, so that

**Condition:** if, provided, provided that, unless

**Concession:** although, though, even if

**Cause:** as, because, since

## Ideas Expressed by Adverbial Clauses

**Time:** I watched the crowd while I was waiting for you.

**Place:** Put the notice where it can be seen.

**Manner:** The soldier walks as if he were lame.

**Degree:** Marvin is not so industrious <u>as his brother (is industrious)</u>.

**Comparison:** The train was later <u>than it usually is</u>.

**Purpose:** Ted practiced every day <u>so that he might win the contest</u>.

**Result:** The salesman was so persuasive <u>that I finally bought the car</u>.

**Condition:** I shall attend the meeting <u>if I have the time</u>.

**Concession:** Frances will sing at the concert <u>although she has a cold</u>.

**Cause or Reason:** Gerald read the book <u>because I recommended it</u>.


## CLAUSES OF DEGREE

An *adverbial clause of degree* that is introduced by the subordinate conjunction *that* usually expresses a **result** idea as well as the idea of **degree.** The degree idea is expressed by words like *such, such a,* and *so* which precede the subordinate clause.

Jane practiced <u>so</u> long <u>that she became very tired</u>.

Harold made <u>such</u> a poor sales record <u>that he lost his position</u>.

In both these sentences, the adverbial clauses introduced by *that* express a *degree idea* and a *result idea*.

An adverbial clause of degree usually modifies an adjective or an adverb in the main clause.

He talked <u>so</u> loud <u>that he annoyed the speaker</u>.

In this sentence, the adverbial clause *that he annoyed the speaker* is introduced by the subordinate conjunction *that*. The adverbial clause modifies the adverb *so* in the main clause.

## THE POSITION OF THE ADVERBIAL CLAUSE

In all of the preceding illustrations, the adverbial clause follows the main clause. An adverbial clause is often placed at the beginning of the sentence for emphasis, or for variety in sentence patterns. When the subordinate clause precedes the main clause, it is usually set off by a comma.

He went to the office <u>when it was convenient</u>. (follows main clause)
adverbial clause

<u>When it was convenient</u>, he went to the office. (precedes main clause) adverbial clause

The men work overtime <u>whenever it is necessary</u>. (follows main clause) adverbial clause

<u>Whenever it is necessary</u>, the men work overtime. (precedes main clause) adverbial clause

In the first sentence, the adverbial clause *follows* the main clause. In the second sentence, the same adverbial clause *precedes* the main clause. The adverbial clause is placed at the beginning of the sentence for emphasis. Since the adverbial clause is in inverted or transposed order, it is set off by a comma.

The adverbial clause in the third sentence *follows* the main clause. In the fourth sentence, this same clause is placed at the beginning of the sentence for emphasis. The adverbial clause is set off by a comma because it is in transposed order.

Sometimes it is necessary to change the position of a noun and a pronoun when the adverbial clause is placed at the beginning of a sentence:

I shall visit **Margaret** in Texas if she sends me her address.

If Margaret sends me her address, I shall visit **her** in Texas.

## EXERCISE 2

Underline the **adverbial clauses.** On the line to the right, indicate whether the clause expresses *time, place, manner, degree,* or *cause* (*reason*).

Example: I will find her <u>wherever she is.</u>

place

1. Everybody spoiled Nancy because she was frail.   1. ...................

2. Whenever the senator spoke, he made a favorable impression.   2. ...................

3. Wherever we looked, we saw evidences of destruction.   3. ...................

4. Present your credentials when you apply for the position.   4. ...................

5. The soprano sings as if she were well-trained.   5. ...................

6. A telegram arrived after you left.   6. ...................

7. He was so startled by the strange noise that he could not speak.   7. ...................

8. Since you have always helped me, I will secure the loan for you.   8. ...................

9. Put the manuscript where the editor can find it.   9. ...................

10. The woman walks as if she were weary.   10. ...................

11. The actress is as beautiful as she is talented.   11. ...................

12. We knew Father was home because his traveling bags were in the hall.   12. ...................

13. The day was so cold that the officers postponed the trip.   13. ...................

**EXERCISE 3**

Underline the **adverbial clauses.** On the line to the right, indicate whether the clause expresses *condition, concession, comparison, purpose,* or *result.*

Example: <u>If it rains,</u> I shall not go.          condition
....................

1.  The bill was passed although several congress-
    men were opposed to it.                           1. ...................

2.  He is taller than I (am tall).                    2. ...................

3.  The nurse opened the window so that the
    patient might have more air.                      3. ...................

4.  If it rains, we shall take another route.         4. ...................

5.  Unless the schedule is changed, the directors
    will meet tomorrow.                               5. ...................

6.  Will you please remove your hat so that those
    behind you can see the speaker?                   6. ...................

7.  We were so late that we missed the concert.       7. ...................

8.  Mary will sing provided the club will pay for
    her services.                                     8. ...................

9.  The book was so technical that I could not
    understand it.                                    9. ...................

10. Silk is more expensive than cotton
    (is expensive).                                   10. ...................

11. The accident would not have occurred if the
    driver had been more careful.                     11. ...................

12. It was so warm in the room that I was
    uncomfortable.                                    12. ...................

13. Her house is larger than ours (is large).         13. ...................

## CLAUSES OF COMPARISON

In both speaking and writing, words are often omitted that are necessary to the grammatical completeness of the sentence. Certain words are sometimes omitted because the meaning of the sentence is perfectly clear without them. Sometimes they are omitted in order to avoid using a sentence that is awkward or monotonous.

Certain words are usually omitted in an *adverbial clause of comparison* for the reasons just given. The verb is often omitted because it can be readily supplied. It is important to realize that the verb has been omitted in order to decide upon the correct form of the pronoun that should be used as the subject of the verb. We often hear sentences like the following, which are incorrect:

> I am younger than **him.** (incorrect)

> John can run as fast as **us.** (incorrect)

In both sentences the *incorrect form* of the pronoun is used in the adverbial clause of comparison. If the speaker had finished the clause, he would have used the correct form of the pronoun. When the clause is finished, it becomes evident that the pronoun is the *subject* of the clause. A pronoun used as the subject should be in the *nominative case.*

> I am younger than **he** (is young). (*he*—subject)

> John can run as fast as **we** (can run). (*we*—subject)

In the unfinished clause of comparison the word *than* is a conjunction, and not a preposition. The word *than* introduces a clause which must be finished grammatically. When we supply the words that are necessary to complete the clause, we realize that the form of the pronoun should be *he* and not *him. He* is the correct form to use for the subject. The subject requires the *nominative case.*

Study the following illustrations carefully. Pay special attention to the form of the pronoun used in the *adverbial clause of comparison.*

The filling in of the words that have been omitted shows what the proper form of the pronoun should be:

You have lived longer than *I* (have lived). (not *me*)

Martha sews as well as *she* (sews). (not *her*)

Some of the men worked harder than *we* (worked). (not *us*)

I speak as correctly as *he* (does). (not *him*)

## "As—As" and "Not So—As" in Comparisons

The connectives *as—as* and *not so—as* are often used in sentences that contain adverbial clauses of comparison. Careful writers and speakers make a distinction in the use of these combinations. They use *as—as* when the comparison is **positive,** and *not so—as* when the comparison is **negative.**

The comparison is said to be positive when the two things compared are approximately the same or equal. The comparison is said to be negative when there is an inequality between the two things compared. An illustration will help make this clear.

John is **as** tall **as** his brother. (positive comparison)

John is **not so** tall **as** his father. (negative comparison)

In the first sentence, the comparison is *positive.* The two persons compared are approximately *equal* in height. The combination *as—as* is used to indicate this type of comparison. In the second sentence, the combination *not so—as* is used to show an *inequality* in height, or a *negative* comparison.

In speaking and in informal writing *as—as* is commonly used to show both types of comparison—positive and negative. However, in formal writing it is advisable to observe the distinctions that discriminating writers make.

## Incorrect Use of "Like" in Clauses

The word *like* is commonly used as a preposition. When the word *like* is used as a preposition, it should be followed by an object. If the object is a pronoun, the pronoun should be in the *objective case.* The word *like* is not a conjunction and should not be used to introduce a subordinate clause of manner or comparison. The words *as, as if,* and *as though* should be used to introduce this type of clause.

I shall write the letter *like* you advised me. (incorrect)

I shall write the letter *as* you advised me. (correct)

You look *like* you were tired. (incorrect)

You look *as if* you were tired. (correct)

It looks *like* it might snow. (incorrect)

It looks *as if* it might snow. (correct)

In the last few years, the colloquial use of *like* as a conjunction has greatly increased in certain sections of the country. This use occasionally appears in print. We often hear the word *like* used as a conjunction in popular radio programs. However, it has not been accepted as standard English.

When *like* is used as a preposition, it means *similar to,* or *in a similar manner to.*

Mary's hat is *like* the one I bought in Paris. (*like*—preposition)

John is *like* his father in temperament. (*like*—preposition)

## EXERCISE 4

Cross out the *incorrect form* of the pronoun enclosed in parentheses. Complete the unfinished clause before you decide which form is the correct one to use.

Example: Grace is taller than (~~me~~, I).

1. They are much better prepared than (we, us).

2. We are more fortunate than (they, them).

3. I hope that you will study as hard as (she, her).

4. They play a better game of golf than (we, us).

5. You are not so industrious as (he, him).

6. We drove faster than (them, they).

7. I can't add figures so rapidly as (he, him).

8. Her mother is more attractive than (she, her).

9. They have more money than (we, us).

10. He cannot swim so well as (I, me).

11. Allen has more ambition than (he, him).

12. The veterans made better grades in college than (we, us).

13. Peter is not so keen a business man as (he, him).

14. The head of the department did not sell so many suits as (she, her).

15. My friend has a larger factory than (we, us).

## EXERCISE 5

Cross out any *incorrect forms* that are used in the following sentences. If the sentence is correct, write the word *correct* after it. Four sentences are correct.

Example: I am not ~~as~~ <sup>so</sup> ill as you think.

1. We walked as far as him.

2. Peter writes like he was well-trained in composition.

3. It is not as cold as it seems.

4. They did not come so soon as we expected.

5. That woman looks like she might be ill.

6. Jane is older than me.

7. John looks like his father.

8. Susan is not as friendly today as she was at the reception.

9. The workmen talk like they were angry about something.

10. The president is not so active as he was five years ago.

11. I am two inches taller than her.

12. Are you as interested in television as them?

13. Your work is not as difficult as mine.

14. Your car is like the one that I sold yesterday.

15. Arrange the files like the manager directed.

## DIAGRAMMING THE ADVERBIAL CLAUSE

Like the adjective clause, the adverbial clause is diagrammed to show that it is a modifier. When words like *when* and *where* introduce adverbial clauses, they serve a double function. They introduce the clause and also modify the verb in the subordinate clause. Both functions must be shown in the diagram. This is done by drawing a slanted, dotted line from the verb to the subordinate conjunction *when* or *where*.

*Sentence:* We left the house <u>when the rain stopped.</u>
                                    adverbial clause

*Sentence:* Ted could not hear the speaker <u>because he sat in the last row.</u>
adverbial clause

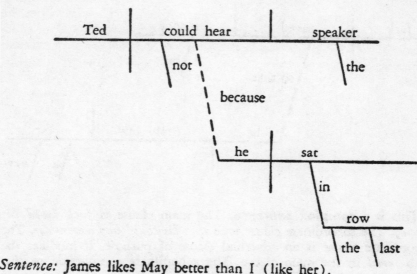

*Sentence:* James likes May better <u>than I (like her).</u>
adverbial clause of comparison

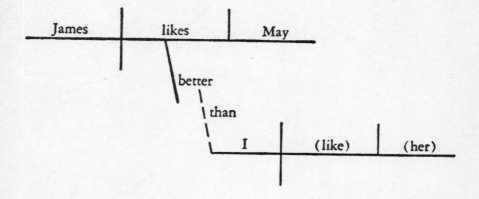

In this sentence, there is an unfinished clause of comparison. The diagram shows the completed clause by enclosing the verb and the object in parentheses. The adverbial clause is a clause of comparison. It modifies the adverb *better* in the main clause.

*Sentence:* Jack saved his money <u>so that he could buy a new car.</u>
adverbial clause of purpose

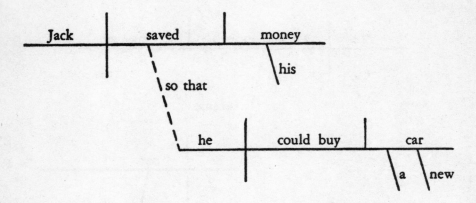

    This is a **complex sentence.** The main clause is *Jack saved his money.* The subordinate clause is *so that he could buy a new car.* The subordinate clause is an adverbial clause of purpose. It modifies the verb *saved* in the main clause. The subordinate conjunction *so that* introduces the adverbial clause.

## EXERCISE 6

Diagram the following sentences. Follow the methods presented in this unit.

1. Jane is older than I (am old).

2. Before we left the hotel, I paid all the bills.

3. The members of the band played as if they liked the music.

## SUMMARY OF GRAMMAR UNIT TWENTY

An *adverbial clause* is a **subordinate clause** that functions as an adverb. An adverbial clause may modify a verb, an adjective, or an adverb.

An *adverbial clause* is usually introduced by a **subordinate conjunction**. A *subordinate conjunction* is a conjunction that is used to connect a subordinate clause to the main clause.

An adverbial clause may express any one of the following ideas: *time, place, manner, degree, comparison, purpose, result, condition, concession, cause (reason)*.

An adverbial clause may follow the main clause or precede it. If the adverbial clause precedes the main clause, it is usually set off by a comma.

An **adverbial clause of degree** introduced by the word *that* usually expresses the idea of *result* as well as the idea of *degree*. A clause of degree modifies an adjective or an adverb in the main clause.

**Adverbial clauses of comparison** are often grammatically incomplete. It is necessary to supply the missing words in order to determine the case of the pronoun that is used as the subject of the clause of comparison.

The combination *as—as* is used to express a **positive comparison**. The combination *not so—as* is used to express a **negative comparison**.

The word *like* is sometimes used as a preposition. It should not be used as a conjunction to introduce an adverbial clause of manner. Use *as, as if*, or *as though* to introduce that type of clause.

## SELF-GRADING ASSIGNMENT 1

Directions: Underline the **adverbial clauses**. On the line to the right, indicate the *subordinate conjunction* that introduces the clause.

1. James will remain in college until he finishes the law course.

    1. ................

2. He likes her better than (he likes) me.

    2. ................

3. The day was so hot that we stayed indoors.

    3. ................

4. Whenever I see Lila, she is wearing a red hat.

    4. ................

5. If the play comes to Chicago, I shall attend the opening performance.

    5. ................

6. Since traveling by air is quicker, we decided to take a plane.

    6. ................

7. Although the manager interviewed many applicants for the position, he did not employ one of them.

    7. ................

8. The quartet will sing unless one of the group is drafted.

    8. ................

9. The officer studied the situation carefully before he issued any orders.

    9. ................

10. Because he was under age, Norman could not join the Marine Corps.

    10. ................

11. We did not hear from the captain after the boat docked.

    11. ................

12. James parked the car where we could locate it easily after the concert.

    12. ................

13. When the water flowed over the dike, the people fled from the city.

    13. ................

*Caution: Check your answers to each assignment with the answer key at the back of the booklet before proceeding with the next assignment.*

**SELF-GRADING ASSIGNMENT 2**

Directions: Underline the **adverbial clauses.** On the line to the right, indicate whether the clause expresses *time, place, manner, degree, comparison, purpose, result, condition, concession, cause (reason).*

1. The boys like to swim where the water is deep.

1. ................

2. Before you buy a car, let me show you our latest model.

2. ................

3. If this program is successful, we shall schedule another series.

3. ................

4. John is a much better dancer than Alice.

4. ................

5. Before you register, you must present your credentials.

5. ................

6. Arthur is not so ambitious as his father.

6. ................

7. The child talks as if he had a speech difficulty.

7. ................

8. We walk home every day because the doctor recommended fresh air and exercise.

8. ................

9. Although we cannot afford it, we are going to buy a new car.

9. ................

10. His writing is more legible than mine.

10. ................

11. He bought a home so that the children might have a playroom.

11. ................

12. Douglas made such an excellent sales record that he was promoted.

12. ................

13. The play is so popular that we cannot get tickets at the box office.

13. ................

14. I could not park my car because there was no available space anywhere.

14. ................

## SELF-GRADING ASSIGNMENT 3

Directions: Cross out any *incorrect forms* that are used in the following sentences. If the sentence is correct, write the word *correct* after it. Five sentences are correct.

as if
Example: The boys played ~~like~~ they were tired.

1. Our business is not as good this year as it was last year.

2. The boy works like a man.

3. Harold is more industrious than me.

4. Ernest is as stubborn as his sister.

5. Jane is not so charming as her mother.

6. The men recently appointed have had more training than us.

7. It looks like Henry will be the next president of our club.

8. He is as well-informed as they.

9. If you were as slender as her, you could wear the new styles.

10. The new secretary is not as dependable as Judith was.

11. Are you as tactful as him?

12. He runs the business like his father ran it twenty years ago.

13. Father, like I, is fond of mystery stories.

14. My friend is not so young as I.

15. The professor is not as critical as he seems to be.

### SELF-GRADING ASSIGNMENT 4

Directions: Diagram the following sentences. This exercise includes both *adjective* and *adverbial clauses*.

1. We sent notices to all the customers who have charge accounts.

2. A pilot does not receive a license until he has passed the tests.

3. Although we do not like the location, we shall buy the house.

## PROGRESS TEST TWENTY

This progress test should not be taken until a day or two after you have completed the assignments. The score you make on the test will then more clearly reflect your understanding of the material in the unit.

Directions: Underline the **subordinate clauses**. In the first column on the right, indicate the word the clause *modifies*. In the second column, indicate whether the clause is an *adjective clause* or an *adverbial clause*. (60 *points*)

| | Modifies | Kind of Clause |
|---|---|---|
| 1. Some of the men worked longer than we (worked). | 1. ................. | ................. |
| 2. Janson put the papers where his partner could find them. | 2. ................. | ................. |
| 3. I do not know the reason why our sales are so low this month. | 3. ................. | ................. |
| 4. The lawyer is not so confident as he was yesterday. | 4. ................. | ................. |
| 5. Since Mr. Adams has had charge of the advertising, business has increased. | 5. ................. | ................. |
| 6. He was so angry that he became speechless. | 6. ................. | ................. |
| 7. The chairman opened the meeting promptly so that there would be time for discussion. | 7. ................. | ................. |
| 8. This is the hotel where I stayed in Rome. | 8. ................. | ................. |
| 9. Lawrence is called in whenever the books of the firm are audited. | 9. ................. | ................. |

## PROGRESS TEST TWENTY (continued)

10. This is the season when you should always be prepared for rain.

10. ................    ................

11. The store was remodeled after the last tenant moved out.

11. ................    ................

12. The gossip that she repeated is false.

12. ................    ................

13. We paid a deposit so that the landlord would hold the apartment for us.

13. ................    ................

14. He still lives in the house where he was born.

14. ................    ................

15. Although Marvin has had the training, he does not want the position.

15. ................    ................

16. I did not hear the remarks which were made after the meeting.

16. ................    ................

17. Constance is the girl whom I invited to the music festival.

17. ................    ................

18. After Alex returned from Brazil, he secured a position with a wholesale firm.

18. ................    ................

19. The house that the famous architect built was sold recently.

19. ................    ................

20. This is the intersection where the accident occurred.

20. ................    ................

## ANSWER KEY

for

## EXERCISES, ASSIGNMENTS, AND PROGRESS TEST
### *Grammar Unit Twenty*

---

### CORRECT ANSWERS TO EXERCISE 1

1. Ned will show you his paintings **while you are waiting for the doctor.**

    1. while

2. I opened the door **when I heard his footsteps.**

    2. when

3. Fred's health has improved **since I saw him in June.**

    3. since

4. David accepted the position **although the salary was inadequate.**

    4. although

5. The men work overtime **whenever it is necessary.**

    5. whenever

6. We didn't take the trip **because we couldn't afford it.**

    6. because

7. Alex is a much better worker **than I am.**

    7. than

8. Listen carefully **so that you will not miss any of the details.**

    8. so that

9. Mrs. Brown sold her home **after the estate was settled.**

    9. after

10. We purchased the book **before we heard the professor's review of it.**

    10. before

11. Your account will be cancelled **unless you pay your bills more promptly.**

    11. unless

12. You will be able to keep your appointment **if you hurry.**

    12. if

13. I would not accept the position **even if they offered me a bonus.**

    13. even if

### CORRECT ANSWERS TO EXERCISE 2

1. Everybody spoiled Nancy **because she was frail.**

    1. *cause (reason)*

2. **Whenever the senator spoke,** he made a favorable impression.

    2. *time*

3. **Wherever we looked,** we saw evidences of destruction.

    3. *place*

4. Present your credentials **when you apply for the position.**

    4. *time*

5. The soprano sings **as if she were well-trained.**    5. *manner*

6. A telegram arrived **after you left.**    6. *time*

7. He was so startled by the strange noise **that he could not speak.**    7. *degree (result)*

8. **Since you have always helped me,** I will secure the loan for you.    8. *cause (reason)*

9. Put the manuscript **where the editor can find it.**    9. *place*

10. The woman walks **as if she were weary.**    10. *manner*

11. The actress is as beautiful **as she is talented.**    11. *degree*

12. We knew Father was home **because his traveling bags were in the hall.**    12. *cause (reason)*

13. The day was so cold **that the officers postponed the trip.**    13. *degree (result)*

## CORRECT ANSWERS TO EXERCISE 3

1. The bill was passed **although several congressmen were opposed to it.**    1. *concession*

2. He is taller **than I (am tall).**    2. *comparison*

3. The nurse opened the window **so that the patient might have more air.**    3. *purpose*

4. **If it rains,** we shall take another route.    4. *condition*

5. **Unless the schedule is changed,** the directors will meet tomorrow.    5. *condition*

6. Will you please remove your hat **so that those behind you can see the speaker?**    6. *purpose*

7. We were so late **that we missed the concert.**    7. *result (degree)*

8. Mary will sing **provided the club will pay for her services.**    8. *condition*

9. The book was so technical **that I could not understand it.**    9. *result (degree)*

10. Silk is more expensive **than cotton (is expensive).**    10. *comparison*

11. The accident would not have occurred **if the driver had been more careful.**    11. *condition*

12. It was so warm in the room **that I was uncomfortable.**    12. *result (degree)*

13. Her house is larger **than ours (is large).**    13. *comparison*

## CORRECT ANSWERS TO EXERCISE 4

1. They are much better prepared than **we** (are).
2. We are more fortunate than **they** (are).
3. I hope that you will study as hard as **she** (studies).
4. They play a better game of golf than **we** (play).
5. You are not so industrious as **he** (is).
6. We drove faster than **they** (drove).
7. I can't add figures so rapidly as **he** (can).
8. Her mother is more attractive than **she** (is).
9. They have more money than **we** (have).
10. He cannot swim so well as **I** (can swim).
11. Allen has more ambition than **he** (has).
12. The veterans made better grades in college than **we** (made).
13. Peter is not so keen a business man as **he** (is).
14. The head of the department did not sell so many suits as **she** (sold).
15. My friend has a larger factory than **we** (have).

## CORRECT ANSWERS TO EXERCISE 5

1. We walked as far as **he**.
2. Peter writes **as if** he **were** well-trained in composition.
3. It is not **so** cold as it seems.
4. They did not come so soon as we expected. (*correct*)
5. That woman looks **as if** she might be ill.
6. Jane is older than **I**.
7. John looks like his father. (*correct*)
8. Susan is not **so** friendly today as she was at the reception.
9. The workmen talk **as if** they were angry about something.
10. The president is not so active as he was five years ago. (*correct*)
11. I am two inches taller than **she**.
12. Are you as interested in television as **they?**
13. Your work is not **so** difficult as mine.
14. Your car is like the one that I sold yesterday. (*correct*)
15. Arrange the files **as** the manager directed.

## CORRECT ANSWERS TO EXERCISE 6

*Sentence:* Jane is older than I (am old).
clause of comparison

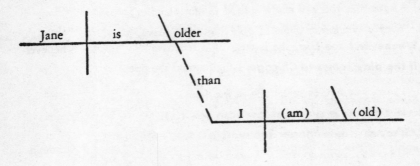

*Sentence:* Before we left the hotel, I paid all the bills.
clause of time

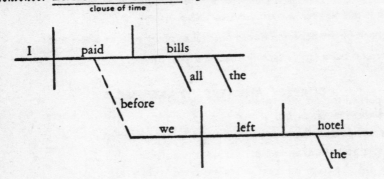

*Sentence:* The members of the band played as if they liked the music.
clause of manner

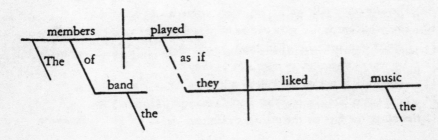

## CORRECT ANSWERS TO ASSIGNMENT 1

1. James will remain in college *until he finishes the law course.*

2. He likes her better *than (he likes) me.*

3. The day was so hot *that we stayed indoors.*

4. *Whenever I see Lila,* she is wearing a red hat.

5. *If the play comes to Chicago,* I shall attend the opening performance.

6. *Since traveling by air is quicker,* we decided to take a plane.

7. *Although the manager interviewed many applicants for the position,* he did not employ one of them.

8. The quartet will sing *unless one of the group is drafted.*

9. The officer studied the situation carefully *before he issued any orders.*

10. *Because he was under age,* Norman could not join the Marine Corps.

11. We did not hear from the captain *after the boat docked.*

12. James parked the car *where we could locate it easily after the concert.*

13. *When the water flowed over the dike,* the people fled from the city.

1. until
2. than
3. that
4. Whenever
5. If
6. Since
7. Although
8. unless
9. before
10. Because
11. after
12. where
13. When

## CORRECT ANSWERS TO ASSIGNMENT 2

1. The boys like to swim *where the water is deep.*

2. *Before you buy a car,* let me show you our latest model.

3. *If this program is successful,* we shall schedule another series.

4. John is a much better dancer *than Alice (is).*

5. *Before you register,* you must present your credentials.

6. Arthur is not so ambitious *as his father (is ambitious).*

1. *place*
2. *time*
3. *condition*
4. *comparison*
5. *time*
6. *comparison*

7. The child talks **as if he had a speech difficulty.**      7. *manner*

8. We walk home every day **because the doctor recommended fresh air and exercise.**      8. *cause (reason)*

9. **Although we cannot afford it,** we are going to buy a new car.      9. *concession*

10. His writing is more legible **than mine (is).**      10. *comparison*

11. He bought a home **so that the children might have a playroom.**      11. *purpose*

12. Douglas made such an excellent sales record **that he was promoted.**      12. *result (degree)*

13. The play is so popular **that we cannot get tickets at the box office.**      13. *result (degree)*

14. I could not park my car **because there was no available space anywhere.**      14. *cause (reason)*

## CORRECT ANSWERS TO ASSIGNMENT 3

1. Our business is not **so** good this year as it was last year.

2. The boy works like a man. (*correct*)

3. Harold is more industrious than **I.**

4. Ernest is as stubborn as his sister. (*correct*)

5. Jane is not so charming as her mother. (*correct*)

6. The men recently appointed have had more training than **we.**

7. It looks **as if** Henry will be the next president of our club.

8. He is as well-informed as they. (*correct*)

9. If you were as slender as **she,** you could wear the new styles.

10. The new secretary is not **so** dependable as Judith was.

11. Are you as tactful as **he?**

12. He runs the business **as** his father ran it twenty years ago.

13. Father, like **me,** is fond of mystery stories.

14. My friend is not so young as I. (*correct*)

15. The professor is not **so** critical as he seems to be.

### CORRECT ANSWERS TO SELF-GRADING ASSIGNMENT 4

*Sentence:* We sent notices to all the customers who have charge accounts.

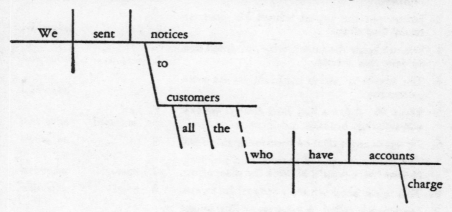

*Sentence:* A pilot does not receive a license until he has passed the tests.

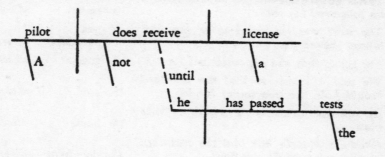

*Sentence:* Although we do not like the location, we shall buy the house.

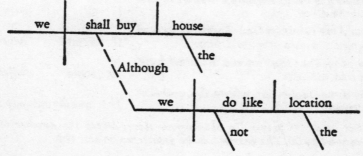

## CORRECT ANSWERS TO PROGRESS TEST TWENTY

1. Some of the men worked longer **than we (worked).**

   1. longer     *adverbial*

2. Janson put the papers **where his partner could find them.**

   2. put     *adverbial*

3. I do not know the reason **why our sales are so low this month.**

   3. reason     *adjective*

4. The lawyer is not so confident **as he was yesterday.**

   4. so     *adverbial*

5. **Since Mr. Adams has had charge of the advertising,** business has increased.

   5. has increased     *adverbial*

6. He was so angry **that he became speechless.**

   6. so     *adverbial*

7. The chairman opened the meeting promptly **so that there would be time for discussion.**

   7. opened     *adverbial*

8. This is the hotel **where I stayed in Rome.**

   8. hotel     *adjective*

9. Lawrence is called in **whenever the books of the firm are audited.**

   9. is called     *adverbial*

10. This is the season **when you should always be prepared for rain.**

    10. season     *adjective*

11. The store was remodeled **after the last tenant moved out.**

    11. was remodeled     *adverbial*

12. The gossip **that she repeated** is false.

    12. gossip     *adjective*

13. We paid a deposit **so that the landlord would hold the apartment for us.**

    13. paid     *adverbial*

14. He still lives in the house **where he was born.**

    14. house     *adjective*

15. **Although Marvin has had the training,** he does not want the position.

    15. does want     *adverbial*

16. I did not hear the remarks **which were made after the meeting.**

    16. remarks     *adjective*

17. Constance is the girl **whom I invited to the music festival.**

    17. girl     *adjective*

18. **After Alex returned from Brazil,** he secured a position with a wholesale firm.

    18. secured     *adverbial*

19. The house **that the famous architect built** was sold recently.

    19. house     *adjective*

20. This is the intersection **where the accident occurred.**

    20. intersection     *adjective*

*The test totals 60 points. To obtain your score, divide the number of your correct answers by 60. The answer will be your score on this test.*

### Practical English Grammar

## OUTLINE OF UNIT TWENTY-ONE

# NOUN CLAUSES

                                                                Page

1. FUNCTION OF THE NOUN CLAUSE.................................... 5

2. OMISSION OF THE CONNECTING WORD....................... 9

3. THE NOUN CLAUSE USED AS AN APPOSITIVE................ 11

4. THE NOUN CLAUSE AND THE INTRODUCTORY "IT".... 12

5. WORDS THAT INTRODUCE NOUN CLAUSES................ 14

6. DIAGRAMMING THE NOUN CLAUSE................................ 18

7. SUMMARY OF GRAMMAR UNIT TWENTY-ONE............ 23

*Self-Grading Assignments* ................................................. 24

*Progress Test Twenty-One* ............................................. 28

*Key to Correct Answers* ................................................. 31

# NOUN CLAUSES

IN GRAMMAR UNITS NINETEEN AND TWENTY you became familiar with the form and function of two types of subordinate clauses—the *adjective clause* and the *adverbial clause*. In this unit you will study the form and function of another type of subordinate clause—the *noun clause*.

You have learned that adjective clauses and adverbial clauses are used as *modifiers* in the same way that adjectives and adverbs are used as modifiers. Noun clauses are not used as modifiers. They perform the same functions that a *noun* performs.

## FUNCTION OF THE NOUN CLAUSE
### Noun Clause—Subject of a Sentence

A noun is commonly used as the *subject* of a sentence. A *noun clause* may also be used as the **subject** of a sentence. The following illustrations show how the noun clause is used as the subject of a sentence:

What the chairman proposed was not practical.
<u>noun clause—subject</u>

How you manage on your income is a puzzle to me.
<u>noun clause—subject</u>

That their house is for sale is a well-known fact.
<u>noun clause—subject</u>

Where we could find an apartment was our problem.
<u>noun clause—subject</u>

The subject of a sentence usually tells what we are talking about. The noun clause in the first sentence tells *what* was not practical; namely, *What the chairman proposed*. In the second sentence, the subject, or the noun clause, tells *what* it is that is a puzzle to me; namely, *How you manage on your income*. In the third sentence, the noun clause tells *what* is a well-known fact; namely, *That their house is for sale*. The noun clause in the last sentence tells *what our problem was*.

If you examine the preceding illustrations, you will see that the following words introduce the noun clauses: *what, how, that,* and *where.* These same words are often used to introduce adjective or adverbial clauses. The only way to be sure that you are dealing with a *noun clause* is to determine how the clause is used in the sentence. If it functions in the way that a noun functions, it is a noun clause.

## Noun Clause—Direct Object of a Verb

A *noun clause* is frequently used as the **direct object** of a verb. A noun used as an object completes the meaning of the verb and answers the question *What?* A noun clause used as the direct object of a verb completes the verb and in almost all cases answers the question *What?* Study the following illustrations. They show how noun clauses are used as objects of verbs:

I hope (*what?*) that you will be promoted. (object of *hope*)

We knew (*what?*) where we could park the car. (object of *knew*)

Tell the manager (*what?*) why you are leaving. (object of *tell*)

I believe (*what?*) that it is going to rain. (object of *believe*)

He understood (*what?*) what we were trying to do. (object of *understood*)

The noun clause in the first sentence tells *what I hope.* It is used as the object of the verb *hope.* The noun clause in the second sentence tells *what we knew.* It is the object of the verb *knew.* The noun clause in the third sentence tells *what you should tell the manager.* It is the object of the verb *tell.* The noun clause in the fourth sentence tells *what I believe.* The noun clause in the last sentence tells *what he understood.*

## EXERCISE 1

Underline the **noun clauses** in the following sentences. On the line to the right indicate whether the clause is used as the *subject,* or as the *direct object* of the verb.

Example: I know <u>what he reads</u>.          *direct obj.*
..................

1.  I will show you where he lives.          1. ................

2.  Martha usually enjoys whatever she does.          2. ................

3.  That she is a famous singer is a well-known fact.  3. ................

4.  No one knew what the outcome would be.          4. ................

5.  Do you remember what you gave her?          5. ................

6.  How it is done should be explained in detail.          6. ................

7.  What the result will be is a debatable question.  7. ................

8.  She revealed where the fugitive had gone.          8. ................

9.  Where the meeting will be held is a secret.          9. ................

10. What we have done should be an incentive
    for others.          10. ................

11. I did not know what law he had violated.          11. ................

12. She did not understand why they were planning
    an investigation.          12. ................

13. Why he left the city is still a mystery.          13. ................

14. Show me what you are reading.          14. ................

15. What he will do depends upon circumstances.  15. ................

*Note: The correct answers to exercises will be found at the back of this booklet. Correct your mistakes and, if necessary, re-read the text material before going on to the next section.*

## Noun Clause—Predicate Noun

A *noun clause* may be used as a **predicate noun** after one of the linking verbs. Like the predicate noun, a noun clause used after a linking verb means the same as the subject. It is also used to complete the verb. The noun clauses in the following sentences are used' as *predicate nouns* after linking verbs:

The rumor was that he had left the city. (means the same as *rumor*)

That is what we agreed to do. (means the same as *that*)

My first impression was that I had seen him before. (means the same as *impression*)

The report was that he was drowned. (means the same as *report*)

The noun clause in the first sentence is *that he had left the city.* It completes the verb *was* and means the same as the subject *rumor.* The noun clause in the second sentence is *what we agreed to do.* It completes the linking verb *is* and means the same as the subject *that.* The noun clause in the third sentence is *that I had seen him before.* It completes the linking verb *was* and means the same as the subject *impression.* The noun clause in the last sentence means the same as *report* and completes the linking verb *was.*

## Noun Clause—Object of a Preposition

Like the noun, a *noun clause* is sometimes used as the **object of a preposition.** You may often find it difficult to determine whether the noun clause is the object of the preposition or whether some word in the clause is the object of the preposition. If you study the following illustrations carefully, you will see why an entire *clause* is the object of the preposition.

Give the message to whoever is in the office. (noun clause—object of the preposition *to*)

We did not agree about <u>what the doctor ordered</u>. (noun clause —object of the preposition *about*)

Do the job in <u>whatever way you wish</u>. (noun clause—object of *in*)

In the first sentence, the noun clause *whoever is in the office* is the object of the preposition *to. Whoever* could not be the object of the preposition because it is the subject of the clause. In addition, the sentence does not mean that you should give the message to *whoever.* It means that you should give the message to *whoever is in the office.* The entire clause is the object of the preposition *to.*

In the second sentence, the noun clause *what the doctor ordered* is the object of the preposition *about.* The sentence does not mean that we did not agree about *what.* It means that we did not agree about *what the doctor ordered.* The word *what* could not be the object of the preposition because it has another function to perform in the clause. It is the object of the verb *ordered.*

The noun clause in the third sentence must be the object of the preposition. The word *way* could not be the object of the preposition because that is not the meaning intended. The sentence does not mean that you should do the job in *whatever way,* but it means that you should do the job in *whatever way you wish.* The entire clause is the object of the preposition *in.*

## OMISSION OF THE CONNECTING WORD

Sometimes the word that introduces a subordinate clause is omitted. The reason for this omission is to bring the main idea and the subordinate idea closer together. Although the best writers and speakers often omit the connecting word, you should supply it whenever there is any doubt about the construction of the clause.

I believe <u>that</u> you will be promoted. (*that*—subordinate conjunction)

I believe you will be promoted. (subordinate conjunction omitted)

## EXERCISE 2

Underline the **noun clauses** in the following sentences. On the line to the right, indicate whether the clause is used as a *predicate noun* or as the *object of a preposition*.

Example: The truth is <u>that we have no funds.</u>    *pred. noun*
....................

1. The truth was that the man had disappeared.    1. ...................

2. The report is that there will be an increase in production.    2. ...................

3. Buy the materials at whichever store is nearest.    3. ...................

4. The criticism was that the presentation was inadequate.    4. ...................

5. Choose your gift from whatever remains on the table.    5. ...................

6. Pay more attention to what the manager tells you.    6. ...................

7. I know nothing except what you told me.    7. ...................

8. His difficulty was that he was not trained for the position.    8. ...................

9. The fact is that the boat was full of holes.    9. ...................

10. He will give help to whoever needs it.    10. ...................

11. The reason was that we lacked the money.    11. ...................

12. Harold does well in whatever position he is placed.    12. ...................

13. We built a cabin with whatever material was available.    13. ...................

14. My fear is that we shall be late.    14. ...................

15. Our conclusion was that we could trust him.    15. ...................

## NOUN CLAUSE USED AS AN APPOSITIVE

A noun is often used *in apposition* with another noun. The word **apposition** comes from two Latin words which mean *"placed by"* or *"put near to."* A word in *apposition* is placed near another word to explain it or to identify it in some way. We often speak of a person and then add something to explain who the person is, or to identify him in some way.

Mike, our *janitor,* is very accommodating.

We called on Dr. Allen, a famous *scientist.*

Paris, a *city* in France, is famous as a fashion center.

In the first sentence, the noun *janitor* is in apposition with the noun *Mike.* It explains who Mike was. In the second sentence, *scientist* is in apposition with *Dr. Allen.* It identifies him as a scientist. In the third sentence, *city* is in apposition with *Paris.*

In all three sentences the nouns that are in apposition with other nouns are set off by commas. Sometimes the appositive is so closely connected with the noun that no commas are required. It is not good practice to set off the appositive by commas in sentences like the following:

My brother Andrew is in London.

The poet Whittier wrote "Snowbound."

Like the noun, a *noun clause* is often used in **apposition** with a word or a group of words. When the noun clause is used in apposition, it usually explains such words as *idea, fact, belief, report, rumor,* etc. Noun clauses used in apposition are not set off by commas.

The rumor that John would be elected spread rapidly.
<small>apposition with rumor</small>

The fact that the contract was signed was important.
<small>apposition with fact</small>

The announcement <u>that the strike was over</u> was received with
apposition with *announcement*

cheers.

We entertained the hope <u>that the crew had survived.</u>
apposition with *hope*

## NOUN CLAUSE AND THE INTRODUCTORY "IT"

Sometimes a sentence begins with the introductory word *it*. In
sentences of this type the word *it* is not the real subject of the sentence.
The grammatical or real subject appears later. The real subject is often
a *noun clause*. Sentences are arranged in this way either for emphasis or
for smoothness.

*It* is obvious <u>that you do not have the money.</u>
noun clause—subject

*(It)* That you do not have the money is obvious. (*transposed
order*)

This sentence begins with the introductory word *it*. The real or
grammatical subject appears later in the sentence. The subject is the
noun clause, *that you do not have the money.* When the sentence was
transposed, the word *it,* which has no grammatical connection with any
part of the sentence, was dropped, and the real subject was put in its
proper place.

The word *it* has only one purpose in sentences of this type. It fills
in the place normally occupied by the subject. Its function is similar
to that of the introductory word *there,* which was explained in Grammar Unit Four. When the word *it* is used in this way, it is called an
**expletive.**

Sentences that begin with *it* as an expletive, or "filling in" word,
are easily recognized because they always follow the same pattern:

It is important <u>that you see him at once.</u>
expletive          noun clause—subject

(It) <u>That you see him at once</u> is important. (*transposed order*)
expletive    noun clause—subject

## EXERCISE 3

Underline the **noun clauses** in the following sentences. On the line to the right, indicate whether the clause is used as the *delayed subject,* or whether it is in *apposition* with some word in the sentence.

Example: It is true <u>that she is ill.</u>                *delayed sub.*
.................

1. The fact that he could not find work unnerved him.                                              1. .................

2. It is true that he could not find work.        2. .................

3. The rumor that prices were going up worried her. 3. .................

4. It is obvious that the typist is incompetent.   4. .................

5. The hope that help was near comforted them.    5. .................

6. It soon became evident that help was near.      6. .................

7. The report that his children were safe relieved his anxiety.                                        7. .................

8. We accepted the proposal that members might invite guests to the lecture.                        8. .................

9. It was certain that she was implicated in the plot.  9. .................

10. It is my belief that you will return to America.  10. .................

11. It is obvious that the cost of living has risen.  11. .................

12. The fact that he was well-trained gave him the opportunity to advance.                          12. .................

## WORDS THAT INTRODUCE NOUN CLAUSES

A *noun clause* may be introduced by a **subordinate conjunction.**
The subordinate conjunctions commonly used in this way are *that,
whether,* and *whether - or.* The sole duty of the subordinate conjunction
is to connect the noun clause to the main clause.

I wonder <u>whether</u> they will recognize me.
          subordinate conjunction

John knows <u>that</u> he will be nominated for an office.
           subordinate conjunction

*Whether* (not *if*) should be used to introduce noun clauses used as
the direct object of the verbs *say, learn, understand, know, doubt,
wonder,* etc.

Ask John **if** he has washed the car. (incorrect)

Ask John **whether** he has washed the car. (correct)

I did not know **if** he would leave or stay. (incorrect)

I did not know **whether** he would leave or stay. (correct)

A noun clause is often introduced by a **relative pronoun:** *who,
what, whatever, whoever, whomever, whichever. Whoever* and *whomever* are seldom used in informal writing and speaking.

The agent does not know <u>what</u> he should do about repairs.
                        relative pronoun

Give to the fund <u>whatever</u> you can afford.
                 relative pronoun

A copy of the speech was given to <u>whoever</u> wanted it.
                                  relative pronoun

The relative pronoun that introduces a noun clause is sometimes called an **indefinite relative pronoun** because it does not have an antecedent expressed in the sentence.

Sometimes the relative pronoun is used as an *adjective* in the noun clause. A pronoun used in this way is called a **relative adjective,** or an **indefinite relative adjective** because it has no antecedent.

I shall accept whatever salary is offered me. (*whatever*—adjective)
modifies salary

The manager always knows what course to follow. (*what*—adjective)
modifies course

Noun clauses are also introduced by the adverbs *how, when, why,* and *where.* The introductory adverb also modifies the verb in the noun clause.

How we should invest the money is the question. (*how*—adverb)
noun clause

He asked where the president lived. (*where*—adverb)
noun clause

I do not know when the speaker will arrive. (*when*—adverb)
noun clause

He did not tell why he left the firm. (*why*—adverb)
noun clause

## EXERCISE 4

Underline the **noun clauses**. In the first column to the right, indicate the word which *introduces* the noun clause. In the second column, indicate whether the introductory word is a *subordinate conjunction*, a *relative pronoun*, a *relative adjective*, or an *adverb*.

|  |  | Relative |
|---|---|---|
| Example: <u>Whatever he does</u> is successful. | *Whatever* | *Pronoun* |

1. I believe that the boat has docked. 1. ............... ...............

2. Why he accepted the position was evident to all of us. 2. ............... ...............

3. The child could not tell where he lived. 3. ............... ...............

4. We shall support whichever side wins. 4. ............... ...............

5. I doubt whether he will be able to secure a passport. 5. ............... ...............

6. Whomever the committee recommends will be given the position. 6. ............... ...............

7. We shall publish whatever material the scientist sends us. 7. ............... ...............

8. He did not know which mathematics course he should take. 8. ............... ...............

9. Sue would not tell what she paid for the mink coat. 9. ............... ...............

10. The students were wondering who would pass the army tests. 10. ............... ...............

## EXERCISE 5

Underline the **noun clauses** in the following sentences. On the line to the right, indicate whether the clause is used as the *subject*, *object of the verb*, *object of a preposition*, as a *predicate noun*, in *apposition*, or as the *delayed subject* after the introductory word *it*.

Example: He is proud of what he did.                *obj. of prep.*

1. I knew that the goods were imperfect.              1. .................

2. It is true that the goods are imperfect.           2. .................

3. The fact is that the goods are imperfect.          3. .................

4. The fact that the goods were imperfect caused general dissatisfaction with the firm.              4. .................

5. That the goods were imperfect is a well-known fact.                                                5. .................

6. We did not agree about what caused the imperfections.                                             6. .................

7. Whatever he recommends will be adopted.            7. .................

8. Pay attention to what he tells you.                8. .................

9. I believe that the train will arrive soon.         9. .................

10. My opinion is that the governor will veto the bill.                                               10. .................

11. I hold the opinion that the governor will veto the bill.                                          11. .................

12. It is true that the governor has vetoed the bill. 12. .................

13. Why he sold his factory is a mystery to all of us. 13. .................

14. The members of the club wondered whether an election would be held.                              14. .................

## DIAGRAMMING THE NOUN CLAUSE

### 1. *Noun Clause Used as the Subject of the Sentence*

*Sentence:* How they will raise the money is their problem.
<u>noun clause—subject</u>

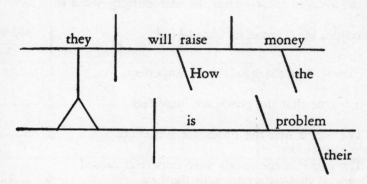

This sentence is a **complex sentence.** The noun clause, *How they will raise the money* is used as the **subject** of the sentence. In the diagram, the noun clause is placed in the position of the subject and is raised on "stilts" so that it will be possible to show the subject and the predicate of the subordinate clause.

### 2. *Noun Clause Used as the Direct Object of the Verb*

*Sentence:* Mary declared that her report was correct.
<u>noun clause—direct object</u>

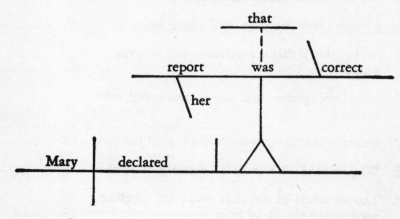

### 3. Noun Clause Used as a Predicate Noun

*Sentence:* My impression was that I had seen him before.

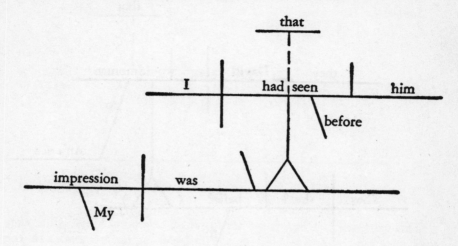

### 4. Noun Clause Used as Object of a Preposition

*Sentence:* I have nothing except what Father has given me.

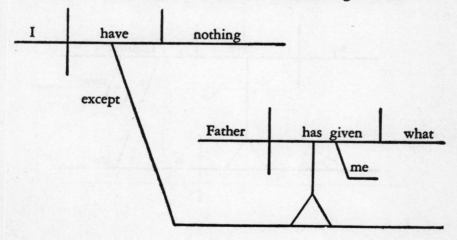

**5. *Noun Clause Used as an Appositive***

*Sentence:* They held the belief that David would return to America.

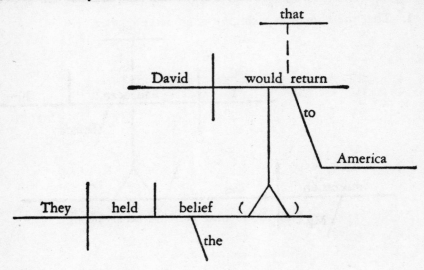

**6. *Noun Clause Used after the Expletive "It"***

*Sentence:* It is true that we have a new Cadillac.

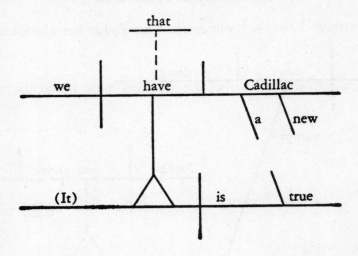

## EXERCISE 6

Diagram the following **complex sentences** containing noun clauses.

1.  That the climate is changing is an accepted fact.

2.  She explained how the furniture should be arranged.

3.  The implication was that the members could attend the meeting.

**EXERCISE 6 (continued)**

4. He held the belief that most men are honest.

5. The agency will give help to whoever needs it.

6. It is evident that you do not know the facts.

## SUMMARY OF GRAMMAR UNIT TWENTY-ONE

A **noun clause** is a subordinate clause that is used as a *noun*. A noun clause may function as the **subject** of the sentence, as the **direct object** of a *verb*, as the **object** of a *preposition*, as a **predicate noun** after a linking verb, as an **appositive,** or as the **delayed subject** after the introductory word *"it."*

A *noun clause* may be introduced by a **subordinate conjunction,** by a **relative pronoun,** a **relative adjective,** or an **adverb.** The relative pronoun that introduces a noun clause is sometimes called an *indefinite relative pronoun* because it has no antecedent expressed in the sentence. The relative adjective is called an *indefinite relative adjective* for the same reason.

The only function of a *subordinate conjunction* in a noun clause is to connect the noun clause to the main clause. The *relative pronoun* has a special function in the noun clause, such as *subject, object,* etc. The *relative adjective* and the *adverb* not only introduce the noun clause, but also modify some word in it.

The word that introduces a subordinate clause is often omitted. The reason for this omission is to bring the main clause and the subordinate clause closer together.

The subordinate conjunction *whether* (not *if*) should be used to introduce a noun clause that is used as the direct object of the verbs *say, learn, know, doubt, wonder, understand,* etc.

A *noun clause* is often the real subject of a sentence that begins with the expletive *it.* Such sentences should be transposed and put in normal or grammatical order. The *noun clause* is the logical subject of the sentence.

## SELF-GRADING ASSIGNMENT 1

Directions: Underline the **noun clauses** in the following sentences. On the line to the right, indicate whether the clause is used as the *subject, direct object* of the verb, or as a *predicate noun.*

1. How to settle the argument was a problem.  1. ..................

2. We believe that we should be prepared for any emergency.  2. ..................

3. The fact is that we have never met him.  3. ..................

4. Where we could put the new furniture was our problem.  4. ..................

5. They proposed that we take certain precautions.  5. ..................

6. The physician decided when the child should have the operation.  6. ..................

7. My fear is that we shall arrive too late.  7. ..................

8. Tell the new employee when he should report.  8. ..................

9. Our reason for leaving was that the weather was too cold.  9. ..................

10. I thought that you had made our reservations.  10. ..................

11. What he accomplished amazed his friends.  11. ..................

12. That conditions would improve was evident.  12. ..................

13. I know that he has several thousand shares of stock.  13. ..................

14. Our hope was that the man would recover.  14. ..................

15. Why he was dismissed was never explained.  15. ..................

*Caution: Check your answers to each assignment with the answer key at the back of the booklet before proceeding with the next assignment.*

## SELF-GRADING ASSIGNMENT 2

Directions: Underline the **noun clauses** in the following sentences. On the line to the right, indicate whether the clause is used as the *object* of a preposition, as an *appositive,* or as the *delayed subject* after the expletive *it*.

Example: It is my belief <u>that he is safe.</u>          *delayed sub.*
...................

1. The fact that the weather was cold was our reason for leaving.                                   1. ...................

2. The stenographer made a list of what we needed.   2. ...................

3. It is obvious that you do not like the plans for a new building.                                   3. ...................

4. I know nothing about him except that he is a lawyer.                                            4. ...................

5. It is inevitable that he will be drafted.          5. ...................

6. The criticism that we were incompetent caused bitter resentment.                              6. ...................

7. We shall rely upon whatever he advises.           7. ...................

8. It is true that the driver was injured in the crash.   8. ...................

9. The decision that every tenant must move caused considerable excitement.                   9. ...................

10. The radio announcement that the strike was over was received with cheers.              10. ...................

11. The old man told his story to whomever he met.   11. ...................

12. The statement that he sold his stock is untrue.   12. ...................

## SELF-GRADING ASSIGNMENT 3

This is a test to show whether you can distinguish between *adjective clauses, adverbial clauses,* and *noun clauses.*

Directions: Underline the **subordinate clauses** in the following sentences. On the line to the right, indicate whether the clause is an *adjective* clause, an *adverbial* clause, or a *noun* clause.

Example: Wait <u>until you are called.</u>     *adverbial*
.................

1. We learned <u>how the parts were assembled.</u>     1. ...................

2. Put the television set <u>where everyone can see the screen.</u>     2. ...................

3. I did not know <u>where I could put the television set.</u>     3. ...................

4. <u>Where I could put the television set</u> was my problem.     4. ...................

5. This is the place <u>where Lincoln was born.</u>     5. ...................

6. He always does his writing at a time <u>when the house is quiet.</u>     6. ...................

7. I never know <u>when the house will be quiet.</u>     7. ...................

8. He lived in an old mansion <u>which was surrounded by an iron fence.</u>     8. ...................

9. The men <u>who were engaged to paint the hall</u> were excellent workmen.     9. ...................

10. We visited many of the art galleries <u>when we traveled in Europe.</u>     10. ...................

11. Do you know a man <u>who can drive a car?</u>     11. ...................

12. People will buy luxuries <u>if the prices are not too high.</u>     12 ...................

## SELF-GRADING ASSIGNMENT 4

Directions: This is a test to show whether you can distinguish between *simple, complex,* and *compound sentences.* On the line to the right, indicate whether the sentence is *simple, complex,* or *compound.*

1. I regret that you must leave early.                     1. ................

2. When I reached the library, I looked up a number of references.                                   2. ................

3. Temporary houses and tents sheltered the immigrants.                                                  3. ................

4. Philip is an excellent worker; nevertheless, he is not as skilled as Robert.                              4. ................

5. Wait in the lobby; I'll get the car.                     5. ................

6. If you need money, write to me at once.                  6. ................

7. The position that he wanted was not available.           7. ................

8. The lights went out, and the room was in total darkness.                                                 8. ................

9. *The Saturday Evening Post, Collier's, and Look* are popular weekly magazines.                         9. ................

10. The speaker received very little attention; in fact, no one spoke to him after the lecture.           10. ................

11. The play was very interesting; it was written by George Bernard Shaw.                               11. ................

12. The road that we chose was very difficult to follow.                                                   12. ................

13. He gave me excellent advice at a time when I needed it.                                               13. ................

14. The manager received the reports and checked them.                                                    14. ................

## PROGRESS TEST TWENTY-ONE

This progress test should not be taken until a day or two after you have completed the assignments. The score you make on the test will then more clearly reflect your understanding of the material in the unit.

### A.

Directions: Underline the **subordinate clauses** in the following sentences. On the line to the right, indicate whether the clause is a *noun* clause, an *adjective* clause, or an *adverbial* clause.    (*30 points*)

**Kind of Clause**

1. Do you like the flowers that I sent to you?        1. ..................

2. Whoever comes first will be served first.        2. ..................

3. The locket that Adele wears belonged to her grandmother.        3. ..................

4. I will tell you where she works.        4. ..................

5. After you have answered these questions, you may go.        5. ..................

6. Since you object to our plan, you should suggest another.        6. ..................

7. Boats which are owned by the residents of the club are anchored in the harbor.        7. ..................

8. The girl whom I selected for the position is a college graduate.        8. ..................

9. I closed the door because it was making a creaking sound.        9. ..................

10. Report what you heard at the meeting.        10. ..................

11. It is a question whether Alex will be promoted.        11. ..................

## PROGRESS TEST TWENTY-ONE (continued)

12. I could not understand why there was so much dissension among the members.

12. ..................

13. The books which you read have a marked influence on your life.

13. ..................

14. Is this the gown that you wore to the reception?

14. ..................

15. When the last patient left, the doctor gave a sigh of relief.

15. ..................

## B.

Directions: On the line to the right, indicate whether the following sentences are *simple sentences, complex sentences,* or *compound sentences.* (*15 points*)

1. Stanley did not enroll in college because he was drafted.

1. ..................

2. If you do not know the meaning of a word, consult a reliable dictionary.

2. ..................

3. Marian baked some cookies and sent them to the service center.

3. ..................

4. Since the weather is stormy, we shall stay home and listen to a radio program.

4. ..................

5. He willed half of his estate to his daughter, but he did not leave anything to the other heirs; he willed the rest to the university.

5. ..................

6. In his perplexity, he went to his lawyer for advice; but the lawyer could not solve the problem for him.

6. ..................

## PROGRESS TEST TWENTY-ONE (continued)

7. It was an excellent speech, but it was entirely too long.

7. ..................

8. A distinguished looking old gentleman mounted the platform and began to speak in a foreign tongue.

8. ..................

9. My friend can handle a canoe as skillfully as an Indian.

9. ..................

10. While we are waiting for the manager, let us examine these blueprints.

10. ..................

11. The soldiers did the work that was assigned to them by the officer in charge.

11. ..................

12. Mr. Allen, who discovered oil on his farm, consulted several engineers.

12. ..................

13. A new car will cost a great deal more this year; however, it will be worth the price.

13. ..................

14. We cannot accept your entire plan, but we shall adopt your suggestions for increasing the output.

14. ..................

15. Experts believe that there are many opportunities in the field of chemical engineering.

15. ..................

## ANSWER KEY

for

## EXERCISES, ASSIGNMENTS, AND PROGRESS TEST

### *Grammar Unit Twenty-one*

---

### CORRECT ANSWERS TO EXERCISE 1

Noun Clauses are printed in **heavy type.**

1. I will show you **where he lives.**     1. *direct object*
2. Martha usually enjoys **whatever she does.**     2. *direct object*
3. **That she is a famous singer** is a well-known fact.     3. *subject*
4. No one knew **what the outcome would be.**     4. *direct object*
5. Do you remember **what you gave her?**     5. *direct object*
6. **How it is done** should be explained in detail.     6. *subject*
7. **What the result will be** is a debatable question.     7. *subject*
8. She revealed **where the fugitive had gone.**     8. *direct object*
9. **Where the meeting will be held** is a secret.     9. *subject*
10. **What we have done** should be an incentive for others.     10. *subject*
11. I did not know **what law he had violated.**     11. *direct object*
12. She did not understand **why they were planning an investigation.**     12. *direct object*
13. **Why he left the city** is still a mystery.     13. *subject*
    Show me **what you are reading.**     14. *direct object*
15. **What he will do** depends upon circumstances.     15. *subject*

### CORRECT ANSWERS TO EXERCISE 2

Noun clauses are printed in **heavy type.**

1. The truth was **that the man had disappeared.**     1. *predicate noun*
2. The report is **that there will be an increase in production.**     2. *predicate noun*

3. Buy the materials at **whichever store is nearest.**

       3. *object of preposition*

4. The criticism was **that the presentation was inadequate.**

       4. *predicate noun*

5. Choose your gift from **whatever remains on the table.**

       5. *object of preposition*

6. Pay more attention to **what the manager tells you.**

       6. *object of preposition*

7. I know nothing except **what you told me.**

       7. *object of preposition*

8. His difficulty was **that he was not trained for the position.**

       8. *predicate noun*

9. The fact is **that the boat was full of holes.**

       9. *predicate noun*

10. He will give help to **whoever needs it.**

       10. *object of preposition*

11. The reason was **that we lacked the money.**

       11. *predicate noun*

12. Harold does well in **whatever position he is placed.**

       12. *object of preposition*

13. We built a cabin with **whatever material was available.**

       13. *object of preposition*

14. My fear is **that we shall be late.**

       14. *predicate noun*

15. Our conclusion was **that we could trust him.**

       15. *predicate noun*

## CORRECT ANSWERS TO EXERCISE 3

Noun clauses are printed in **heavy type.**

1. The fact **that he could not find work** unnerved him.

       1. *apposition*

2. It is true **that he could not find work.**

       2. *delayed subject*

3. The rumor **that prices were going up** worried her.

       3. *apposition*

4. It is obvious **that the typist is incompetent.**

       4. *delayed subject*

5. The hope **that help was near** comforted them.

       5. *apposition*

6. It soon became evident **that help was near.**

       6. *delayed subject*

7. The report **that his chidren were safe** relieved his anxiety.

       7. *apposition*

8. We accepted the proposal *that members might invite guests to the lecture.*

8. *apposition*

9. It was certain *that she was implicated in the plot.*

9. *delayed subject*

10. It is my belief *that you will return to America.*

10. *delayed subject*

11. It is obvious *that the cost of living has risen.*

11. *delayed subject*

12. The fact *that he was well trained* gave him the opportunity to advance.

12. *apposition*

## CORRECT ANSWERS TO EXERCISE 4

Noun clauses are printed in *heavy type.*

1. I believe *that the boat has docked.*

1. that — *subordinate conjunction*

2. *Why he accepted the position* was evident to all of us.

2. Why — *adverb*

3. The child could not tell *where he lived.*

3. where — *adverb*

4. We shall support *whichever side wins.*

4. whichever — *relative adjective*

5. I doubt *whether he will be able to secure a passport.*

5. whether — *subordinate conjunction*

6. *Whomever the committee recommends* will be given the position.

6. Whomever — *relative pronoun*

7. We shall publish *whatever material the scientist sends us.*

7. whatever — *relative adjective*

8. He did not know *which mathematics course he should take.*

8. which — *relative adjective*

9. Sue would not tell *what she paid for the mink coat.*

9. what — *relative pronoun*

10. The students were wondering *who would pass the army tests.*

10. who — *relative pronoun*

## CORRECT ANSWERS TO EXERCISE 5

Noun clauses are printed in *heavy type.*

1. I knew *that the goods were imperfect.*

1. *object of verb*

2. It is true *that the goods are imperfect.*

2. *delayed subject*

3. The fact is *that the goods are imperfect.*

3. *predicate noun*

4. The fact *that the goods were imperfect* caused general dissatisfaction with the firm.

    4. *apposition*

5. *That the goods were imperfect* is a well-known fact.

    5. *subject*

6. We did not agree about *what caused the imperfections.*

    6. *object of preposition*

7. *Whatever he recommends* will be adopted.

    7. *subject*

8. Pay attention to *what he tells you.*

    8. *object of preposition*

9. I believe *that the train will arrive soon.*

    9. *object of verb*

10. My opinion is *that the governor will veto the bill.*

    10. *predicate noun*

11. I hold the opinion *that the governor will veto the bill.*

    11. *apposition*

12. It is true *that the governor has vetoed the bill.*

    12. *delayed subject*

13. *Why he sold his factory* is a mystery to all of us.

    13. *subject*

14. The members of the club wondered *whether an election would be held.*

    14. *object of verb*

## CORRECT ANSWERS TO EXERCISE 6

1. That the climate is changing is an accepted fact.
       noun clause—subject

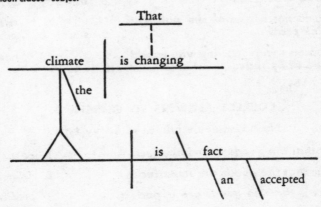

**2. She explained how the furniture should be arranged.**
noun clause—object of the verb

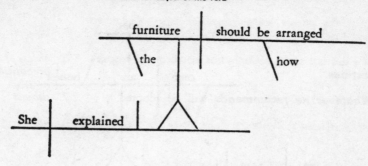

**3. The implication was that the members could attend the meeting.**
noun clause—predicate noun

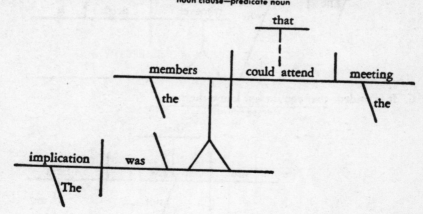

**4. He held the belief that most men are honest.**
<u>noun clause—apposition</u>

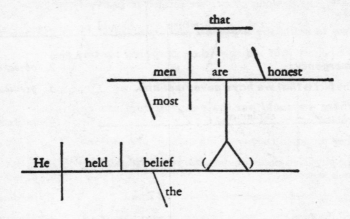

**5. The agency will give help to whoever needs it.**
<u>noun clause—object of preposition</u>

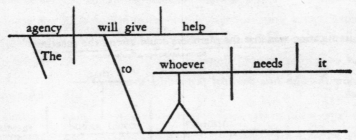

**6. It is evident that you do not know the facts.**
<u>delayed subject</u>

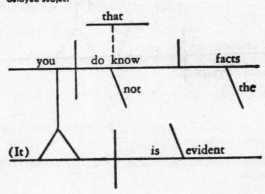

## CORRECT ANSWERS TO ASSIGNMENT 1

Noun clauses are printed in **heavy type.**

1. **How to settle the argument** was a problem.    1. *subject*

2. We believe **that we should be prepared for any emergency.**    2. *object of verb*

3. The fact is **that we have never met him.**    3. *predicate noun*

4. **Where we could put the new furniture** was our problem.    4. *subject*

5. They proposed **that we take certain precautions.**    5. *object of verb*

6. The physician decided **when the child should have the operation.**    6. *object of verb*

7. My fear is **that we shall arrive too late.**    7. *predicate noun*

8. Tell the new employee **when he should report.**    8. *object of verb*

9. Our reason for leaving was **that the weather was too cold.**    9. *predicate noun*

10. I thought **that you had made our reservations.**    10. *object of verb*

11. **What he accomplished** amazed his friends.    11. *subject*

12. **That conditions would improve** was evident.    12. *subject*

13. I know **that he has several thousand shares of stock.**    13. *object of verb*

14. Our hope was **that the man would recover.**    14. *predicate noun*

15. **Why he was dismissed** was never explained.    15. *subject*

## CORRECT ANSWERS TO ASSIGNMENT 2

Noun clauses are printed in **heavy type.**

1. The fact **that the weather was cold** was our reason for leaving.    1. *in apposition*

2. The stenographer made a list of **what we needed.**    2. *object of preposition*

3. It is obvious **that you do not like the plans for a new building.**    3. *delayed subject*

4. I know nothing about him except **that he is a lawyer.**    4. *object of preposition*

5. It is inevitable *that he will be drafted.*                5. *delayed subject*

6. The criticism *that we were incompetent* caused
   bitter resentment.                                         6. *in apposition*

7. We shall rely upon *whatever he advises.*                  7. *object of
                                                                 preposition*

8. It is true *that the driver was injured in the crash.*     8. *delayed subject*

9. The decision *that every tenant must move* caused
   considerable excitement.                                   9. *in apposition*

10. The radio announcement *that the strike was over*
    was received with cheers.                                 10. *in apposition*

11. The old man told his story to *whomever he met.*          11. *object of
                                                                  preposition*

12. The statement *that he sold his stock* is untrue.         12. *in apposition*


## CORRECT ANSWERS TO ASSIGNMENT 3

Subordinate clauses are printed in *heavy type.*

1. We learned *how the parts were assembled.*                 1. *noun*

2. Put the television set *where everyone can see the
   screen.*                                                   2. *adverbial*

3. I did not know *where I could put the television set.*     3. *noun*

4. *Where I could put the television set* was my problem.     4. *noun*

5. This is the place *where Lincoln was born.*                5. *adjective*

6. He always does his writing at a time *when the house
   is quiet.*                                                 6. *adjective*

7. I never know *when the house will be quiet.*               7. *noun*

8. He lived in an old mansion *which was surrounded by
   an iron fence.*                                            8. *adjective*

9. The men *who were engaged to paint the hall* were
   excellent workmen.                                         9. *adjective*

10. We visited many of the art galleries *when we traveled
    in Europe.*                                               10. *adverbial*

11. Do you know a man *who can drive a car?*                  11. *adjective*

12. People will buy luxuries *if the prices are not too high.*  12. *adverbial*

## CORRECT ANSWERS TO ASSIGNMENT 4

1. **complex sentence**—one main clause and one subordinate clause
2. **complex sentence**—one main clause and one subordinate clause
3. **simple sentence** with a compound subject
4. **compound sentence**—two main clauses
5. **compound sentence**—two main clauses
6. **complex sentence**—one main clause and one subordinate clause
7. **complex sentence**—one main clause and one subordinate clause
8. **compound sentence**—two main clauses
9. **simple sentence** with a compound subject
10. **compound sentence**—two main clauses
11. **compound sentence**—two main clauses
12. **complex sentence**—one main clause and one subordinate clause
13. **complex sentence**—one main clause and one subordinate clause
14. **simple sentence** with a compound predicate

## CORRECT ANSWERS TO PROGRESS TEST TWENTY-ONE

Subordinate clauses are printed in **heavy type.**

### A.—(*30 points*)      Kind of Clause

1. Do you like the flowers **that I sent to you?**    1. *adjective*
2. **Whoever comes first** will be served first.    2. *noun clause*
3. The locket **that Adele wears** belonged to her grandmother.    3. *adjective*
4. I will tell you **where she works.**    4. *noun clause*
5. **After you have answered these questions,** you may go.    5. *adverbial*
6. **Since you object to our plan,** you should suggest another.    6. *adverbial*
7. Boats **which are owned by the residents of the club** are anchored in the harbor.    7. *adjective*
8. The girl **whom I selected for the position** is a college graduate.    8. *adjective*

9. I closed the door **because it was making a creaking sound.**     9. *adverbial*

10. Report **what you heard at the meeting.**     10. *noun clause*

11. It is a question **whether Alex will be promoted.**     11. *noun clause*

12. I could not understand **why there was so much dissension among the members.**     12. *noun clause*

13. The books **which you read** have a marked influence on your life.     13. *adjective*

14. Is this the gown **that you wore to the reception?**     14. *adjective*

15. **When the last patient left,** the doctor gave a sigh of relief.     15. *adverbial*

### B.—(*15 points*)

1. **complex sentence**—one main clause and one subordinate clause

2. **complex sentence**—one main clause and one subordinate clause

3. **simple sentence** with a compound predicate

4. **complex sentence**—one main clause and one subordinate clause

5. **compound sentence**—three main clauses

6. **compound sentence**—two main clauses

7. **compound sentence**—two main clauses

8. **simple sentence** with a compound predicate

9. **complex sentence**—one main clause and one subordinate clause

10. **complex sentence**—one main clause and one subordinate clause

11. **complex sentence**—one main clause and one subordinate clause

12. **complex sentence**—one main clause and one subordinate clause

13. **compound sentence**—two main clauses

14. **compound sentence**—two main clauses

15. **complex sentence**—one main clause and one subordinate clause

### HOW TO OBTAIN YOUR SCORE

*The test totals 45 points. To obtain your score, divide the number of your correct answers by 45. The answer will be your score on this test. For example, if you have 40 points correct, your score is 40 divided by 45 which is 89 per cent. In other words, your score on this test is 89. You can obtain your score on any of the exercises or assignments by following the same procedure.*

**Practical English Grammar**

## OUTLINE OF UNIT TWENTY-TWO

# PARTICIPLES

Page

1. THE NATURE OF VERBALS............................................ 5

2. FORMS OF THE PARTICIPLE........................................ 8

3. THE PARTICIPIAL PHRASE ........................................ 12

4. MODIFIERS OF PARTICIPLES...................................... 12

5. COMPLEMENTS OF PARTICIPLES.............................. 13

6. PARTICIPLES USED IN INDEPENDENT
   CONSTRUCTIONS .................................................... 14

7. DANGLING PARTICIPLES ........................................ 16

8. MISPLACED MODIFIERS .......................................... 17

9. PARTICIPLES USED IN VERB PHRASES........................ 19

10. DIAGRAMMING THE PARTICIPIAL PHRASE.............. 22

11. SUMMARY OF GRAMMAR UNIT TWENTY-TWO...... 25

*Self-Grading Assignments* ................................................ 26

*Progress Test Twenty-Two*................................................ 30

*Key to Correct Answers*.................................................... 32

# PARTICIPLES

## THE NATURE OF VERBALS

THERE are three verb forms in English that are known as **verbals:** *participles, infinitives,* and *gerunds.* These verb forms are called *verbals* because they are derived from verbs and retain many of the characteristics of the verb.

A **verbal** may take any kind of modifier or any kind of complement that a verb might take. In addition to this verb-like function, a verbal has a special function of its own. A verbal usually performs the work of two parts of speech at the same time.

There is one function that a *verbal* cannot perform. It cannot function as the predicate verb in a sentence because it is an incomplete form of the verb. A verbal cannot make a statement or ask a question.

A **participle** is a verbal (verb form) which is *used as an adjective.* Since a participle is a verb form and partakes of the nature of a verb, it may take modifiers and complements.

*Participles* do not always take modifiers or complements. Very often they are used as **pure adjectives** and are placed directly before the nouns which they modify. Sometimes they are used as **predicate adjectives** after linking verbs. The following illustrations show the participle used as a simple adjective:

He conducts a <u>flourishing</u> business. (*flourishing* — modifies *business*)
participle<br>or<br>adjective

The reports were <u>discouraging.</u> (*discouraging*—modifies *reports*)
participle<br>or<br>predicate adjective

We are reading an <u>interesting</u> book. (*interesting*—modifies *book*)
participle<br>or<br>adjective

The participle that is most commonly used as an adjective is the participle that ends in *ing*. This is called the **present participle.** In the following illustrations the *present participles* are placed directly before the nouns which they modify. When used in this way, they are generally regarded as pure adjectives.

| | |
|---|---|
| *running* water | *singing* brook |
| *shaking* knees | *rustling* leaves |
| *murmuring* pines | *dangling* modifiers |
| *coming* events | *whistling* boy |
| *soaring* prices | *sleeping* child |

The participles found in the preceding illustrations are *running, shaking, murmuring, coming, soaring, singing, rustling, dangling, whistling,* and *sleeping.* All these forms are derived from verbs.

Many participles are used as pure adjectives. When the participle is used as a pure adjective, it is usually placed directly before the noun which it modifies. When the participle is used as a **predicate adjective,** it is found in the predicate and modifies the subject.

The game was exciting. (*exciting*—used as a predicate adjective)
participle

The book is interesting. (*interesting*—predicate adjective)
participle

The rumors were startling. (*startling*—used as a predicate adjective)
participle

In the first sentence, the participle *exciting* is used as a predicate adjective, modifying the noun *game.* The participle *interesting,* in the second sentence modifies the noun *book.* In the third sentence, the participle *startling* is used as a predicate adjective, modifying the subject noun *rumors.* The participles *exciting, interesting,* and *startling* are forms of verbs.

---

**A participle is a verb form which is used as an adjective**

---

## EXERCISE 1

Underline the **participles** in the following sentences On the line to the right, indicate the word which the participle *modifies*.

Example: His attitude was <u>irritating.</u>

**Modifies**
attitude
..................

1. Shouting, the men walked down the street.          1. ...............

2. He manages a thriving business.                    2. ...............

3. The men, shouting, walked down the street.         3. ...............

4. The woman, weeping, told her story to the judge.   4. ...............

5. He walked to the cottage in his dripping clothes.  5. ...............

6. Weeping, the woman told her story to the judge.    6. ...............

7. The barking dog frightened the child.              7. ...............

8. The dog, barking, frightened the child.            8. ...............

9. Grumbling, the old man sat down on the bench.      9. ...............

10. The senator's speech was stimulating.             10. ...............

11. The leaves, fluttering, dropped to the ground.    11. ...............

12. The limping child tried to follow the parade.     12. ...............

*Note: The correct answers to exercises will be found at the back of this booklet. Correct your mistakes, and if necessary, re-read the text material before going on to the next section.*

## FORMS OF THE PARTICIPLE

There are three participles that are commonly used as adjectives: the *present participle* (active voice); the *past participle* (passive voice); and the *perfect participle* (active voice). There is no active past participle in English.

These participles are easily recognized. The **present participle** always ends in *ing;* the **past participle** usually ends in *ed, d, t, n,* or *en.* The past participles of some of the irregular verbs do not have distinctive endings: *swum, drunk, gone, sung,* etc. The **perfect participle** is always formed by prefixing the word *having* to the past participle: *having sung, having called, having driven, having seen,* etc.

| Present Participle | Past Participle | Perfect Participle |
|---|---|---|
| (*active*) | (*passive*) | (*active*) |
| singing | sung | having sung |
| driving | driven | having driven |
| calling | called | having called |
| building | built | having built |
| going | gone | having gone |
| watching | watched | having watched |

### PAST PARTICIPLES AND PERFECT PARTICIPLES

The past participle ending in *ed* is commonly used as an adjective. The following illustrations show how *past participles* function as *adjectives*:

A doctor, **called** to the scene, examined the injured man.

The **neglected** and **forgotten** child was picked up by an officer.

The army, **surprised** by the attack, fled into the woods.

The street was littered with paper, **thrown** from the windows.

In the first sentence, the past participle, which is used as an adjective, is the word *called*. The participle is modified by the adverbial phrase, *to the scene*. There are two past participles in the second sentence, *neglected* and *forgotten*. One ends in *ed* and the other ends in *en*. These participles modify the noun *child*. In this sentence, the participles are placed directly before the noun *child*, which they modify.

The past participle *surprised* in the third sentence is modified by the adverbial phrase *by the attack*. The past participle *thrown* in the last sentence is modified by the adverbial phrase *from the windows*. The participle *thrown* modifies the noun paper.

The following sentences show the adjective use of the *perfect participle*:

Having finished the dress, Mary packed it carefully in a box.

Having completed the job, the men left early.

Having accomplished his mission, the ambassador returned home.

Having recovered completely, Ted left the hospital.

The perfect participles in the preceding illustrations are *having finished, having completed, having accomplished,* and *having recovered*. The first three take direct objects—*dress, job,* and *mission*. The last one, *having recovered*, is modified by the adverb *completely*. They are all in the active voice.

The perfect participle, *having finished*, modifies the noun *Mary*. *Having completed* modifies the noun *men; having accomplished* modifies *ambassador,* and *having recovered* modifies *Ted*. These participles are used as adjectives.

## EXERCISE 2

Fill in the table by giving the *present participles*, the *past participles*, and the *perfect participles* of the following verbs:

| Verb | Present Participle (*active*) | Past Participle | Perfect Participle (*active*) |
|---|---|---|---|
| 1. meet | ..................... | ..................... | ..................... |
| 2. break | ..................... | ..................... | ..................... |
| 3. sing | ..................... | ..................... | ..................... |
| 4. drive | ..................... | ..................... | ..................... |
| 5. keep | ..................... | ..................... | ..................... |
| 6. cut | ..................... | ..................... | ..................... |
| 7. catch | ..................... | ..................... | ..................... |
| 8. pay | ..................... | ..................... | ..................... |
| 9. tell | ..................... | ..................... | ..................... |
| 10. leave | ..................... | ..................... | ..................... |
| 11. lie (recline) | ..................... | ..................... | ..................... |
| 12. finish | ..................... | ..................... | ..................... |

## EXERCISE 3

Underline the *past participles* and the *perfect participles* in the following sentences. On the line to the right, indicate the word which the participle *modifies*.

**Modifies**

Example: <u>Having finished</u> our work, we went home.        we
        *perfect participle*
.................

1. Fascinated by the speaker, I forgot my errand.    1. .................

2. Designed by a famous architect, the new office
   building is very beautiful.                        2. .................

3. The mended nets were returned to the fishermen.  3. .................

4. The girl, having swum to the shore, came out
   of the water.                                      4. .................

5. The curtains, soiled and torn, lay in a heap
   on the floor.                                      5. .................

6. Stephen took all the required courses in science. 6. .................

7. Having been a stenographer, she knew how to
   cut a stencil.                                     7. .................

8. The men in the factory became discouraged.        8. .................

9. Having made his decision, Jack prepared to
   leave.                                             9. .................

10. The wrecked automobile was taken to the
    garage.                                          10. .................

11. The defeated team resolved to play again.       11. .................

12. Having gained sufficient skill, Mae secured
    a position as a typist.                          12. .................

## THE PARTICIPIAL PHRASE

Since the participle is derived from a verb, it retains many of the characteristics of a verb. Like the verb, a participle may take **modifiers** and **complements**. The participle with its *modifiers* or *complements*, or with both complements and modifiers is called a **participial phrase.**

## MODIFIERS OF PARTICIPLES

A participle is often modified by an adverb or an adverbial phrase:

Looking up suddenly, Robert saw a rainbow in the sky.
        adv.   adv.

Coming close to the rock, we saw a strange sight.
       adv.  adv. ph.

In the first sentence, the participle *looking* modifies the noun *Robert.* The participle *looking* is modified by the adverb *up* and the adverb *suddenly. Looking up suddenly* is a **participial phrase.**

In the second sentence, the participle *coming* modifies the pronoun *we.* The participle *coming* is modified by the adverb *close* and the adverbial phrase *to the rock. Coming close to the rock* is a **participial phrase.**

The participles in the following sentences also take *adverbial modifiers*:

Trembling with excitement, Sara waited for her friends.
          participial phrase
(Participial phrase modifies the noun *Sara.*)

The house, remodeled recently, is very attractive.
          participial phrase
(Participial phrase modifies the noun *house.*)

We saw an old man lying on the road.
                  participial phrase
(Participial phrase modifies the noun *man.*)

In the first sentence the participial phrase consists of the participle *trembling* and its modifier, the adverbial phrase *with excitement.* The phrase, taken as a whole, modifies the noun *Sara*. The participial phrase *trembling with excitement* is used as an adjective, modifying *Sara*.

In the second sentence, the participial phrase consists of the participle *remodeled* and the adverbial modifier, the adverb *recently*. The entire phrase, *remodeled recently,* is used as an adjective, modifying the noun *house*.

In the third sentence, the participial phrase is *lying on the road*. It consists of the participle *lying* and the adverbial phrase *on the road*. The entire phrase, *lying on the road,* modifies the noun *man*.

## COMPLEMENTS OF PARTICIPLES

**1. Like the verb, a participle may take a direct object if the verb expresses action.**

Carrying a suitcase, the porter entered the train.
participle    dir. obj.
participial phrase

Realizing the danger, the captain ordered a retreat.
participle    dir. obj.
participial phrase

In the first sentence, the noun *suitcase* is the direct object of the participle *Carrying*. The entire expression, *Carrying a suitcase,* is a participial phrase. The participial phrase modifies the noun *porter*.

In the second sentence, the noun *danger* is the direct object of the participle *realizing*. The entire expression, *Realizing the danger,* is a participial phrase. The participial phrase modifies the noun *captain*.

**2. Like the verb, a participle may be followed by a predicate noun or a predicate adjective.**

Participles that take predicate nouns or predicate adjectives as complements are forms of *linking verbs*.

Being an invalid, he could not climb the steep hill.
participle    pred. noun
participial phrase

Becoming weary, the traveler sat down to rest.
participle    pred. adj.
participial phrase

In the first sentence, the participle *being* is followed by the predicate noun *invalid*. The noun *invalid* refers to the same person as the subject *he*. The entire expression, *being an invalid,* is a participial phrase. The participial phrase modifies the subject pronoun *he*. *Being* is a form of the linking verb *to be*.

In the second sentence, the participle *becoming* is followed by the predicate adjective *weary*. The entire expression, *becoming weary,* is a participial phrase, modifying the noun *traveler*. *Becoming* is a form of the linking verb *to become*.

## PARTICIPLES USED IN INDEPENDENT CONSTRUCTIONS

Sometimes a participle is used with a noun in an independent construction; that is, the participle and the noun which it modifies are not related grammatically to any other part of the sentence. Such a construction is called the **nominative absolute construction.**

The term *absolute* is used because the entire expression is an *independent construction*. It forms part of a sentence, but is not connected with the rest of the sentence grammatically. The term *nominative* is used because the noun which the participle modifies is in the *nominative case*. The following illustrations will make this use of the participle clear:

<u>The sun having set</u>, we decided to return home.
     independent construction

<u>The train being late</u>, the soldiers missed the boat.
     independent construction

In the first sentence, the expression, *The sun having set,* consists of the perfect participle *having set* and the noun *sun* with its modifier *The*. The entire expression, *The sun having set,* is used *absolutely* or independently. It has no grammatical connection with the rest of the sentence. The noun *sun* is in the nominative case.

The expression, *The train being late,* in the second sentence is also a *nominative absolute construction;* that is, it has no grammatical relation to the rest of the sentence. The noun *train* is in the nominative case. It is modified by the expression *being late,* which consists of the participle *being* and the predicate adjective *late*.

## EXERCISE 4

Underline the **participial phrases** in the following sentences. On the line to the right, indicate the word the participial phrase *modifies*.

**Modifies**

Example: I found Jack <u>polishing the car.</u>                    Jack
participial phrase                    .....................

1. Leaping over the wall, the young man disappeared from sight.                    1. ...................

2. Weakened by the loss of blood, the boy fainted.                    2. ...................

3. Having finished the job, the painters left early.                    3. ...................

4. Approaching quietly, the deer startled the hunter.                    4. ...................

5. Walking along the highway, I met a band of gypsies.                    5. ...................

6. Having discovered the error, the accountant corrected it immediately.                    6. ...................

7. The road, winding in and out, was not easy to follow.                    7. ...................

8. The tourists, standing on top of the mountain, admired the wonderful view.                    8. ...................

9. Having settled our business affairs, we adjourned.                    9. ...................

10. The planes, flying overhead, attracted our attention.                    10. ...................

11. The captain, being an excellent swimmer, rescued the drowning man.                    11. ...................

12. The ship, driven by the wind, crashed on a rock.                    12. ...................

## DANGLING PARTICIPLES

Participles are often used incorrectly in speaking and writing. One of the most common mistakes in English is to use what is commonly referred to as the **dangling participle**. Anything that dangles is said *to hang loosely*, without secure attachment. A participle "dangles" when there is no word in the sentence which it could properly modify, or when it seems to be related to a word which does not convey the meaning intended.

It is easy to detect these loose participial modifiers. Sometimes the use of a *dangling modifier* gives a ridiculous or a humorous slant to the meaning of the sentence. You can avoid this error if you think through your sentences carefully and relate the participle to the proper word.

When the participial phrase is placed at the beginning of a sentence, it should refer to the subject. When it could not possibly modify the subject from the standpoint of meaning, the sentence must be rewritten and a suitable subject supplied which it could logically modify.

Walking through the tunnel, a wallet was picked up.
dangling modifier

Entering the harbor, the Statue of Liberty came into view.
dangling modifier

After taking the test, the teacher gave me a passing grade.
dangling modifier

In the first sentence, the participial phrase *walking through the tunnel* modifies the subject of the sentence, which is *tunnel*. A participle used at the beginning of a sentence modifies the subject. It is evident that the wallet was not walking through the tunnel; however, that is the meaning conveyed by the sentence as it is written. Very often the best way to get rid of a dangling participle is to substitute a clause for it.

While we were walking through the tunnel, we picked up a wallet.

In the second sentence, the participial phrase modifies *Statue of Liberty*. But it was not the *Statue of Liberty* that was entering the harbor. The phrase seems to be related to a word which it could not modify. The word which the participial phrase really modifies is not in the sentence. The sentence might be revised as follows:

<u>As we entered the harbor</u>, the Statue of Liberty came into view.

In the last sentence, the participial phrase modifies the word *teacher*. If you read the sentence carefully, you will readily see that it was not the teacher who took the test. The sentence would be correctly written if a clause were substituted for the dangling phrase.

<u>After I took the test</u>, the teacher gave me a passing grade.

## MISPLACED MODIFIERS

Sometimes there is a word in the sentence which the participial phrase properly modifies, but the participle is not placed correctly. As a result, the meaning is confused. This error is commonly referred to as a **misplaced modifier.**

<u>Jumping into the water</u>, the children were rescued by the life guard. misplaced modifier

Several soldiers passed by in their uniforms <u>recently drafted</u>.
misplaced modifier

If you read the first sentence carefully, you will see that the word which the participle modifies is in the sentence. It is the word *lifeguard*. It was the *lifeguard* who jumped into the water. It was not the *children*. The trouble with the sentence is that the participial phrase should modify the subject. As the sentence is written, the subject is *children*. The subject should be the word *lifeguard*. The sentence might be rewritten as follows:

<u>Jumping into the water</u>, the lifeguard rescued the children.
participial phrase

In the second sentence, a participial modifier is also misplaced. As the sentence is written, the participial phrase modifies the word *uniforms*. But it was not the *uniforms* that were recently drafted; it was the *soldiers*. The sentence might be rewritten as follows:

Several <u>recently drafted</u> soldiers passed by in their uniforms.
participial phrase

## EXERCISE 5

Underline the **dangling participial phrases** and the **misplaced modifiers.** Write the words *dangling modifier* or *misplaced modifier* under the phrase that you underlined.

Example: <u>Entering the stadium,</u> the game started.
<br>dangling modifier

1.  Crossing the desert, the stretches of sand seemed endless.

2.  Wearing our raincoats and galoshes, the storm did not stop us.

3.  Having stopped for refreshments, the journey was continued.

4.  I found my keys returning to my room.

5.  Driving along the deserted road, the radio was a comfort to me.

6.  Having eaten our lunch, the taxi driver took us home.

7.  Being alone, an officer assisted the old man across the street.

8.  Having played golf all morning, our appetites were enormous.

9.  Lying on the beach, our thoughts went back to other days.

10. Searching among the records, his will was found.

11. I left my purse on the bus containing my money and keys.

12.  Lying on the table, I found John's hat.

13. Working alone at night, the plan was worked out successfully.

14. Looking at the sunset, an airplane passed overhead.

15. Not having a road map, the town was difficult to find.

## PARTICIPLES USED IN VERB PHRASES

*Participles* are not always used as adjectives. One of their most important uses is to help form a *verb phrase.* When the participle forms part of a verb phrase, it is not considered as a separate word, but as part of the verb phrase.

A participle is never used alone as the predicate verb in a sentence because it is an incomplete form of the verb. It is used as part of a verb phrase. The following illustrations show how the participle is used as part of a verb phrase:

The janitor is washing the windows. (*washing*—part of verb phrase)
<u>verb phrase</u>

The gardener has planted the shrubs. (*planted*—part of verb phrase)
<u>verb phrase</u>

In the first sentence, the verb phrase *is washing* is made up of the auxiliary verb *is* and the present participle of the verb *wash,* or the *ing* participle, *washing.* In the second sentence, the verb phrase *has planted* is made up of the auxiliary *has* and the past participle of the verb *plant,* which is *planted.*

Sometimes it is difficult to determine whether the participle is part of the verb phrase, or whether it is used as an adjective modifying the subject. This is often true when a participle follows a linking verb. The meaning of the sentence will help you determine which use is intended by the speaker or writer. Study the following sentences carefully:

The talk was **inspiring.** (participle, used as an *adjective*)

We **were inspired** by his talk. (participle, part of *verb phrase*)

In the first sentence, the verb is *was,* not *was inspiring.* The verb *was* is a linking verb and requires a complement. In this sentence the complement is *inspiring,* which is used as a predicate adjective modifying the noun *talk.* The sentence means *inspiring talk. Inspiring* is a participle used as an adjective.

In the second sentence, the verb is *were inspired.* In this sentence, the past participle *inspired* is part of the verb phrase, *were inspired.* Study the following sentences carefully. Try to determine whether the participle is used as an adjective or is part of the verb phrase:

Robert was elected secretary at our last meeting. (*elected*—part
<u>verb phrase</u>
of the verb phrase)

The old man looked neglected. (*neglected*—participle used as
adjective)        modifies man

The milk seems frozen. (*frozen*—participle used as adjective)

modifies milk

The house was furnished by an interior decorator. (*furnished*—
<u>verb phrase</u>
part of verb phrase)

I have been sitting here for an hour. (*sitting*—part of verb
phrase) verb phrase

We were exhausted after the swim. (*exhausted*—participle used

modifies we
as adjective)

When the participle follows a linking verb, it is used as an adjective
if it describes the state or the condition of the subject. In the second
sentence, the participle *neglected* describes the condition of the old
man. In the third sentence, the participle *frozen* describes the condition
of the milk. Both participles are used as adjectives. In the last sentence,
the participle *exhausted* also describes the condition of the subject, *we.*

## EXERCISE 6

Underline the **participles** in the following sentences. On the line to the right, indicate whether the participle is used as an *adjective,* or as part of a *verb phrase.*

**Adjective or Part of Verb Phrase**

Example: The men are <u>mixing</u> the cement.   *part of verb phrase*

1. The girl in the blue dress is charming.   1. ...................

2. We were charmed by her manner.   2. ...................

3. The reports were discouraging.   3. ...................

4. We were discouraged by the recent reports.   4. ...................

5. We are planning a trip to Hawaii.   5. ...................

6. A man in the crowd was whistling a tune.   6. ...................

7. The adventure proved fascinating.   7. ...................

8. We were fascinated by the magician.   8. ...................

9. The detective has examined everything in the room.   9. ...................

10. They are trying a new experiment.   10. ...................

11. The food was tempting.   11. ...................

12. Jack was throwing a fast ball.   12. ...................

13. The dress was torn.   13. ...................

14. The houses were painted by inexperienced men.   14. ...................

15. The river was rising steadily.   15. ...................

## DIAGRAMMING THE PARTICIPIAL PHRASE

When a participle is used as a pure adjective, it is usually diagrammed in the same way as an adjective is diagrammed. This applies when it is placed directly before the noun which it modifies, or when it is used as a predicate adjective after a linking verb.

The following is the method that is used in diagramming the *participial phrase:*

*Sentence:* The colonel, carrying an American flag, led the parade.
                        participial phrase

In this sentence, *carrying an American flag*, is a participial phrase modifying the noun *colonel*. The participle *carrying* takes the direct object *flag*. The noun *flag* is modified by the article *an* and the proper adjective *American*.

### DIAGRAM

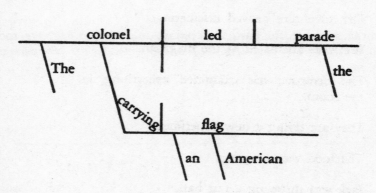

In this diagram, the participle is placed on an angle between a slanted line which joins a horizontal line. The participle is placed so that it slants across and touches the two lines. Note the position of the participle *carrying* in the diagram. The direct object *flag* is placed on the horizontal line and is diagrammed in the same way as the object of a verb is always diagrammed.

*Sentence:* Being an ambassador, my uncle entertained lavishly.
<u>participial phrase</u>

In this sentence, *Being an ambassador,* is a participial phrase, modifying the noun *uncle.* The participle *being* takes the predicate noun *ambassador* to complete the meaning. The noun *ambassador* is modified by the article *an.*

**DIAGRAM**

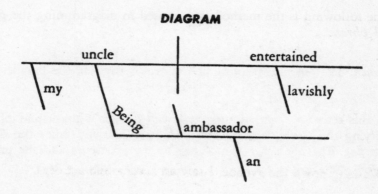

*Sentence:* Loaded with baggage, the truck moved out of the station.
<u>participial phrase</u>

In this sentence, the participial phrase, *loaded with baggage,* modifies the noun *truck.* The participle *loaded* is modified by the adverbial phrase *with baggage.*

**DIAGRAM**

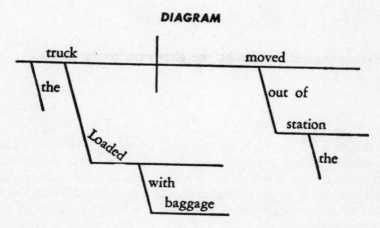

### EXERCISE 7

Diagram the following sentences, using the methods of diagramming that have been presented in this unit.

1.  The man wearing a military uniform is my brother.

2.  Walking down the avenue, I saw an automobile accident.

3.  Having finished their tasks, the girls went to the theater.

## SUMMARY OF GRAMMAR UNIT TWENTY-TWO

A **verbal** is a form of a verb which is used as another part of speech. There are three verbals in English—*participles, gerunds,* and *infinitives.*

A *verbal* retains many of the characteristics of a verb, but it cannot function as the predicate verb in a sentence because it is an incomplete verb form. A verbal cannot make a statement, ask a question, or express a command.

A *verbal* may take any **complement** or any adverbial **modifier** that a verb may take. When verbals take complements or modifiers, they function as two parts of speech at the same time.

A **participle** is a verbal (verb form) which is used as an *adjective.*

A **participial phrase** consists of a participle and any modifiers or complements that the participle may have in the sentence. A participial phrase functions as an *adjective.*

A **dangling participle** is a participle which does not modify any word in the sentence. *Dangling participles* usually appear at the beginning of a sentence. When a participle is placed at the beginning of a sentence, it logically modifies the subject. If the subject is not the word which the participle properly modifies, the participle "dangles."

A **misplaced modifier** is a modifier that is incorrectly placed in the sentence. The modifier must be attached to the word which it modifies and not to some other word. When a modifier is misplaced, it often leads to a wrong interpretation of the sentence.

A participle or a participial phrase is often used with a noun or a pronoun in an independent construction. Such an expression is often called a **nominative absolute.** An absolute expression is one that is *grammatically independent* of the rest of the sentence. A noun or a pronoun used in a *nominative absolute* construction is in the *nominative case.*

### SELF-GRADING ASSIGNMENT 1

Directions: Underline the **participles** used as *simple adjectives* in the following sentences. On the line to the right, indicate the word the adjective *modifies*.

**Modifies**

Example: I spoke to the <u>defeated</u> candidate.          candidate

1. His new job is interesting.                                    1. ..................

2. The sobbing woman was led from the courtroom. 2. ..................

3. He worried about the declining value
   of his property.                                               3. ..................

4. The remodeled house is very attractive.           4. ..................

5. We did not meet the defeated candidate.          5. ..................

6. Many colored flowers grow in her garden.         6. ..................

7. The contract is binding.                                    7. ..................

8. On his desk they found a revised manuscript.   8. ..................

9. The situation looks encouraging.                       9. ..................

10. We discovered a number of winding roads.     10. ..................

11. Apply the method in a given situation.           11. ..................

12. A barking dog ran down the street.               12. ..................

13. The judge was an interested listener.            13. ..................

14. Joe's antics were tantalizing.                        14. ..................

15. The discouraged athlete gave up the contest.  15. ..................

*Caution: Check your answers to each assignment with the answer key at the back of the booklet before proceeding with the next assignment.*

## SELF-GRADING ASSIGNMENT 2

Directions: Underline the **participial phrases** in the following sentences. On the line to the right, indicate the word that the participial phrase *modifies*.

**Modifies**

Example: <u>Returning to the office,</u> I finished the report.      I
...............

1. The hamper, filled with food, suddenly disappeared.

   1. ...............

2. The senator, urging immediate action, concluded his speech.

   2. ...............

3. Spurred by ambition, Andrew entered the university.

   3. ...............

4. Withdrawing quietly, Jim hastened to the news office.

   4. ...............

5. Encouraged by her success, Mary bought a home.   5. ...............

6. Having lost his fortune, Richard looked for a job.

   6. ...............

7. Mrs. Oakes, polishing the silverware, complained about the work.

   7. ...............

8. Screaming loudly, the child ran to his mother.   8. ...............

9. Listening to the radio, Raymond heard the entire opera.

   9. ...............

10. The doctor, operating immediately, saved Henry's life.

    10. ...............

11. Having lost his ticket, John returned home.   11. ...............

12. This is a copy of the letter sent to the president.   12. ...............

13. Having eaten our lunch, we continued our journey.

    13. ...............

14. The detective, listening to the men, recognized Miller's voice.

    14. ...............

## SELF-GRADING ASSIGNMENT 3

Directions: Each of the following sentences contains a participial phrase used as a modifier. If the phrase dangles, write *dangling modifier* in the blank space to the right. If it does not dangle, write *correct* on the line. Underline the **participial phrases**.

Example: <u>Eating my lunch</u>, the room seemed very
attractive.                                          *dangling modifier*
........................................

1. Walking up the hill, the road was very slippery.

    1. ...................

2. Driving down town, the icy roads made me nervous.

    2. ...................

3. Arriving at the inn, the beautiful mountain scenery thrilled us.

    3. ...................

4. Listening to the radio, an hour passed by.

    4. ...................

5. Being of Irish stock, my parents had a sense of humor.

    5. ...................

6. Highly spiced, Jane could not eat the food.

    6. ...................

7. The driver suddenly noticed an officer standing near him.

    7. ...................

8. Leaving Chicago in the morning, our trip was very exciting.

    8. ...................

9. Being very active, the extra work did not tire our manager.

    9. ...................

10. Entering the shop, a television set was turned on for a demonstration.

    10. ...................

11. Being done, the cook removed the cake from the oven.

    11. ...................

12. Having finished the letter, it was posted.

    12. ...................

13. Glancing through the editorials, the newspaper impressed me favorably.

    13. ...................

14. Arriving home late, my supper was on the table.

    14. ...................

## SELF-GRADING ASSIGNMENT 4

Directions: Diagram the following sentences, using the methods of diagramming that have been presented in this unit.

1. Driving recklessly, Tom had a serious accident.

2. Carrying a heavy suitcase, James walked to the station.

3. Being a delegate, Father attended every meeting.

## PROGRESS TEST TWENTY-TWO

This progress test should not be taken until a day or two after you have completed the assignments. The score you make on the test will then more clearly reflect your understanding of the material in the unit.

Directions: Each of the following sentences contains a participial phrase. If the phrase dangles, write *dangling modifier* in the blank space. If the phrase is a misplaced modifier, write *misplaced modifier* in the blank space. If the sentence is correct, write *correct* on the line. Underline the **participial phrase.** *(44 points)*

Example: <u>Having seen the play</u>, my money
was refunded.                  *dangling modifier*
.......................................

1. I found a wallet walking down the street.    1. ................

2. Seeking an answer, the problem was solved.    2. ................

3. Being interested in poetry, the lecture
   appealed to me.    3. ................

4. Answering the telephone, the book lay
   unopened.    4. ................

5. Commencing to rain, we turned back.    5. ................

6. Entering the room, Jack turned on the lights.    6. ................

7. Knowing the owner, our rent was not raised.    7. ................

8. Leaving her ironing, Mary answered the
   telephone.    8. ................

9. The tower is easily seen walking down
   Michigan Avenue.    9. ................

10. Having a heavy suitcase, the conductor
    assisted me.    10. ................

## PROGRESS TEST TWENTY-TWO (continued)

11. One of the little refugees hid behind her mother, crying bitterly.

11. ................

12. Floating on the surface of the pond, we saw some beautiful water lilies.

12. ................

13. Walking toward the pictures, the names of the artists could be clearly seen.

13. ................

14. Arriving at the bank, we found that it was closed.

14. ................

15. Mother found an old trunk looking for something in the attic.

15. ................

16. Being alone, I turned on the radio for company.

16. ................

17. Having reached home, I dressed for dinner.

17. ................

18. I saw a strange looking man enter the house wearing a leather jacket.

18. ................

19. Checking the car, the engine stopped.

19. ................

20. Waiting for an hour, Martha finally arrived.

20. ................

21. Having finished our work, the outdoors seemed refreshing.

21. ................

22. Made of silk and lace, she found her grandmother's dress in an old trunk.

22. ................

## ANSWER KEY
for
## EXERCISES, ASSIGNMENTS, AND PROGRESS TEST
### Grammar Unit Twenty-two

---

### CORRECT ANSWERS TO EXERCISE 1

1.  *Shouting*, the men walked down the street.        1. men
2.  He manages a *thriving* business.                  2. business
3.  The men, *shouting*, walked down the street.       3. men
4.  The woman, *weeping*, told her story to the judge. 4. woman
5.  He walked to the cottage in his *dripping* clothes. 5. clothes
6.  *Weeping*, the woman told her story to the judge.  6. woman
7.  The *barking* dog frightened the child.            7. dog
8.  The dog, *barking*, frightened the child.          8. dog
9.  *Grumbling*, the old man sat down on the bench.    9. man
10. The senator's speech was *stimulating*.            10. speech
11. The leaves, *fluttering*, dropped to the ground.   11. leaves
12. The *limping* child tried to follow the parade.    12. child

### CORRECT ANSWERS TO EXERCISE 2

| | | | |
|---|---|---|---|
| 1. meet | meeting | met | having met |
| 2. break | breaking | broken | having broken |
| 3. sing | singing | sung | having sung |
| 4. drive | driving | driven | having driven |
| 5. keep | keeping | kept | having kept |
| 6. cut | cutting | cut | having cut |
| 7. catch | catching | caught | having caught |
| 8. pay | paying | paid | having paid |
| 9. tell | telling | told | having told |
| 10. leave | leaving | left | having left |
| 11. lie (recline) | lying | lain | having lain |
| 12. finish | finishing | finished | having finished |

## CORRECT ANSWERS TO EXERCISE 3

1. *Fascinated* by the speaker, I forgot my errand.

2. *Designed* by a famous architect, the new office building is very beautiful.

3. The *mended* nets were returned to the fishermen.

4. The girl, *having swum* to the shore, came out of the water.

5. The curtains, *soiled* and *torn*, lay in a heap on the floor.

6. Stephen took all the *required* courses in science.

7. *Having been* a stenographer, she knew how to cut a stencil.

8. The men in the factory became *discouraged*.

9. *Having made* his decision, Jack prepared to leave.

10. The *wrecked* automobile was taken to the garage.

11. The *defeated* team resolved to play again.

12. *Having gained* sufficient skill, Mae secured a position as a typist.

1. I

2. building

3. nets

4. girl

5. curtains

6. courses

7. she

8. men

9. Jack

10. automobile

11. team

12. Mae

## CORRECT ANSWERS TO EXERCISE 4

1. *Leaping over the wall,* the young man disappeared from sight.

2. *Weakened by the loss of blood,* the boy fainted.

3. *Having finished the job,* the painters left early.

4. *Approaching quietly,* the deer startled the hunter.

5. *Walking along the highway,* I met a band of gypsies.

6. *Having discovered the error,* the accountant corrected it immediately.

7. The road, *winding in and out,* was not easy to follow.

8. The tourists, *standing on top of the mountain,* admired the wonderful view.

9. *Having settled our business affairs,* we adjourned.

10. The planes, *flying overhead,* attracted our attention.

11. The captain, *being an excellent swimmer,* rescued the drowning man.

12. The ship, *driven by the wind,* crashed on a rock.

1. man

2. boy

3. painters

4. deer

5. I

6. accountant

7. road

8. tourists

9. we

10. planes

11. captain

12. ship

## CORRECT ANSWERS TO EXERCISE 5

1. Crossing the desert, the stretches of sand seemed endless.
   *dangling modifier*

2. Wearing our raincoats and galoshes, the storm did not stop us.
   *dangling modifier*

3. Having stopped for refreshments, the journey was continued.
   *dangling modifier*

4. I found my keys returning to my room.
   *misplaced modifier*

5. Driving along the deserted road, the radio was a comfort to me.
   *dangling modifier*

6. Having eaten our lunch, the taxi driver took us home.
   *dangling modifier*

7. Being alone, an officer assisted the old man across the street.
   *misplaced modifier*

8. Having played golf all morning, our appetites were enormous.
   *dangling modifier*

9. Lying on the beach, our thoughts went back to other days.
   *dangling modifier*

10. Searching among the records, his will was found.
    *dangling modifier*

11. I left my purse on the bus containing my money and keys.
    *misplaced modifier*

12. Lying on the table, I found John's hat.
    *misplaced modifier*

13. Working alone at night, the plan was worked out successfully.
    *dangling modifier*

14. Looking at the sunset, an airplane passed overhead.
    *dangling modifier*

15. Not having a road map, the town was difficult to find.
    *dangling modifier*

## CORRECT ANSWERS TO EXERCISE 6

| | |
|---|---|
| 1. The girl in the blue dress is charming. | 1. *adjective* |
| 2. We were charmed by her manner. | 2. *part of verb phrase* |
| 3. The reports were discouraging. | 3. *adjective* |

4. We were <u>discouraged</u> by the recent reports.

    4. *part of verb phrase*

5. We are <u>planning</u> a trip to Hawaii.

    5. *part of verb phrase*

6. A man in the crowd was <u>whistling</u> a tune.

    6. *part of verb phrase*

7. The adventure proved <u>fascinating</u>.

    7. *adjective*

8. We were <u>fascinated</u> by the magician.

    8. *part of verb phrase*

9. The detective has <u>examined</u> everything in the room.

    9. *part of verb phrase*

10. They are <u>trying</u> a new experiment.

    10. *part of verb phrase*

11. The food was <u>tempting</u>.

    11. *adjective*

12. Jack was <u>throwing</u> a fast ball.

    12. *part of verb phrase*

13. The dress was <u>torn</u>.

    13. *adjective*

14. The houses were <u>painted</u> by inexperienced men.

    14. *part of verb phrase*

15. The river was <u>rising</u> steadily.

    15. *part of verb phrase*

## CORRECT ANSWERS TO EXERCISE 7

1. The man <u>wearing a military uniform</u> is my brother.
              participial phrase

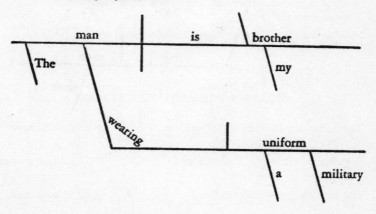

2. <u>Walking down the avenue</u>, I saw an automobile accident.
   **participial phrase**

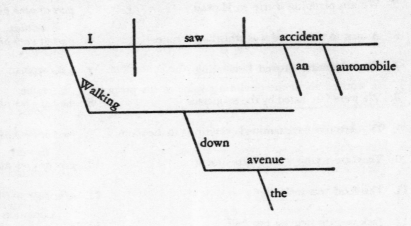

8. <u>Having finished their tasks</u>, the girls went to the theater.
   **participial phrase**

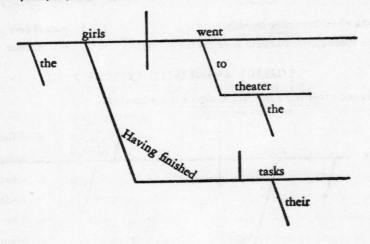

## CORRECT ANSWERS TO ASSIGNMENT 1

Participles are printed in **heavy type**.

**Modifies**

1. His new job is **interesting**.　　　　　　　　1. job
2. The **sobbing** woman was led from the courtroom.　　2. woman
3. He worried about the **declining** value of his property.　3. value
4. The **remodeled** house is very attractive.　　　4. house
5. We did not meet the **defeated** candidate.　　5. candidate
6. Many **colored** flowers grow in her garden.　　6. flowers
7. The contract is **binding**.　　　　　　　　7. contract
8. On his desk they found a **revised** manuscript.　8. manuscript
9. The situation looks **encouraging**.　　　　　9. situation
10. We discovered a number of **winding** roads.　10. roads
11. Apply the method in a **given** situation.　　11. situation
12. A **barking** dog ran down the street.　　　12. dog
13. The judge was an **interested** listener.　　13. listener
14. Joe's antics were **tantalizing**.　　　　　14. antics
15. The **discouraged** athlete gave up the contest.　15. athlete

## CORRECT ANSWERS TO ASSIGNMENT 2

Participial phrase are printed in **heavy type**.

**Modifies**

1. The hamper, **filled with food**, suddenly disappeared.　1. hamper
2. The senator, **urging immediate action**, concluded his speech.　2. senator
3. **Spurred by ambition**, Andrew entered the university.　3. Andrew
4. **Withdrawing quietly**, Jim hastened to the news office.　4. Jim
5. **Encouraged by her success**, Mary bought a home.　5. Mary
6. **Having lost his fortune**, Richard looked for a job.　6. Richard
7. Mrs. Oaks, **polishing the silverware**, complained about the work.　7. Mrs. Oaks
8. **Screaming loudly**, the child ran to his mother.　8. child

9. **Listening to the radio,** Raymond heard the entire opera.    9. Raymond

10. The doctor, **operating immediately,** saved Henry's life.    10. doctor

11. **Having lost his ticket,** John returned home.    11. John

12. This is a copy of the letter **sent to the president.**    12. letter

13. **Having eaten our lunch,** we continued our journey.    13. we

14. The detective, **listening to the men,** recognized Miller's voice.    14. detective

## CORRECT ANSWERS TO ASSIGNMENT 3

Participial phrases are printed in **heavy type.**

1. **Walking up the hill,** the road was very slippery.    1. *dangling modifier*

2. **Driving down town,** the icy roads made me nervous.    2. *dangling modifier*

3. **Arriving at the inn,** the beautiful mountain scenery thrilled us.    3. *dangling modifier*

4. **Listening to the radio,** an hour passed by.    4. *dangling modifier*

5. **Being of Irish stock,** my parents had a sense of humor.    5. correct-phrase modifies *parents*

6. **Highly spiced,** Jane could not eat the food.    6. *dangling modifier*

7. The driver suddenly noticed an officer **standing near him.**    7. correct-phrase modifies *officer*

8. **Leaving Chicago in the morning,** our trip was very exciting.    8. *dangling modifier*

9. **Being very active,** the extra work did not tire our manager.    9. *dangling modifier*

10. **Entering the shop,** a television set was turned on for a demonstration.    10. *dangling modifier*

11. **Being done,** the cook removed the cake from the oven.    11. *dangling modifier*

12. **Having finished the letter,** it was posted.    12. *dangling modifier*

13. **Glancing through the editorials,** the newspaper impressed me favorably.    13. *dangling modifier*

14. **Arriving home late,** my supper was on the table.,    14. *dangling modifier*

## CORRECT ANSWERS TO ASSIGNMENT 4

1. <u>Driving recklessly</u>, Tom had a serious accident.
   **participial phrase**

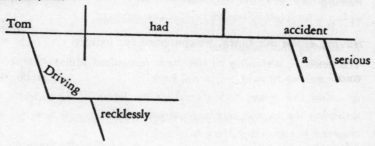

2. <u>Carrying a heavy suitcase</u>, James walked to the station.
   **participial phrase**

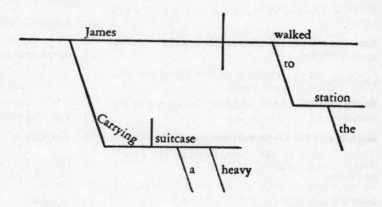

3. <u>Being a delegate</u>, Father attended every meeting.
   **participial phrase**

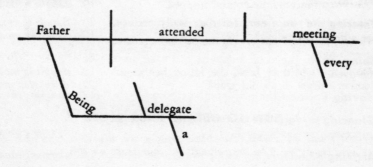

## CORRECT ANSWERS TO PROGRESS TEST TWENTY-TWO

1. I found a wallet **walking down the street.**
    1. *misplaced modifier*

2. **Seeking an answer,** the problem was solved.
    2. *dangling modifier*

3. **Being interested in poetry,** the lecture appealed to me.
    3. *dangling modifier*

4. **Answering the telephone,** the book lay unopened.
    4. *dangling modifier*

5. **Commencing to rain,** we turned back.
    5. *dangling modifier*

6. **Entering the room,** Jack turned on the lights.
    6. correct

7. **Knowing the owner,** our rent was not raised.
    7. *dangling modifier*

8. **Leaving her ironing,** Mary answered the telephone.
    8. correct

9. The tower is easily seen **walking down Michigan Avenue.**
    9. *dangling modifier*

10. **Having a heavy suitcase,** the conductor assisted me.
    10. *dangling modifier*

11. One of the little refugees hid behind her mother, **crying bitterly.**
    11. *misplaced modifier*

12. **Floating on the surface of the pond,** we saw some beautiful water lilies.
    12. *misplaced modifier*

13. **Walking toward the pictures,** the names of the artists could be clearly seen.
    13. *dangling modifier*

14. **Arriving at the bank,** we found that it was closed.
    14. correct

15. Mother found an old trunk **looking for something in the attic.**
    15. *misplaced modifier*

16. **Being alone,** I turned on the radio for company.
    16. correct

17. **Having reached home,** I dressed for dinner.
    17. correct

18. I saw a strange looking man enter the house **wearing a leather jacket.**
    18. *misplaced modifier*

19. **Checking the car,** the engine stopped.
    19. *dangling modifier*

20. **Waiting for an hour,** Martha finally arrived.
    20. *dangling modifier*

21. **Having finished our work,** the outdoors seemed refreshing.
    21. *dangling modifier*

22. **Made of silk and lace,** she found her grandmother's dress in an old trunk.
    22. *misplaced modifier*

## HOW TO OBTAIN YOUR SCORE

*The test totals 44 points. To obtain your score, divide the number of your correct answers by 44. The answer will be your score on this test.*

**Practical English Grammar**

## OUTLINE OF UNIT TWENTY-THREE

# GERUNDS

Page

1. NATURE OF THE GERUND ............................................... 5

2. THE GERUND PHRASE ..................................................... 7

3. COMPLEMENTS OF GERUNDS ......................................... 7

4. ADVERBIAL MODIFIERS OF GERUNDS ........................ 8

5. ADJECTIVE MODIFIERS OF GERUNDS ........................... 11

6. THE POSSESSIVE CASE BEFORE THE GERUND............... 12

7. THE DANGLING GERUND ............................................... 14

8. DIAGRAMMING THE GERUND ....................................... 17

9. DIAGRAMMING THE GERUND PHRASE ........................ 19

10. SUMMARY OF GRAMMAR UNIT TWENTY-THREE...... 22

*Self-Grading Assignments* ............................................................... 23

*Progress Test Twenty-Three* .............................................................. 27

*Key to Progress Test*............................................................................ 29

# GERUNDS

## Nature of the Gerund

IF you understand the dual nature of the participle, you will have little difficulty in understanding the dual nature of the **gerund.** You have already learned that the participle is both *verb* and *adjective.* The gerund is both *verb* and *noun.*

Gerunds are like participles in many respects. Gerunds and participles are *verbals;* that is, they are *forms derived from verbs.* Both participles and gerunds have the same *"ing"* forms. Both take the same kinds of complements and modifiers that verbs take.

Gerunds differ from participles in one fundamental respect. **Gerunds are verb forms used as nouns.** Participles are verb forms used as adjectives. Because a gerund functions as a noun, it can take certain modifiers that a participle cannot take. Like the noun, a gerund is often modified by an *adjective* or by an *adjective phrase.* Participles cannot take adjective modifiers.

Since the gerund functions as a noun, it may be used as the *subject* of a sentence, the *direct object* of a verb, the *object of a preposition,* or as a *predicate noun* after one of the linking verbs. Gerunds are often called *verbal nouns* because they are derived from verbs.

<u>Painting</u> is Martha's hobby. ( gerund used as *subject* )
subject

Martha enjoys <u>painting</u>. ( gerund used as *direct object* )
direct object

Martha earns a living by <u>painting</u>. (gerund used as *object of a preposition)*
object of preposition

Martha's hobby is <u>painting</u>. ( gerund used as a *predicate noun* )
predicate noun

In the first sentence, the word *painting* is a gerund. It is a verb form that is used as a noun. *Painting* is the subject of the sentence. In the second sentence the same verb form *painting* is used as the direct object of the verb *enjoys.* In the third sentence *painting* is used as the object of the preposition *by,* and in the fourth sentence it is used as a predicate noun after the linking verb *is.*

## EXERCISE 1

Underline the **gerunds** in the following sentences. On the line to the right, indicate whether the gerund is used as the *subject, direct object, object of a preposition,* or as a *predicate noun.*

1. His profession is teaching.     1. ................

2. Swimming is good exercise.     2. ................

3. Are you sure about his leaving?     3. ................

4. I enjoy walking.     4. ................

5. The instructor praised her writing.     5. ................

6. I am sure of returning.     6. ................

7. Speeding is very dangerous.     7. ................

8. Did you read the new regulation about speeding?     8. ................

9. Father prefers motoring.     9. ................

10. Jean does not like typing.     10. ................

11. Through traveling, he became very well informed.     11. ................

12. We spent the evening in reading.     12. ................

13. The professor dislikes lecturing.     13. ................

14. The campers talked about fishing.     14. ................

15. The banker's favorite recreation was bowling.     15. ................

*Note: The correct answers to exercises will be found at the back of this booklet. Correct your mistakes and, if necessary, re-read the text material before going on to the next section.*

# THE GERUND PHRASE

Like the participle, the gerund retains many of the characteristics of a verb. Because the gerund is a verb form, it may take any of the complements or any of the modifiers that a verb might take. The gerund with its complements and modifiers is called a **gerund phrase.**

# COMPLEMENTS OF GERUNDS

Like the verb, a *gerund* may take a **direct object.** Study the following sentence carefully. You will readily see that although the gerund is used as a noun, it retains the characteristics of a verb because it takes a *direct object.*

Sweeping the floor was one of Jack's duties.
gerund      dir. object
    gerund phrase

In this sentence the word *sweeping* is a gerund. It is used as the *subject* of the sentence. This is its noun function. Since the gerund is a verb form, it retains some of the characteristics of a verb. The verb *sweep* is an action verb and may take a *direct object.* The gerund *sweeping* may also take a direct object. In this sentence the direct object of the gerund *sweeping* is the noun *floor.*

Some verbs take both a direct and an indirect object. Gerunds formed from such verbs may also take a **direct** and an **indirect object.**

Giving the girls a holiday will please them.
gerund    indir. obj.    dir. obj.
    gerund phrase

In this sentence, *giving* is a gerund used as the subject of the sentence. This is its use as a **noun.** As a **verb form,** it takes the direct object *holiday* and the indirect object *girls.* The entire expression, *giving the girls a holiday* is a **gerund phrase.**

If the gerund is a form of a linking verb, it may take a **predicate noun** or a **predicate adjective** as a *complement.* Study the following sentences carefully. In both sentences the gerund requires a complement to complete its meaning. The gerunds are forms of linking verbs.

His <u>becoming</u> a <u>captain</u> involved certain responsibilities.
     gerund    pred. noun
       gerund phrase

I had not heard of Jane's <u>being</u> <u>ill.</u>
        gerund   pred. adj.
        gerund phrase

In the first sentence, the gerund *becoming* takes the predicate noun *captain* as a complement. In the second sentence, the gerund *being* takes the predicate adjective *ill* as a complement.

## ADVERBIAL MODIFIERS OF GERUNDS

The gerund, like the participle, may be modified by an **adverb** or an **adverbial phrase.** You should have no trouble in identifying the adverbial modifiers of the gerunds in the following sentences:

<u>Sitting</u> <u>on a park bench</u> was his favorite pastime.
gerund        adv. ph.
   gerund phrase

<u>Driving</u> a truck <u>in the city</u> is difficult.
gerund        adv. ph.
     gerund phrase

I do not advise your <u>seeing</u> him <u>now.</u>
        gerund    adv.
       gerund phrase

The gerund *sitting* in the first sentence is modified by the adverbial phrase *on a park bench.* The gerund *driving* in the second sentence is modified by the adverbial phrase *in the city.* The gerund *seeing* in the third sentence is modified by the adverb *now.*

## EXERCISE 2

Underline the **gerund phrases** in the following sentences. On the line to the right, indicate the kind of complement the gerund takes: *direct object, indirect object, predicate noun,* or *predicate adjective.*

**Complement of Gerund**

Example: <u>Hunting deer</u> is his favorite sport.     *direct object*

1. Elizabeth dislikes washing dishes.    1. ...................

2. In planning the house, I must consider the cost.    2. ...................

3. Being a counselor requires considerable tact.    3. ...................

4. He attempted combining two jobs.    4. ...................

5. Promoting sales is the job of the sales manager.    5. ...................

6. Margery's worst fault is being late.    6. ...................

7. I had not anticipated your becoming an executive.    7. ...................

8. He entered the house by breaking the lock.    8. ...................

9. Buying Mary a gift was a pleasant task.    9. ...................

10. Reading the comic strips has become a habit.    10. ...................

11. Giving him fencing lessons was difficult.    11. ...................

12. Have you finished reading the article?    12. ...................

13. I had no intention of offering her a ticket.    13. ...................

14. Breaking traffic laws endangers life.    14. ...................

15. He made his expenses by selling magazines.    15. ...................

## EXERCISE 3

Underline the **gerund phrases** in the following sentences. On the line to the right, indicate the kind of modifier the gerund takes: *adverb* or *adverbial phrase*.

**Modifier of Gerund**

Example: He does not like <u>working in a factory.</u>   adverbial phrase
                                gerund phrase   ...........................

1. I did not like his leaving so abruptly.   1. ................

2. Arthur enjoys driving fast.   2. ................

3. He saved himself by staying on the raft.   3. ................

4. Walking through the woods is a delightful experience.   4. ................

5. The campers enjoyed swimming in the lake.   5. ................

6. You will succeed by studying constantly.   6. ................

7. I would not advise opposing him now.   7. ................

8. The agent's job is collecting the rents regularly.   8. ................

9. You might try sending a letter to his office.   9. ................

10. The men did not like working late.   10. ................

11. The children enjoy playing in the sand.   11. ................

12. We considered buying a home in Mexico.   12. ................

13. Mrs. Jones objected to signing the lease at that time.   13. ................

14. Driving carefully at night is a wise procedure.   14. ................

15. We planned seeing him in his office.   15. ................

## ADJECTIVE MODIFIERS OF GERUNDS

Because the gerund functions as a noun, it may be modified by an *adjective,* or by a *noun* or a *pronoun* used as an *adjective.*

The slow driving in the mountains irritated Max.
gerund

(*slow*—adjective, modifying the gerund *driving*)

The dog's barking saved the child's life.
gerund

(*dog's*—noun used as an adjective, modifying *barking*)

The critics praised her wonderful dancing.
gerund

(*her*—pronoun used as an adjective, modifying *dancing*)

(*wonderful*—adjective, modifying *dancing*)

In the first sentence, the gerund *driving* is modified by the adjective *slow.* In the second sentence, the gerund *barking* is modified by the word *dog's,* which is a noun in the possessive case used as an adjective. In the third sentence, the gerund *dancing* is modified by the possessive adjective *her* (pronoun used as an adjective) and the adjective *wonderful.*

Like the noun, a gerund is often modified by an *adjective phrase.* In the following sentences, the gerunds take adjective phrases as modifiers:

We heard the rustling of the leaves.
gerund    adj. ph.

The villagers listened to the tolling of the bell.
gerund    adj. ph.

In the first sentence, the gerund *rustling* is modified by the adjective phrase *of the leaves.* You can readily see that the adjective phrase modifies *rustling* because the sentence means that we heard the *leaves' rustling.* The second sentence means that the villagers listened to the *bell's tolling.*

## THE POSSESSIVE CASE BEFORE THE GERUND

The gerund is frequently modified by a noun or a pronoun in the *possessive case*. A mistake commonly made is to forget to put the noun or pronoun in the possessive case to show that it is a modifier. The important word in such sentences is the *gerund,* and not the modifier. The following illustration will help to make this clear:

The men objected to <u>me</u> <u>playing</u> on the team. (*incorrect*)
pro.  gerund

The men objected to <u>my</u> <u>playing</u> on the team. (*correct*)
pro.  gerund

The first sentence is incorrect because it conveys the wrong meaning. The sentence does not mean that the men objected to *me.* The word *me* is not the object of the preposition *to.* The object of the preposition *to* is the gerund *playing.* The sentence means that the men objected to the *playing.* The use of the form *me* before the gerund is incorrect. The possessive form *my* should be used.

The following sentences are incorrect because the wrong form of the pronoun is used before the gerund:

I am interested in <u>him</u> <u>advancing</u> in his profession. (*incorrect*)
pro.    gerund

Mother did not like <u>me</u> <u>taking</u> part in the contest. (*incorrect*)
pro.  gerund

The first sentence does not mean that I am interested in *him* primarily, but that I am interested in *his advancing.* The object of the preposition *in* is the gerund *advancing,* and not the pronoun *him.* Since the pronoun is a modifier of the gerund, it must be put in the possessive case (*his* advancing).

The second sentence does not mean that Mother does not like *me.* It means that she does not like the *taking part* in the contest. The correct form of the pronoun before the gerund is *my.* (*my* taking part).

**EXERCISE 4**

Correct the error in the case of the **noun** or **pronoun** used before the *gerund*. Cross out the incorrect form and write the correct form above it.

our
Example: Father did not like us taking the car.

1. The club insisted on me taking the office.

2. He left the city without us knowing it.

3. Have you heard of my sister winning the contest?

4. We appreciate you finishing the job for us.

5. I understand Marvin not accepting the position.

6. He had not heard of us finding an apartment.

7. Do you remember him replying to our letter?

8. The men leaving caused considerable commotion.

9. Him playing the part of the villain was excellent acting.

10. I had not heard of you being ill.

11. Do you approve of us naming your successor?

12. There was no hope of him rivaling his brother.

13. Did you hear about me winning a prize?

14. Were you notified about John leaving?

15. We were confident of Jack passing the examination.

## THE DANGLING GERUND

Gerunds are often found in prepositional phrases which are placed at the beginning of the sentence. The gerund or the gerund phrase is the *object of the preposition*. The entire prepositional phrase should modify some word in the main part of the sentence. If there is no such word, the phrase *"dangles"* in the sentence; that is, the phrase is an unattached modifier.

The gerund almost always expresses action. There must be some word in the sentence to indicate the *doer* of this action. That word would logically be the subject of the sentence. Examine the following sentence carefully:

Upon receiving the telegram, the trip was cancelled.
      gerund
                          dangling gerund

This sentence begins with a prepositional phrase. The object of the preposition *upon* is the gerund phrase, *receiving the telegram.* The gerund *receiving* implies that someone received the telegram. The way the sentence is written, the *trip* received the telegram. The trouble with the sentence is that the subject has no logical relation to the gerund. The subject of the sentence should indicate *who* is doing the *receiving.* The following sentences are written correctly:

Upon receiving the telegram, **we** cancelled the trip.
      gerund

or

After we had received the telegram, we cancelled the trip.
       clause substituted for gerund phrase

This error might be corrected in one of two ways as shown in the preceding illustrations:

1. By supplying the word which the prepositional phrase logically refers to.

2. By substituting a subordinate clause for the gerund phrase.

When the gerund phrase at the beginning of a sentence does not have a logical relation to the subject of the sentence, the result is often humorous. The careful study of a sentence like the following will help you understand the error and the reason for the correction:

By <u>pressing a button</u>, the <u>table</u> comes out of the wall. (*incorrect*)
gerund phrase

(*pressing*—dangling gerund)

This sentence clearly indicates that *someone must press a button* before *the table* will come out of the wall. According to the way in which the sentence is written, *the table* performs that function. Such an interpretation would be absurd.

The trouble with the sentence is that the *subject* has no logical relation to the *gerund*. The subject of the sentence should be a word that would indicate the *doer* of the action expressed by the gerund. That word does not appear in the sentence as it is written. The sentence would be correctly written in either one of the following ways:

By <u>pressing a button</u>, *you* will release the table from the wall.
gerund phrase

If <u>you press a button</u>, the table will come out of the wall.
subordinate clause

## EXERCISE 5

Directions: Write *dangling gerund* on the line opposite the sentence that contains a dangling gerund. Write *correct* opposite a sentence that does not contain a dangling gerund.

Example: After <u>riding</u> all day, the hotel
looked inviting.                                    *dangling gerund*
                                                    ...................

1. By working overtime, the entire job was
   finished.                                        1.  ................

2. After discussing the plan, a vote was taken.     2.  ................

3. Before finishing our dinner, the taxi driver sounded his horn.

3. ................

4. After climbing the mountain, a rest was recommended by the guide.

4. ................

5. Upon arriving at the inn, dinner was served.

5. ................

6. After playing golf all day, we went to the hotel to rest.

6. ................

7. Before offering Mr. White the position, the manager made several stipulations.

7. ................

8. Upon returning home, my friend was waiting for me.

8. ................

9. After studying our lessons, the books were collected.

9. ................

10. Before leaving the office, the elevator stopped.

10. ................

11. After searching for an hour, we found the report on the manager's desk.

11. ................

12. By running very fast, the goal was reached.

12. ................

13. After discussing the plan with the committee, the chairman called for a vote.

13. ................

14. Upon arriving in New York, a bus strike was called.

14. ................

15. On investigating the charges, the judge discovered that Jones had stolen the money.

15. ................

## DIAGRAMMING THE GERUND

The simple gerund, without modifiers and without complements, is diagrammed just like any other noun, with this exception: the gerund is placed on a "stepped" line instead of being placed on a straight line.

*Sentence*: <u>Swimming</u> is healthful exercise.
             <small>gerund</small>

In this sentence, the gerund *swimming* is used as the subject of the sentence. The sentence is diagrammed as follows:

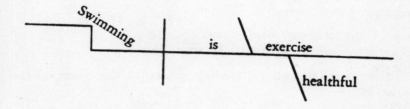

Note the "stepped" line on which the gerund is placed.

*Sentence*: John enjoys <u>swimming</u>.
                   <small>gerund</small>

In this sentence, the gerund *swimming* is used as the direct object of the verb *enjoys*. It is placed on a "stepped" line.

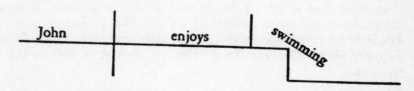

*Sentence*:  My favorite sport is <u>fishing</u>.
gerund

In this sentence, the gerund *fishing* is used as a predicate noun after the linking verb *is*.

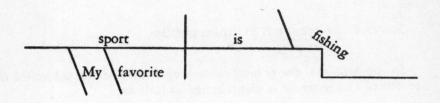

*Sentence*:  I increased my speed in <u>reading</u>.
gerund

In this sentence, the gerund *reading* is used as the object of the preposition *in*.

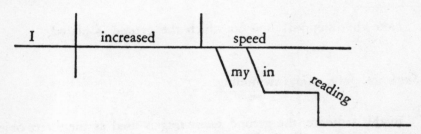

In these four diagrams the gerund is used as a *noun;* it does not show any of the characteristics of a verb. The gerund does not have modifiers or complements in any of these sentences. The next set of diagrams shows the *verb function* of the gerund as well as the noun *function.*

## DIAGRAMMING THE GERUND PHRASE

Like the noun clause, the gerund phrase is raised on "stilts" and placed above the base line of the diagram. This is necessary in order to show the complements and modifiers of the gerund. The gerund is placed on a line that resembles a step. Study the following diagram carefully:

*Sentence*: Driving that car is a great pleasure.
        gerund     obj. of ger.
             gerund phrase

In this sentence, *driving* is a gerund. It takes the direct object *car*. *Driving that car* is a *gerund phrase* used as the subject of the sentence. The predicate verb *is* takes the predicate noun *pleasure* as a complement. *Pleasure* is modified by the article *a* and the adjective *great*. Car is modified by the demonstrative adjective *that*.

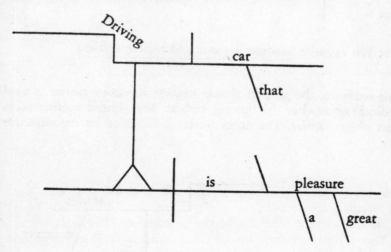

*Sentence*: Marian dislikes singing before a crowd of people.
                             gerund phrase

In this sentence, the gerund phrase *singing before a crowd of people* is the direct object of the verb *dislikes*. The gerund *singing* is modified by the adverbial phrase *before a crowd*. The noun *crowd* is modified by the adjective phrase *of people*.

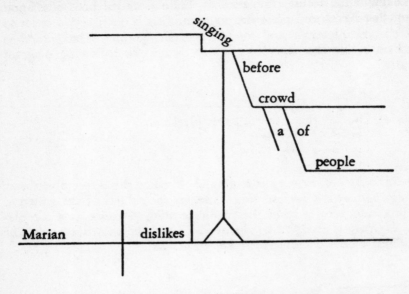

Sentence: His favorite pastime is <u>reading detective stories.</u>
                                   gerund phrase

In this sentence, the gerund phrase *reading detective stories* is used as a predicate noun after the linking verb *is*. The gerund *reading* takes the direct object *stories*. The noun *stories* is modified by the adjective *detective*.

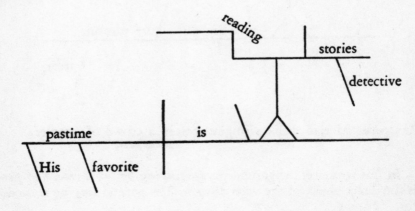

## EXERCISE 6

Diagram the following sentences. Follow the methods of diagramming that have been presented in this unit.

1. Painting is my hobby.

2. Father does not like driving a car.

3. The men were paid well for working overtime.

## SUMMARY OF GRAMMAR UNIT TWENTY-THREE

A **gerund** is a verb form (verbal) that functions as a *noun*. A gerund may function as the *subject* of a sentence, the *direct object* of a verb, the *object of a preposition,* or as a *predicate noun* after a linking verb. It may also be modified by an adjective, an adjective phrase, or by a noun or a pronoun in the possessive case.

Because the gerund retains the characteristics of a verb, it may take a *direct object,* an *indirect object,* a *predicate noun,* or a *predicate adjective* as a complement. It may also be modified by an *adverb* or an *adverbial phrase.*

If the gerund is a form of an action verb, it expresses *action.* If it is a form of a linking verb, it expresses *state of condition.*

The gerund ends in *ing.* The present participle also ends in *ing.* The only way to tell whether a word ending in *ing* is a participle or a gerund, is to study its use in the sentence. If it functions as an **adjective,** it is a **participle.** If it functions as a **noun,** it is a **gerund.**

A gerund is frequently modified by a noun or a pronoun in the *possessive case.* A common error in English is to fail to put the noun or pronoun before the gerund in the possessive case. Failure to do this often leads to statements which are misleading and illogical.

A prepositional phrase containing a gerund should modify some word in the sentence. If there is no word in the sentence which the gerund phrase could logically modify, the phrase is called a *dangling modifier.* The gerund is called a *dangling gerund.*

## SELF-GRADING ASSIGNMENT 1

Directions: Underline the **gerund phrases.** On the line to the right, indicate whether the phrase is used as the *subject, direct object, predicate noun,* or *object of a preposition.*

Example: She likes <u>teaching English to adults.</u>      *direct object*
gerund phrase

1. Traveling in a plane was a new experience.      1. .................

2. Alfred does not like operating that machine.      2. .................

3. Allen's job was interviewing the candidates.      3. .................

4. Henry's favorite sport is skiing in the
   mountains.                                        4. .................

5. My eyes ached after reading the copy.             5. .................

6. In stepping to the platform, the speaker
   dropped his notes.                                6. .................

7. Her most difficult task was helping the refugees.  7. .................

8. The manager recommended making the needed
   improvements.                                     8. .................

9. The gardener enjoyed beautifying the grounds.     9. .................

10. After beautifying the grounds, he painted the
    house.                                           10. .................

11. Seeing my old friend was an unexpected
    pleasure.                                        11. .................

12. We became weary of watching the players.         12. .................

13. Harold enjoys driving in the mountains during
    the summer.                                      13. .................

14. We did not pay any attention to his complain-
    ing about the long hours.                        14. .................

*Caution: Check your answers to each assignment with the answer key at the back of the booklet before proceeding with the next assignment.*

## SELF-GRADING ASSIGNMENT 2

Directions: Underline the **gerunds** in the following sentences. On the line to the right, indicate the kind of complement the gerund takes: *direct object, indirect object, predicate noun,* or *predicate adjective.* Some gerunds take two complements. Indicate both.

Example: His mission is <u>helping</u> crippled <u>children</u>.    *direct object*
                        <sub>gerund</sub>              <sub>dir. obj.</sub>   ........................

1. We made plans for improving our home.        1. ...................

2. They objected to my entering the contest.        2. ...................

3. Buying Alice a radio was a pleasure.        3. ...................

4. I had not heard of his being ill.        4. ...................

5. Father's becoming an ambassador changed our plans.        5. ...................

6. Mrs. Jarvis enjoys weaving rugs.        6. ...................

7. Painting the walls and ceilings preserves them.        7. ...................

8. Sending Jerry the tickets was an obligation.        8. ...................

9. He did not like our becoming so popular.        9. ...................

10. On investigating the case, the officer discovered some new clues.        10. ...................

11. Riding a horse was a thrilling experience for Jane.        11. ...................

12. The men spent their vacation in hunting rabbits.        12. ...................

13. Being an executive involves many responsibilities.        13. ...................

14. The owner permits parking in that empty lot.        14. ...................

15. My friend never dreamed of becoming an architect.        15. ...................

## SELF-GRADING ASSIGNMENT 3

The _possessive case_ of the noun or pronoun should be used before the gerund when the noun or pronoun is clearly a modifier of the gerund.

Directions: Cross out the _incorrect form_ of the noun or pronoun in the parentheses.

his

Example: I had not heard of him becoming a doctor.

1. I cannot understand (Ralph's, Ralph) being so irresponsible.

2. Father would not give his consent to (us, our) driving his car.

3. Mother did not approve of (me, my) taking part in the play.

4. (Him, His) talking during the concert annoyed everybody.

5. Do you remember (me, my) speaking to you about the dinner?

6. I had not heard of the (officer, officer's) recent ruling.

7. He left the city without (them, their) knowing about it.

8. I did not think of (Anne, Anne's) having a car.

9. The dean objected to the (boys, boys') staying out so late.

10. There is no doubt of (it, its) being right.

11. What do you think of (Frank, Frank's) going to Japan?

12. Ted laughed at (Sue, Sue's) being afraid of the thunder.

13. Have you heard of (me, my) inheriting a fortune?

14. We do not like the (manager, manager's) speaking to us in that manner.

15. We appreciated (you, your) waiting for us yesterday.

## SELF-GRADING ASSIGNMENT 4

Directions: Diagram the following sentences:

1. Before closing the office, the stenographer filed all the letters.

2. Reading the latest novels was his favorite pastime.

3. His favorite diversion is listening to the radio.

## PROGRESS TEST TWENTY-THREE

This progress test should not be taken until a day or two after you have completed the assignments. The score you make on the test will then more clearly reflect your understanding of the material in the unit.

This exercise is a test of your ability to distinguish between the two verbals—participles and gerunds. Always keep in mind the fact that participles are used as adjectives and gerunds are used as nouns.

Directions: Underline the **participial phrases** and the **gerund phrases** in the following sentences. Write **ger.ph.** under the gerund phrases and **part.ph.** under the participial phrases.

On the line to the right, indicate the use of the gerund phrase: *subject, direct object, object of a preposition,* or *predicate noun.* Name the word the participial phrase modifies. (*40 points*)

Example: <u>Coming into the room,</u> we saw a strange
part. ph.

      sight.                              modifies *we*

1. Following the example of her friends, Mary signed up for evening classes.

                                          1. ...................

2. Operating that machine is dangerous work.   2. ...................

3. After making a thorough investigation, the judge dismissed the case.

                                          3. ...................

4. We anticipated cooking our dinner outdoors.   4. ...................

5. The scientist, called to the platform, gave an impromptu address.

                                          5. ...................

6. The officer found a man lying on the road.   6. ...................

7. The dress designed by Worth won the award.   7. ...................

8. Excavating for the new building has begun.   8. ...................

## PROGRESS TEST TWENTY-THREE (continued)

9. Hiding his fear, Donald opened the door.    9. ................

10. Delaying the project was approved by the committee.    10. ................

11. The men have stopped working on the project.    11. ................

12. I am opposed to his going to the convention.    12. ................

13. By working overtime, Harold completed the job in a month.    13. ................

14. There were no trains leaving at that hour.    14. ................

15. The man sitting in the second row is my cousin.    15. ................

16. After stopping for a light lunch, we hurried to the studio.    16. ................

17. Everett does not like working in a factory.    17. ................

18. Operating daily, the surgeon acquired remarkable skill.    18. ................

19. Her chief diversion was reading the comic strips.    19. ................

20. Studying all night, James found the solution to the problem.    20. ................

# ANSWER KEY

for

## EXERCISES, ASSIGNMENTS, AND PROGRESS TEST
### Grammar Unit Twenty-three

---

## CORRECT ANSWERS TO EXERCISES

| | EXERCISE 1 | | EXERCISE 2 | |
|---|---|---|---|---|
| | **Gerund** | **Use of Gerund** | **Gerund Phrase** | **Complement of Gerund** |
| 1. | teaching | *predicate noun* | washing **dishes** | *direct object* |
| 2. | Swimming | *subject* | planning the **house** | *direct object* |
| 3. | leaving | *object of preposition* | Being a **counselor** | *predicate noun* |
| 4. | walking | *object of verb* | combining two **jobs** | *direct object* |
| 5. | writing | *object of verb* | Promoting **sales** | *direct object* |
| 6. | returning | *object of preposition* | being **late** | *predicate adjective* |
| 7. | Speeding | *subject* | becoming an **executive** | *predicate noun* |
| 8. | speeding | *object of preposition* | breaking the **lock** | *direct object* |
| 9. | motoring | *object of verb* | Buying **Mary** a **gift** | *indirect object* *direct object* |
| 10. | typing | *object of verb* | Reading the comic **strips** | *direct object* |
| 11. | traveling | *object of preposition* | Giving **him** fencing **lessons** | *indirect object* *direct object* |
| 12. | reading | *object of preposition* | reading the **article** | *direct object* |
| 13. | lecturing | *object of verb* | offering **her** a **ticket** | *indirect object* *direct object* |
| 14. | fishing | *object of preposition* | Breaking traffic **laws** | *direct object* |
| 15. | bowling | *predicate noun* | selling **magazines** | *direct object* |

## CORRECT ANSWERS TO EXERCISE 3

Gerund phrases are printed in **heavy type.**

**Modifier of Gerund**

| | | |
|---|---|---|
| 1. | I did not like his **leaving so abruptly.** | 1. *adverb* |
| 2. | Arthur enjoys **driving fast.** | 2. *adverb* |
| 3. | He saved himself by **staying on the raft.** | 3. *adverbial phrase* |
| 4. | **Walking through the woods** is a delightful experience. | 4. *adverbial phrase* |
| 5. | The campers enjoyed **swimming in the lake.** | 5. *adverbial phrase* |
| 6. | You will succeed by **studying constantly.** | 6. *adverb* |
| 7. | I would not advise **opposing him now.** | 7. *adverb* |
| 8. | The agent's job is **collecting the rents regularly.** | 8. *adverb* |
| 9. | You might try **sending a letter to his office.** | 9. *adverbial phrase* |
| 10. | The men did not like **working late.** | 10. *adverb* |
| 11. | The children enjoy **playing in the sand.** | 11. *adverbial phrase* |
| 12. | We considered **buying a home in Mexico.** | 12. *adverbial phrase* |
| 13. | Mrs. Jones objected to **signing the lease at that time.** | 13. *adverbial phrase* |
| 14. | **Driving carefully at night** is a wise procedure. | 14. *adverb and adverbial phrase* |
| 15. | We planned **seeing him in his office.** | 15. *adverbial phrase* |

## CORRECT ANSWERS TO EXERCISE 4

Correct nouns and pronouns are printed in **heavy type.**

1. The club insisted on **my** taking the office.
2. He left the city without **our** knowing it.
3. Have you heard of my **sister's** winning the contest?
4. We appreciate **your** finishing the job for us.
5. I understand **Marvin's** not accepting the position.
6. He had not heard of **our** finding an apartment.
7. Do you remember **his** replying to our letter?
8. The **men's** leaving caused considerable commotion.
9. **His** playing the part of the villain was excellent acting.
10. I had not heard of **your** being ill.
11. Do you approve of **our** naming your successor?
12. There was no hope of **his** rivaling his brother.
13. Did you hear about **my** winning a prize?
14. Were you notified about **John's** leaving?
15. We were confident of **Jack's** passing the examination.

## CORRECT ANSWERS TO EXERCISE 5

1. dangling gerund
2. dangling gerund
3. dangling gerund
4. dangling gerund
5. dangling gerund

6. (correct)
7. (correct)
8. dangling gerund
9. dangling gerund
10. dangling gerund

11. (correct)
12. dangling gerund
13. (correct)
14. dangling gerund
15. (correct)

## CORRECT ANSWERS TO EXERCISE 6

1. Painting is my hobby.

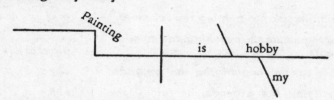

2. Father does not like driving a car.

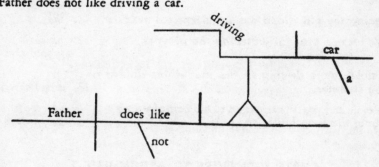

3. The men were paid well for working overtime.

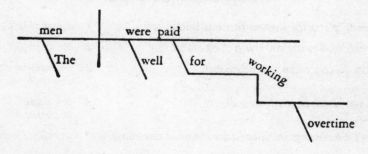

## CORRECT ANSWERS TO ASSIGNMENT 1

Gerund phrases are printed in **heavy type.**

| | |
|---|---|
| 1. **Traveling in a plane** was a new experience. | 1. *subject* |
| 2. Alfred does not like **operating that machine.** | 2. *direct object* |
| 3. Allen's job was **interviewing the candidates.** | 3. *predicate noun* |
| 4. Henry's favorite sport is **skiing in the mountains.** | 4. *predicate noun* |
| 5. My eyes ached after **reading the copy.** | 5. *object of preposition* |
| 6. In **stepping to the platform,** the speaker dropped his notes. | 6. *object of preposition* |
| 7. Her most difficult task was **helping the refugees.** | 7. *predicate noun* |
| 8. The manager recommended **making the needed improvements.** | 8. *direct object* |
| 9. The gardener enjoyed **beautifying the grounds.** | 9. *direct object* |
| 10. After **beautifying the grounds,** he painted the house. | 10. *object of preposition* |
| 11. **Seeing my old friend** was an unexpected pleasure. | 11. *subject* |
| 12. We became weary of **watching the players.** | 12. *object of preposition* |
| 13. Harold enjoys **driving in the mountains during the summer.** | 13. *direct object* |
| 14. We did not pay any attention to **his complaining about the long hours.** | 14. *object of preposition* |

## CORRECT ANSWERS TO ASSIGNMENT 2

Gerunds are printed in **heavy type.**

| | |
|---|---|
| 1. We made plans for **improving** our home. | 1. *direct object* |
| 2. They objected to my **entering** the contest. | 2. *direct object* |
| 3. **Buying** Alice a radio was a pleasure. | 3. *indirect object* *direct object* |
| 4. I had not heard of his **being** ill. | 4. *predicate adjective* |
| 5. Father's **becoming** an ambassador changed our plans. | 5. *predicate noun* |

6. Mrs. Jarvis enjoys **weaving** rugs.

6. *direct object*

7. **Painting** the walls and ceilings preserves them.

7. *compound direct object*

8. **Sending** Jerry the tickets was an obligation.

8. *indirect object direct object*

9. He did not like our **becoming** so popular.

9. *predicate adjective*

10. On **investigating** the case, the officer discovered some new clues.

10. *direct object*

11. **Riding** a horse was a thrilling experience for Jane.

11. *direct object*

12. The men spent their vacation in **hunting** rabbits.

12. *direct object*

13. **Being** an executive involves many responsibilities.

13. *predicate noun*

14. The owner permits **parking** in that empty lot.

14. no complement

15. My friend never dreamed of **becoming** an architect.

15. *predicate noun*

## CORRECT ANSWERS TO ASSIGNMENT 3

Correct nouns and pronouns are printed in **heavy type.**

1. I cannot understand **Ralph's** being so irresponsible.
2. Father would not give his consent to **our** driving his car.
3. Mother did not approve of **my** taking part in the play.
4. **His** talking during the concert annoyed everybody.
5. Do you remember **my** speaking to you about the dinner?
6. I had not heard of the **officer's** recent ruling.
7. He left the city without **their** knowing about it.
8. I did not think of **Anne's** having a car.
9. The dean objected to the **boys'** staying out so late.
10. There is no doubt of **its** being right.
11. What do you think of **Frank's** going to Japan?
12. Ted laughed at **Sue's** being afraid of the thunder.
13. Have you heard of **my** inheriting a fortune?
14. We do not like the **manager's** speaking to us in that manner.
15. We appreciated **your** waiting for us yesterday.

## CORRECT ANSWERS TO ASSIGNMENT 4

1. Before closing the office, the stenographer filed all the letters.
   gerund phrase

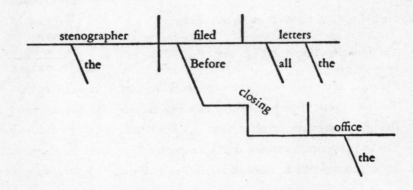

2. Reading the latest novels was his favorite pastime.
   gerund phrase

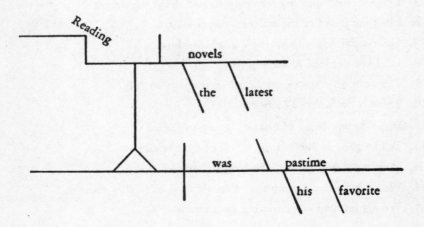

3. His favorite diversion is <u>listening to the radio</u>.
   gerund phrase

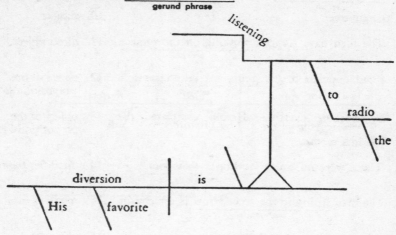

## CORRECT ANSWERS TO PROGRESS TEST TWENTY-THREE

1. <u>Following the example of her friends</u>, Mary
   part. ph.
   signed up for evening classes.

   1. modifies *Mary*

2. <u>Operating that machine</u> is dangerous work.
   ger. ph.

   2. subject

3. After <u>making a thorough investigation</u>,
   ger. ph.
   the judge dismissed the case.

   3. object of preposition *after*

4. We anticipated <u>cooking our dinner outdoors</u>.
   ger. ph.

   4. direct object

5. The scientist, <u>called to the platform</u>, gave an
   part. ph.
   impromptu address.

   5. modifies *scientist*

6. The officer found a man <u>lying on the road</u>.
   part. ph.

   6. modifies *man*

7. The dress <u>designed by Worth</u> won the award.
   part. ph.

   7. modifies *dress*

8. <u>Excavating for the new building</u> has begun.
   ger. ph.

   8. subject

9. <u>Hiding his fear</u>, Donald opened the door.
   part. ph.

   9. modifies *Donald*

10. Delaying the project was approved by the
    <u>ger. ph.</u>
    committee.

      10. subject

11. The men have stopped <u>working on the project</u>.
    <u>ger. ph.</u>

      11. direct object

12. I am opposed to <u>his going to the convention</u>.
    <u>ger. ph.</u>

      12. object of the
    preposition *to*

13. By <u>working overtime</u>, Harold completed the
    <u>ger. ph.</u>
    job in a month.

      13. object of the
    preposition *by*

14. There were no trains <u>leaving at that hour</u>.
    <u>part. ph.</u>

      14. modifies *trains*

15. The man <u>sitting in the second row</u> is my cousin.
    <u>part. ph.</u>

      15. modifies *man*

16. After <u>stopping for a light lunch</u>, we hurried to
    <u>ger. ph.</u>
    the studio.

      16. object of the
    preposition *after*

17. Everett does not like <u>working in a factory</u>.
    <u>ger. ph.</u>

      17. direct object

18. <u>Operating daily</u>, the surgeon acquired remarkable
    <u>part. ph.</u>
    skill.

      18. modifies *surgeon*

19. Her chief diversion was <u>reading the comic strips</u>.
    <u>ger. ph.</u>

      19. predicate noun

20. <u>Studying all night</u>, James found the solution to
    <u>part. ph.</u>
    the problem.

      20. modifies *James*

## HOW TO OBTAIN YOUR SCORE

*The test totals 40 points. To obtain your score, divide the number of your correct answers by 40. The answer will be your score on this test. For example, if you have 36 points correct, your score is 36 divided by 40 which is 90 per cent. In other words, your score on this test is 90. You can obtain your score on any of the exercises or assignments by following the same procedure.*

**Practical English Grammar**

## OUTLINE OF UNIT TWENTY-FOUR

# INFINITIVES

Page

1. NATURE OF THE INFINITIVE ............................................. 5

2. USES OF THE INFINITIVE ..................................... 6

3. INFINITIVES USED AS ADJECTIVES ............................... 8

4. INFINITIVES USED AS ADVERBS ...................................... 9

5. COMPLEMENTS OF INFINITIVES ..................................... 12

6. MODIFIERS OF INFINITIVES .............................................. 13

7. THE INFINITIVE PHRASE ..................................... 14

8. THE OMISSION OF THE SIGN "TO"...................................... 16

9. SUMMARY OF GRAMMAR UNIT TWENTY-FOUR.......... 18

*Self-Grading Assignments* ................................................. 19

*Progress Test Twenty-Four* ............................................. 23

*Key to Correct Answers* ................................................. 25

# INFINITIVES

## Nature of the Infinitive

EVERY verb has *three forms* that are called *verbals*. Verbals are forms of the verb that are used as other parts of speech. In Grammar Unit Twenty-Two you studied the adjective use of the participle, and in Unit Twenty-Three you studied the noun uses of the gerund. In this unit you will study the various uses of the **infinitive**.

*Participles, gerunds,* and *infinitives* are called **verbals** because they are derived from verbs and function like verbs in many respects. They are unlike verbs because they cannot function as the predicate verb in a sentence. They are incomplete forms that cannot be used to make statements, ask questions, or give commands or requests. This is an important fact regarding verbals that you should always keep in mind.

You have learned how to recognize a participle or a gerund by its form. The infinitive is very easy to identify because it carries a definite sign which indicates that it is an infinitive. An infinitive is usually preceded by the word *to,* which is commonly called the *sign of the infinitive.*

When the word *to* is used with a verb form to complete the infinitive, it is *not a preposition.* It is merely the *sign* of the infinitive. The way to be sure that the expression is an infinitive, and not a prepositional phrase, is to look at the word which follows *to.* If this word is a verb form, the expression is an infinitive, and not a prepositional phrase.

Like the gerund, the infinitive is *used as a noun.* It may also function as an *adjective* or as an *adverb.* An infinitive may take any complement or any modifier that a verb might take.

The sign of the infinitive (*to*) is usually omitted after certain verbs in order to avoid awkward or stilted expressions. The *to* is usually omitted after the following verbs: *hear, feel, watch, let, dare, help, see, make, please, bid, need,* etc.

## USES OF THE INFINITIVE

You have already studied the two-sided character of the participle and the gerund. The participle functions as an adjective and retains some of the characteristics of a verb. The gerund functions as a noun and also retains some of the characteristics of a verb. The **infinitive** retains its verb nature, and in addition may function as a *noun,* an *adjective,* or an *adverb.*

The noun function of an infinitive is very similar to the noun function of a gerund. An infinitive may be the *subject* of a sentence, the *direct object* of a verb, the *object of a preposition,* or a *predicate noun* after a linking verb.


<u>To write</u> was his ambition.
   subject


His ambition was <u>to write.</u>
           predicate noun


He did nothing except <u>(to) write.</u>
           object of preposition


He likes <u>to write.</u>
     direct object


In the first sentence, the infinitive *To write* is the subject of the sentence. In the second sentence, the infinitive *to write* is used as a predicate noun after the linking verb *was.* In the third sentence, the infinitive *to write* is used as the object of the preposition *except.* In this sentence, the sign of the infinitive is omitted. In the fourth sentence, the infinitive *to write* is used as the direct object of the verb *likes.*

## EXERCISE 1

Underline the **infinitives** in the following sentences. On the line to the right, indicate whether the infinitive is used as the *subject*, the *direct object*, the *object of a preposition*, or as a *predicate noun*.

Example: I like <u>to sing</u>.       *direct object*
................

1. There was nothing to do except (to) wait.    1. ................

2. The famous contralto promised to sing.    2. ................

3. His plan was to escape.    3. ................

4. The president likes to talk.    4. ................

5. They would do nothing but (to) argue.    5. ................

6. To succeed was his goal.    6. ................

7. He did everything except (to) work.    7. ................

8. Jane likes to skate.    8. ................

9. To sing was her great desire.    9. ................

10. Her great desire was to sing.    10. ................

11. The young man plans to enlist.    11. ................

12. To build is our plan for next year.    12. ................

13. Our plan is to wait.    13. ................

14. Ellen does everything except (to) study.    14. ................

15. We expect to win.    15. ................

*Note: The correct answers to exercises will be found at the back of this booklet. Correct your mistakes and, if necessary, re-read the text material before going on to the next section.*

## INFINITIVES USED AS ADJECTIVES

The infinitive is often used as an *adjective* or an *adverb*. When the infinitive is used as an adjective, it usually modifies a noun which precedes it. It is easy to identify the adjective use of the infinitive because an adjective could be readily substituted for the infinitive. Study the following illustrations carefully:

The desire **to win** was apparent. (the *winning* desire)

They asked permission **to leave.** (*leaving* permission)

He obtained a permit **to build.** (*building* permit)

We had fresh water **to drink.** (*drinking* water)

In the first sentence, the infinitive *to win* is used as an adjective. It modifies the noun *desire*. In the second sentence, the infinitive *to leave* modifies the noun *permission*. In the third sentence, the infinitive *to build* modifies the noun *permit*. In the last sentence, the infinitive *to drink* modifies *water*.

### EXERCISE 2

Underline the **infinitives** used as adjectives. On the line to the right, indicate the word the infinitive modifies.

Example: The sailors wanted fresh water to drink.     *water*

1. There are no apartments to rent.     1. ................

2. I didn't have time to argue.     2. ................

3. The urge to fly was strong.     3. ................

4. To find a way to travel was difficult.     4. ................

5. There are many difficulties to overcome.     5. ................

6. The order to surrender was given.     6. ................

7. His eagerness to co-operate was appreciated.    7. ..................

8. Promises to pay were made regularly.            8. ..................

9. That shop has many foreign products to sell.    9. ..................

10. The sailors had plenty of fresh water to drink. 10. ..................

11. The prisoner was looking for an opportunity
to escape.                                         11. ..................

12. The men wanted a place to meet.                12. ..................

13. This is the road to follow.                    13. ..................

14. The librarian gave me several books to read.   14. ..................

15. His desire to succeed was his incentive to work. 15. ..................

## INFINITIVES USED AS ADVERBS

The infinitive is often used as an *adverb* to modify a verb, an adjective, or an adverb. When the infinitive is used as an adverb, it usually expresses *purpose* or *degree*.

It is easy to identify an infinitive used as an adverb when it modifies a verb. In almost every case, the infinitive expresses *purpose*. It tells why, or for what purpose the action is performed. When an infinitive is used in this way, it is often called the *infinitive of purpose*. The infinitives in the following illustrations express purpose and modify the verb:

The traveler stopped **to rest.** (*to rest*—expresses purpose)

The composer came **to listen.** (*to listen*—expresses purpose)

The officer returned **to help.** (*to help*—expresses purpose)

In the first sentence, the infinitive *to rest* modifies the verb *stopped*. The infinitive expresses purpose; that is, it tells why the traveler stopped. The infinitive *to listen* modifies the verb *came*. This infinitive also expresses purpose. It tells why the composer came. The infinitive in the third sentence tells why the officer returned. It modifies the verb and expresses purpose.

An infinitive used as an adverb frequently modifies an *adjective*. This use of the infinitive is also easy to identify. In most cases, the infinitive modifies an adjective which follows a linking verb. Examine the following illustrations carefully:

The cake was ready **to bake.** (*to bake*—modifies the adjective *ready*)

The men were anxious **to work.** (*to work*—modifies the adjective *anxious*)

We are sorry **to leave.** (*to leave*—modifies the adjective *sorry*)

I shall be glad **to help.** (*to help*—modifies the adjective *glad*)

In the first sentence, the linking verb *was* is followed by the predicate adjective *ready*. The adjective *ready* is modified by the infinitive *to bake* which is used as an adverb. As you have learned, only adverbs can modify adjectives. The sentence means that the cake was ready *for baking*. The infinitive *to bake* could readily be turned into an adverbial phrase. This should make its adverbial function clear.

In the second sentence, the linking verb *were* is followed by the predicate adjective *anxious*. The adjective *anxious* is modified by the infinitive *to work*. In the third sentence, the predicate adjective *sorry* is modified by the infinitive *to leave*. In the last sentence, the predicate adjective *glad* is modified by the infinitive *to help*.

In all of the preceding illustrations a linking verb is followed by a predicate adjective. The predicate adjective is modified by an infinitive which is used as an adverb.

## EXERCISE 3

Underline the **infinitives**. Write **adj.** under the infinitive which is used as an adjective, and **adv.** under the infinitive which is used as an adverb. On the line to the right, indicate the word which the infinitive modifies.

Example: There are many difficulties <u>to overcome.</u>   *difficulties*
                                              adj.        .....................

1. The mountain climbers were eager to start.      1. .................

2. The book is difficult to understand.            2. .................

3. The refugees had plenty of food to eat.         3. .................

4. The firm was ready to expand.                   4. .................

5. I have an opportunity to travel.                5. .................

6. Philip has a boat to rent.                      6. .................

7. We are anxious to go.                            7. .................

8. The reporter wants more time to write.          8. .................

9. The way to operate the camera is described in
   the directions.                                 9. .................

10. The chairman rose to speak.                    10. .................

11. We went to the lake to swim.                   11. .................

12. There were interesting trips to take.          12. .................

13. Here are some magazines to read.               13. .................

14. Margaret went to New York to study.            14. .................

15. The dealer has automobiles to sell.            15. .................

## COMPLEMENTS OF INFINITIVES

Like the gerund and the participle, the infinitive may take any kind of complement a verb might take. Sometimes the infinitive takes a *direct object*. Sometimes it takes both a *direct* and an *indirect object*. If the infinitive is a form of a linking verb, it may take a *predicate noun* or a *predicate adjective* as a complement.

Arlene wanted to buy a fur coat. (*coat*—object of *to buy*)

The tailor promised to make me a suit. (*me*—indirect object)
(*suit*—direct object)

John would like to be an aviator. (*aviator*—predicate noun)

His ambition is to become rich. (*rich*—predicate adjective)

In the first sentence, the infinitive *to buy* takes the direct object *coat*. In the second sentence, the infinitive *to make* takes both an indirect object and a direct object. *Me* is the indirect object and *suit* is the direct object. In the third sentence, the infinitive *to be* takes the predicate noun *aviator* as a complement. In the last sentence, the infinitive *to become* takes the predicate adjective *rich* as a complement.

### EXERCISE 4

Underline the **complements** of the *infinitives* in the following sentences. On the line to the right, indicate whether the complement is a *direct object,* an *indirect object,* a *predicate noun,* or a *predicate adjective.* Some infinitives have both a direct and an indirect object. Indicate both.

Example: I like to read French novels.     *direct object*
..........................

1. We desired to secure our tickets early.     1. ...................

2. To become a professor was his great ambition.     2. .................

3. Several attempted to cross the channel.     3. .................

4.  Allen wanted to give Martha a ring.        4.  ..................

5.  Evelyn forgot to read the directions.      5.  ..................

6.  Every attempt to find the jewels was futile.   6.  ..................

7.  The officer came to inspect the uniforms.   7.  ..................

8.  Alice wants to be popular.                  8.  ..................

9.  Not to be punctual is to be inconsiderate.   9.  ..................

10.  Father promised to send Norman a check.   10.  ..................

11.  To know you has been a pleasure.          11.  ..................

12.  The plan was to raise the necessary funds by
     subscription.                             12.  ..................

13.  I should like to send Marian some orchids.   13.  ..................

14.  Have you the time to see him?             14.  ..................

15.  Horace wants to have a position in a bank.   15.  ..................

## MODIFIERS OF INFINITIVES

1.  Like the verb, an infinitive may be modified by an *adverb* or by an *adverbial phrase.*

The boys like to swim fast. (*fast*—adverb, modifies *to swim*)
<small>adverb</small>

The boys like to swim in Lake Michigan. (adverbial phrase—
<small>adverbial phrase</small>
modifies *to swim*)

To write well is an accomplishment. (*well*—adverb—modifies
<small>adverb</small>
*To write*)

To fish in that stream is a pleasure. (adverbial phrase—modifies
<small>adverbial phrase</small>
*To fish*)

2.   Sometimes the infinitive has both a complement and a modifier.

To do the job properly would require a month's time.
         dir. obj.   adv.

In this sentence the infinitive *To do* takes the direct object *job*. The infinitive is also modified by the adverb *properly*.

## THE INFINITIVE PHRASE

In the preceding illustration, the entire phrase, *To do the job properly,* regarded as a whole, is the **complete subject** of the sentence. This group of words is called an **infinitive phrase.** An *infinitive phrase* consists of an infinitive with its complements or its modifiers, or both, if it takes both.

Ted's aim was to please others. (infinitive with a *direct object*)
               infinitive phrase

We did not want to travel by plane. (infinitive with an *adverbial*
                  infinitive phrase
*phrase* as a modifier)

The men would like to begin the project now. (infinitive with a
                     infinitive phrase
*direct object* and an *adverb* as modifier)

The infinitive phrase in the first sentence is *to please others.* The phrase consists of the infinitive *to please* and its object *others.* The infinitive phrase in the second sentence is *to travel by plane.* It consists of the infinitive *to travel* and the adverbial phrase *by plane,* which modifies the infinitive. The infinitive phrase in the last sentence is *to begin the project now.* The infinitive takes the direct object *project* and the adverbial modifier *now.*

## EXERCISE 5

Underline the **infinitive phrases.** On the line to the right, indicate whether the infinitive takes a *complement* or a *modifier,* or both a *complement* and a *modifier.*

1. The general's plan was to trap the enemy.     1. ................

2. Paul wanted to buy a fur coat for his sister.   2. ................

3. My failure to arrive on time irritated her.     3. ................

4. To buy fruit out of season is extravagant.      4. ................

5. His ambition was to belong to the air force.    5. ................

6. We desired to improve our living conditions.    6. ................

7. The agent promised to reserve our seats.        7. ................

8. We must leave at eight to meet our guests.      8. ................

9. She does nothing but (to) listen to the radio.  9. ................

10. The way to succeed in business is not found
    in books.                                     10. ................

11. We were anxious to start our fall program.    11. ................

12. I didn't have time to argue with her yesterday. 12. ................

13. She went to Europe to visit the art galleries. 13. ................

14. His plan was to raise funds quickly.          14. ................

15. I like to sit in the sun occasionally.        15. ................

## THE OMISSION OF THE SIGN "TO"

You have learned that the sign of the infinitive (*to*) is omitted when the infinitive is used after certain verbs. The sign is not used because the sentence would sound awkward or stilted with the sign placed before the verb form. You should become familiar with the verbs that are followed by the infinitive without the sign "*to*."

The sign of the infinitive is usually omitted when the infinitive is used after the following verbs: *hear, feel, let, watch, dare, help, see, make, please, bid, need,* etc. The following sentences illustrate the use of the infinitive without the sign. The *to* is enclosed in parentheses to show you that you should supply it mentally in order to recognize the infinitive construction.

### INFINITIVES WITHOUT THE SIGN

1. I felt the floor (to) shake under me.

2. We heard him (to) sing some old ballads.

3. I saw her (to) enter the theater.

4. They bid us (to) leave immediately.

5. They dare not (to) cause a riot.

6. Help me (to) carry the luggage.

7. Let his friend (to) help him.

8. They made him (to) wait for an hour.

9. They watched him (to) play.

10. There was nothing to do but (to) read.

11. We watched him (to) climb the ladder.

12. They helped us (to) build the garage.

13. They heard him (to) cry for help.

14. Let the old man (to) have his way.

15. The janitor does everything except (to) clean the windows.

## EXERCISE 6

This exercise will help you recognize the verbs that are followed by an infinitive used without the infinitive sign *to*.

Underline the **infinitives** in the following sentences. On the line to the right, indicate the *verb* that is followed by an infinitive without the sign *to*.

**Verb**

Example: I made him <u>sign</u> the lease. (*to sign*)          *made*
...........................

1. I saw him stop the car.                          1. ...................

2. We heard him call the police.                    2. ...................

3. Hubert helped us paint the fence.                3. ...................

4. I bid you beware.                                4. ...................

5. Help me translate this letter.                   5. ...................

6. I felt the floor shake under me.                 6. ...................

7. Let Marion have the magazine.                    7. ...................

8. The manager made him work overtime.              8. ...................

9. They dare not cause a riot.                      9. ...................

10. We helped him accomplish his mission.           10. ...................

11. We watched him take the pictures.               11. ...................

12. I suddenly felt the train move.                 12. ...................

13. Will you let me speak?                          13. ...................

14. We watched the sun rise.                        14. ...................

15. You need not do it now.                         15. ...................

## SUMMARY OF GRAMMAR UNIT TWENTY-FOUR

An **infinitive** is a verb form (verbal) which is used as a *noun,* an *adjective,* or an *adverb.* An infinitive is usually preceded by the word *to* which is commonly called the sign of the infinitive. When *to* is used in this way, it is *not a preposition.*

An infinitive is often used as a **noun.** Like the noun, an infinitive may be used as the *subject* of a sentence, the *direct object* of a verb, the *object of a preposition,* or as a *predicate noun* after a linking verb.

The infinitive is also used as an **adjective** or an **adverb.** When the infinitive is used as an adjective, it usually modifies a preceding *noun.* When the infinitive is used as an adverb, it modifies a *verb,* an *adjective,* or an *adverb.* When the infinitive modifies a verb, it usually expresses *purpose.*

Like the gerund and the participle, an infinitive may take any kind of **complement** or **modifier** that a verb might take. Sometimes the infinitive takes a *direct object.* Sometimes it takes both an *indirect* and a *direct object.* If the infinitive is a form of a linking verb, it is usually followed by a *predicate noun* or a *predicate adjective.* An infinitive may be modified by an *adverb* or an *adverbial phrase.*

An infinitive with its complement or complements and its modifier or modifiers constitutes an **infinitive phrase.** The infinitive phrase may be used as a *noun,* an *adjective,* or an *adverb.*

Like the participle and the gerund, the infinitive *cannot* function as the **predicate verb** of a sentence.

## SELF-GRADING ASSIGNMENT 1

Directions: Underline the *infinitives* in the following sentences. On the line to the right, indicate whether the infinitive is used as the *subject, direct object, object of a preposition,* or as a *predicate noun.*

Example: The men wanted to play golf.　　*direct object*
................................

1. George tried to telephone Max.　　1. ........................

2. To fail her best friend was never considered.　　2. ........................

3. His plan was to improve working conditions.　　3. ........................

4. Try to check this list carefully.　　4. ........................

5. To build a skyscraper was his dream.　　5. ........................

6. The prisoner wanted to talk to the judge.　　6. ........................

7. We like to study science out-of-doors.　　7. ........................

8. My first impulse was to refuse their offer.　　8. ........................

9. To win the beauty prize was her great desire.　　9. ........................

10. The supervisor's objective was to create harmony among the men.　　10. ........................

11. The servants did little but visit.　　11. ........................

12. The members wanted to practice golf on the new course.　　12. ........................

13. To forgive means to forget.　　13. ........................

14. The agent promised to send the order at once.　　14. ........................

15. To become a pilot requires skill.　　15. ........................

*Caution*: *Check your answers to each assignment with the answer key at the back of the booklet before proceeding with the next assignment.*

### SELF-GRADING ASSIGNMENT 2

Directions: Underline the *infinitives* in the following sentences. On the line to the right, indicate whether the infinitive is used as an *adverb* or as an *adjective*.

Example: We have an apartment to rent.    *adjective*
.............................

1. We had time to interview the candidate.    1. ..................

2. We must leave early to catch the boat.    2. ..................

3. His failure to pass the examination discouraged him.    3. ..................

4. All the attempts to stop the flood proved futile.    4. ..................

5. There are many difficulties to overcome.    5. ..................

6. The Red Cross sent supplies to prevent a famine.    6. ..................

7. The way to build the plane is described in the book.    7. ..................

8. The officer stopped to question the driver.    8. ..................

9. I have an opportunity to study French.    9. ..................

10. The diplomat went to Africa to study the economic conditions.    10. ..................

11. The committee met to arrange the program.    11. ..................

12. Ned was eager to appear well-dressed.    12. ..................

13. The material is difficult to read.    13. ..................

14. The hunter was anxious to set the trap.    14. ..................

15. He left hastily to avoid detection.    15. ..................

## SELF-GRADING ASSIGNMENT 3

Directions: Underline the *infinitives* in the following sentences. On the line to the right, indicate how the infinitive is used: *subject, direct object, object of a preposition, predicate noun, adjective,* or *adverb.*

Example: We planned to leave early.          *direct object*
.........................

1. I went to the city to buy a car.          1. .................

2. We had planned to travel in England.          2. .................

3. It is the time to pay your income tax.          3. .................

4. Apartments to rent are very scarce.          4. .................

5. We are willing to do the work.          5. .................

6. The manager is the one to interview.          6. .................

7. The boys and girls did everything but study.          7. .................

8. We were fortunate to secure passage.          8. .................

9. Her greatest desire is to go to Italy.          9. .................

10. This is your chance to get a better position.          10. .................

11. To become an expert musician requires hours of practice.          11. .................

12. Her job was to read the copy.          12. .................

13. To learn to speak correctly is difficult.          13. .................

14. He made certain contacts to attain his purpose.          14. .................

15. I shall try to follow your directions.          15. .................

## SELF-GRADING ASSIGNMENT 4

In this assignment you are dealing with the infinitive phrase taken as a whole. The infinitive phrase functions as the *complete subject,* the *complete object* of a *verb* or a *preposition,* and the *complete predicate noun.* The infinitive phrase is also the *complete adjective* or *adverbial modifier.*

Directions: Underline the **infinitives phrases** in the following sentences. On the line to the right, indicate the use of the infinitive phrase: *subject, direct object, object of a preposition, predicate noun, adjective modifier,* or an *adverbial modifier.*

Example: <u>To read well</u> is an acccomplishment.    *subject*
.......................

1. To please the customer is our policy.    1. ..................

2. Our policy is to please the customer.    2. ..................

3. To increase the efficiency of the office force was his aim.    3. ..................

4. His aim was to increase the efficiency of the office force.    4. ..................

5. Two typists will be employed to complete the extra work.    5. ..................

6. Andrew was anxious to join the Marines.    6. ..................

7. The president had no time to interview the candidates.    7. ..................

8. The girls did nothing but talk in their spare time.    8. ..................

9. The salesman wants to reserve rooms at the Stevens Hotel.    9. ..................

10. We went to Detroit to buy a new car.    10. ..................

11. We stopped the car to avoid an accident.    11. ..................

12. The reporter had an opportunity to attend the game.    12. ..................

## PROGRESS TEST TWENTY-FOUR

This progress test should not be taken until a day or two after you have completed the assignments. The score you make on the test will then more clearly reflect your understanding of the material in the unit.

Directions: Underline the **infinitives** and the **infinitive phrases** in the following sentences. On the line to the right, indicate the way in which the infinitive or the infinitive phrase is used: *subject, direct object, object of a preposition, predicate noun, adjective modifier,* or *adverbial modifier.* (*50 points*)

Example: The committee met to arrange the program.

*infinitive phrase*

*adverbial use*
......................

1. He blew the whistle to announce the dinner hour.

1. .................

2. Arthur dislikes to work on his father's farm.

2. .................

3. The senator was eager to complete the survey.

3. .................

4. To buy a home in the suburbs was her ambition.

4. .................

5. The most difficult task was to sort the mail.

5. .................

6. I should like to give Kathleen a television set.

6. .................

7. There are many duties to perform.

7. .................

8. We planned to purchase some new typewriters.

8. .................

9. To become an expert stenographer was her goal.

9. .................

10. The president wants to enlarge the factory.

10. .................

11. The committee met to arrange the program.

11. .................

12. Marvin was anxious to succeed.

12. .................

## PROGRESS TEST TWENTY-FOUR (continued)

13. We have many difficulties to surmount.    13. ................

14. To advance is the general's plan.    14. ................

15. Ada always tries to do her best.    15. ................

16. The officer attempted to stop the car.    16. ................

17. Show me the way to putt.    17. ................

18. He does everything but play golf.    18. ................

19. She did nothing except complain.    19. ................

20. He obtained the right to sell his product.    20. ................

21. I hope to meet the new officers of our club.    21. ................

22. Father's plan is to move to New York.    22. ................

23. The landlord did everything except varnish the floors.    23. ................

24. Mr. Jones was eager to secure his license.    24. ................

25. The president likes to talk to the employees.    25. ................

## ANSWER KEY

for

## EXERCISES, ASSIGNMENTS, AND PROGRESS TEST

### *Grammar Unit Twenty-four*

---

### CORRECT ANSWERS TO EXERCISE 1

1. There was nothing to do except *(to)* **wait**.
2. The famous contralto promised **to sing**.
3. His plan was **to escape**.
4. The president likes **to talk**.
5. They would do nothing but *(to)* **argue**.

6. **To succeed** was his goal.
7. He did everything except *(to)* **work**.

8. Jane likes **to skate**.
9. **To sing** was her great desire.
10. Her great desire was **to sing**.
11. The young man plans **to enlist**.
12. **To build** is our plan for next year.
13. Our plan is **to wait**.
14. Ellen does everything except *(to)* **study**.

15. We expect **to win**.

1. *object of preposition*

2. *direct object*

3. *predicate noun*

4. *direct object*

5. *object of preposition*

6. *subject*

7. *object of preposition*

8. *direct object*

9. *subject*

10. *predicate noun*

11. *direct object*

12. *subject*

13. *predicate noun*

14. *object of preposition*

15. *direct object*

### CORRECT ANSWERS TO EXERCISE 2

1. There are no apartments **to rent**.
2. I didn't have time **to argue**.
3. The urge **to fly** was strong.
4. To find a way **to travel** was difficult.
5. There are many difficulties **to overcome**.

1. apartments

2. time

3. urge

4. way

5. difficulties

6. The order *to surrender* was given.                6. order
7. His eagerness *to co-operate* was appreciated.     7. eagerness
8. Promises *to pay* were made regularly.             8. promises
9. That shop has many foreign products *to sell*.     9. products
10. The sailors had plenty of fresh water *to drink*. 10. water
11. The prisoner was looking for an opportunity *to escape*. 11. opportunity
12. The men wanted a place *to meet*.                 12. place
13. This is the road *to follow*.                     13. road
14. The librarian gave me several books *to read*.    14. books
15. His desire *to succeed* was his incentive *to work*. 15. desire
                                                          incentive

## CORRECT ANSWERS TO EXERCISE 3

1. The mountain climbers were eager to start.
                                         adv.
   1. eager

2. The book is difficult to understand.
                          adv.
   2. difficult

3. The refugees had plenty of food to eat.
                                    adj.
   3. food

4. The firm was ready to expand.
                       adv.
   4. ready

5. I have an opportunity to travel.
                         adj.
   5. opportunity

6. Philip has a boat to rent.
                     adj.
   6. boat

7. We are anxious to go.
                  adv.
   7. anxious

8. The reporter wants more time to write.
                                 adj.
   8. time

9. The way to operate the camera is described in
          adj.
   the directions.
   9. way

10. The chairman rose to speak.
                       adv.
    10. rose

11. We went to the lake to swim.
                        adv.
    11. went

12. There were interesting trips to take.
                                 adj.
    12. trips

13. Here are some magazines to read.
                            adj.
    13. magazines

14. Margaret went to New York to study.
                               adv.
    14. went

15. The dealer has automobiles to sell.
                               adj.
    15. automobiles

## CORRECT ANSWERS TO EXERCISE 4

1. We desired to secure our tickets early.
   　　　　　　　　　　　　dir. obj.

2. To become a professor was his great ambition.
   　　　　　pred. noun

3. Several attempted to cross the channel.
   　　　　　　　　　　　　dir. obj.

4. Allen wanted to give Martha a ring.
   　　　　　　　　indir. obj.　dir. obj.

5. Evelyn forgot to read the directions.
   　　　　　　　　　　　dir. obj.

6. Every attempt to find the jewels was futile.
   　　　　　　　　　dir. obj.

7. The officer came to inspect the uniforms.
   　　　　　　　　　　　　dir. obj.

8. Alice wants to be popular .
   　　　　　　　pred. adj.

9. Not to be punctual is to be inconsiderate.
   　　　pred. adj.　　　　　pred. adj.

10. Father promised to send Norman a check.
    　　　　　　　　　indir. obj.　dir. obj.

11. To know you has been a pleasure.
    　　　dir. obj.

12. The plan was to raise the necessary funds by subscription.
    　　　　　　　　　　　　dir. obj.

13. I should like to send Marian some orchids.
    　　　　　　　　indir. obj.　　dir. obj.

14. Have you the time to see him?
    　　　　　　　　　dir. obj.

15. Horace wants to have a position in a bank.
    　　　　　　　　　　dir. obj.

## CORRECT ANSWERS TO EXERCISE 5

1. The general's plan was **to trap the enemy.**　　1. *enemy*—complement

2. Paul wanted **to buy a fur coat for his sister.**　2. *coat*—complement
   　　　　　　　　　　　　　　　　　　　　　　　*for his sister*—
   　　　　　　　　　　　　　　　　　　　　　　　modifier

3. My failure **to arrive on time** irritated her.　　3. *on time*—modifier

4. **To buy fruit out of season** is extravagant.

    4. *out of season—* modifier
    *fruit—*complement

5. His ambition was **to belong to the air force.**

    5. *to the air force—* modifier

6. We desired **to improve our living conditions.**

    6. *conditions—* complement

7. The agent promised **to reserve our seats.**

    7. *seats—*complement

8. We must leave at eight **to meet our guests.**

    8. *guests—*complement

9. She does nothing but **(to) listen to the radio.**

    9. *to the radio—* modifier

10. The way **to succeed in business** is not found in books.

    10. *in business—* modifier

11. We were anxious **to start our fall program.**

    11. *program—* complement

12. I didn't have time **to argue with her yesterday.**

    12. *with her—*modifier
    *yesterday—*modifier

13. She went to Europe **to visit the art galleries.**

    13. *galleries—* complement

14. His plan was **to raise funds quickly.**

    14. *funds—*complement
    *quickly—*modifier

15. I like **to sit in the sun occasionally.**

    15. *in the sun—*modifier
    *occasionally—* modifier

## CORRECT ANSWERS TO EXERCISE 6

1. I saw him **(to) stop** the car.

    1. saw

2. We heard him **(to) call** the police.

    2. heard

3. Hubert helped us **(to) paint** the fence.

    3. helped

4. I bid you **(to) beware.**

    4. bid

5. Help me **(to) translate** this letter.

    5. help

6. I felt the floor **(to) shake** under me.

    6. felt

7. Let Marian **(to) have** the magazine.

    7. let

8. The manager made him **(to) work** overtime.

    8. made

9. They dare not **(to) cause** a riot.

    9. dare

10. We helped him *(to)* **accomplish** his mission.          10. helped

11. We watched him *(to)* **take** the pictures.          11. watched

12. I suddenly felt the train *(to)* **move.**          12. felt

13. Will you let me *(to)* **speak?**          13. will let

14. We watched the sun *(to)* **rise.**          14. watched

15. You need not *(to)* **do** it now.          15. need

## CORRECT ANSWERS TO ASSIGNMENT 1

1. George tried **to telephone** Max.          1. *direct object*

2. **To fail** her best friend was never considered.          2. *subject*

3. His plan was **to improve** working conditions.          3. *predicate noun*

4. Try **to check** this list carefully.          4. *direct object*

5. **To build** a skyscraper was his dream.          5. *subject*

6. The prisoner wanted **to talk** to the judge.          6. *direct object*

7. We like **to study** science out-of-doors.          7. *direct object*

8. My first impulse was **to refuse** their offer.          8. *predicate noun*

9. **To win** the beauty prize was her great desire.          9. *subject*

10. The supervisor's objective was **to create** harmony among the men.          10. *predicate noun*

11. The servants did little but *(to)* **visit.**          11. *object of the preposition* **but**

12. The members wanted **to practice** golf on the new course.          12. *direct object*

13. **To forgive** means **to forget.**          13. *subject* *direct object*

14. The agent promised **to send** the order at once.          14. *direct object*

15. **To become** a pilot requires skill.          15. *subject*

## CORRECT ANSWERS TO ASSIGNMENT 2

1. We had time **to interview** the candidate.          1. *adjective*

2. We must leave early **to catch** the boat.          2. *adverb*

3. His failure **to pass** the examination discouraged him.          3. *adjective*

4. All the attempts **to stop** the flood proved futile.          4. *adjective*

5. There are many difficulties **to overcome**.                5. *adjective*

6. The Red Cross sent supplies **to prevent** a famine.        6. *adverb*

7. The way **to build** the plane is described in the book.    7. *adjective*

8. The officer stopped **to question** the driver.             8. *adverb*

9. I have an opportunity **to study** French.                  9. *adjective*

10. The diplomat went to Africa **to study** the
economic conditions.                                          10. *adverb*

11. The committee met **to arrange** the program.             11. *adverb*

12. Ned was eager **to appear** well-dressed.                 12. *adverb*

13. The material is difficult **to read**.                    13. *adverb*

14. The hunter was anxious **to set** the trap.               14. *adverb*

15. He left hastily **to avoid** detection.                   15. *adverb*


## CORRECT ANSWERS TO ASSIGNMENT 3

1. I went to the city **to buy** a car.                        1. *adverb*

2. We had planned **to travel** in England.                    2. *direct object*

3. It is the time **to pay** your income tax.                  3. *adjective*

4. Apartments **to rent** are very scarce.                     4. *adjecitve*

5. We are willing **to do** the work.                          5. *adverb*

6. The manager is the one **to interview**.                    6. *adjective*

7. The boys and girls did everything but **(to) study**.       7. *object of the preposition* **but**

8. We were fortunate **to secure** passage.                    8. *adverb*

9. Her greatest desire is **to go** to Italy.                  9. *predicate noun*

10. This is your chance **to get** a better position.         10. *adjective*

11. **To become** an expert musician requires hours
of practice.                                                  11. *subject*

12. Her job was **to read** the copy.                         12. *predicate noun*

13. **To learn to speak** correctly is difficult.             13. *to learn*—subject *to speak*—object of *to learn*

14. He made certain contacts **to attain** his purpose.       14. *adverb*

15. I shall try **to follow** your directions.                15. *direct object*

## CORRECT ANSWERS TO ASSIGNMENT 4

| Infinitive Phrase | Use in the Sentence |
|---|---|
| 1. To please the customer | *subject* |
| 2. to please the customer | *predicate noun* |
| 3. To increase the efficiency of the office force | *subject* |
| 4. to increase the efficiency of the office force | *predicate noun* |
| 5. to complete the extra work | *adverb*—expresses purpose modifies **will be employed** |
| 6. to join the Marines | *adverb*—modifies **anxious** |
| 7. to interview the candidates | *adjective*—modifies **time** |
| 8. (to) talk in their spare time | *object of the preposition* **but** |
| 9. to reserve rooms at the Stevens Hotel | *direct object of* **wants** |
| 10. to buy a new car | *adverb*—expresses purpose modifies **went** |
| 11. to avoid an accident | *adverb*—expresses purpose modifies **stopped** |
| 12. to attend the game | *adjective*—modifies **opportunity** |

## CORRECT ANSWERS TO PROGRESS TEST TWENTY-FOUR

1. He blew the whistle to announce the dinner hour.
   infinitive phrase
   1. *adverbial use*

2. Arthur dislikes to work on his father's farm.
   infinitive phrase
   2. *direct object*

3. The senator was eager to complete the survey.
   infinitive phrase
   3. *adverbial use*

4. To buy a home in the suburbs was her ambition.
   infinitive phrase
   4. *subject*

5. The most difficult task was to sort the mail.
   infinitive phrase
   5. *predicate noun*

6. I should like to give Kathleen a television set.
   infinitive phrase
   6. *direct object*

7. There are many duties to perform.
   infinitive
   7. *adjective use*

8. We planned to purchase some new typewriters.
   infinitive phrase
   8. *direct object*

9. To become an expert stenographer was her goal.
   <br>infinitive phrase

9. *subject*

10. The president wants to enlarge the factory.
    <br>infinitive phrase

10. *direct object*

11. The committee met to arrange the program.
    <br>infinitive phrase

11. *adverbial use*

12. Marvin was anxious to succeed.
    <br>infinitive

12. *adverbial use*

13. We have many difficulties to surmount.
    <br>infinitive

13. *adjective use*

14. To advance is the general's plan.
    <br>infinitive

14. *subject*

15. Ada always tries to do her best.
    <br>infinitive phrase

15. *direct object*

16. The officer attempted to stop the car.
    <br>infinitive phrase

16. *direct object*

17. Show me the way to putt.
    <br>infinitive

17. *adjective use*

18. He does everything but (to) play golf.
    <br>infinitive phrase

18. *object of preposition*

19. She did nothing except (to) complain.
    <br>infinitive

19. *object of preposition*

20. He obtained the right to sell his product.
    <br>infinitive phrase

20. *adjective use*

21. I hope to meet the new officers of our club.
    <br>infinitive phrase

21. *direct object*

22. Father's plan is to move to New York.
    <br>infinitive phrase

22. *predicate noun*

23. The landlord did everything except (to) varnish the floors.
    <br>infinitive phrase

23. *object of preposition*

24. Mr. Jones was eager to secure his license.
    <br>infinitive phrase

24. *adverbial use*

25. The president likes to talk to the employees.
    <br>infinitive phrase

25. *direct object*

## HOW TO OBTAIN YOUR SCORE

*The test totals 50 points. To obtain your score, divide the number of your correct answers by 50. The answer will be your score on this test. For example, if you have 47 points correct, your score is 47 divided by 50 which is 94 per cent. In other words, your score on this test is 94. You can obtain your score on any of the exercises or assignments by following the same procedure.*

## Practical English Grammar

## OUTLINE OF UNIT TWENTY-FIVE

# PROBLEMS IN THE USE OF INFINITIVES

Page

1. THE INFINITIVE CLAUSE ...................................................... 5

2. VERB "TO BE" IN AN INFINITIVE CLAUSE.................... 8

3. THE SPLIT INFINITIVE ......................................... 11

4. SPECIAL USES OF THE INFINITIVE.............................. 14

5. THE THREE-SIDED CHARACTER OF THE INFINITIVE.. 16

6. DIAGRAMMING INFINITIVES ........................................... 17

7. SUMMARY OF GRAMMAR UNIT TWENTY-FIVE........... 23

*Self-Grading Assignments* ................................................. 24

*Progress Test Twenty-Five* ............................................. 27

*Key to Correct Answers* ................................................. 29

# PROBLEMS IN THE USE OF INFINITIVES

## THE INFINITIVE CLAUSE

IN GRAMMAR UNIT TWENTY-ONE you learned that the noun clause is often used as the direct object of a verb. The infinitive is often used in a construction which is similar to this use of a noun clause.

Sometimes the infinitive has its own *subject*. With this subject, the infinitive is used in a construction which is commonly called the **"infinitive clause."** *The infinitive clause is not a true clause* because the infinitive cannot function as a predicate verb. An infinitive cannot function as the predicate verb in a clause because it is an incomplete verb form. The following illustrations will help make this clear:

The officers want the men to sing at the Rotary Club.
<u>infinitive clause</u>

We believed him to be capable.
<u>infinitive clause</u>

In the first sentence, the group of words, *the men to sing at the Rotary Club,* is called an **"infinitive clause."** This expression is called a clause because the infinitive has a subject, and the entire group of words functions in the same way as a **noun clause** would function. The *infinitive clause* is used as the direct object of the verb *want.*

In the second sentence, the group of words *him to be capable* is an infinitive clause. The subject of the infinitive is the pronoun *him.* The entire expression *him to be capable* is used as the direct object of the verb *believed,* but it is not a true clause. The infinitive *to be* is not a predicate verb.

Jean asked me to go with her. (*me*—subject of the infinitive *to go*)
<u>infinitive clause</u>

Father advised him to buy the bonds. (*him*—subject of the infinitive *to buy*)
<u>infinitive clause</u>

He believed her to be honest. (*her*—subject of the infinitive
*to be*)
<small>infinitive clause</small>

We want them to build a house. (*them*—subject of the infinitive
*to build*)
<small>infinitive clause</small>

The underlined expression in each of the preceding sentences is the
**object** of the preceding verb. In the first sentence, *me to go with her*
is the object of the verb *asked.* The sentence does not mean that she
asked *me.* It means that she asked *me to go with her.* The entire expression, *me to go with her,* is the object of the verb *asked.*

The group of words, *me to go with her,* is called an "infinitive clause."
It consists of the subject *me* and the infinitive *to go* with the modifier
of the infinitive, the adverbial phrase *with her.* You can readily see
that this is not a true clause because the infinitive *to go* is an incomplete verb form and cannot function as the predicate verb.

The important fact to keep in mind about this construction is that
the *subject* of the infinitive is always in the **objective case.** This is an
*exception* to the rule that subjects of sentences and subjects of clauses
are always in the nominative case.

Examine the preceding illustrations again. In the second sentence,
*him* is the subject of the infinitive clause, *him to buy the bonds. Him*
is in the objective case. In the third sentence, *her* is the subject of the
infinitive clause, *her to be honest. Her* is in the objective case. In the
last sentence, *them* is the subject of the infinitive clause *them to go
with us. Them* is in the objective case.

You will not have any difficulty with the **case** of the subject of the
infinitive. No one would think of saying, "Jean asked *I* to go with her,"
or "Father advised *he* to buy the bonds." It is natural to use the *objective
case* as the subject of the infinitive. However, it is important to keep
the following rule in mind. It will help you understand some of the
other problems connected with the use of infinitives.

---

**The subject of an infinitive is always in the objective case.**

---

Sometimes the sign of the infinitive is omitted in the "infinitive clause." You must learn how to recognize such "clauses" even if the sign is omitted.

The manager made <u>Mary copy the report again.</u>
infinitive clause

The manager made <u>Mary (to) copy the report again.</u>
infinitive clause

I saw <u>her dance at the carnival.</u>
infinitive clause

I saw <u>her (to) dance at the carnival.</u>
infinitive clause

In the first sentence, the infinitive clause, *Mary (to) copy the report again,* is the direct object of the verb *made.* The sign of the infinitive *(to)* is omitted in this sentence. In the second sentence, the infinitive clause *her (to) dance at the carnival* is the object of the verb *saw.* The sign of the infinitive is omitted before *dance.*

### EXERCISE 1

Underline the **infinitive clauses** in the following sentences. On the line to the right, indicate the word that is used as the *subject* of the infinitive.

|  | Subject of the Infinitive |
|---|---|
| Example: I asked <u>the janitor to wash the windows.</u> | janitor |

1. We invited <u>them to stay at the lodge.</u>      1. ...................

2. I knew <u>it to be true.</u>      2. ...................

3. Robert expects <u>Mary to go to the dance.</u>      3. ...................

4. The manager urged <u>Norman to remain with the firm.</u>      4. ...................

5. We believed Jack to be the best tennis player.    5. .................

6. The professor advised me to study Spanish.    6. .................

7. I mistook Florence to be my sister.    7. .................

8. I considered her to be my best friend.    8. .................

9. I never heard him make a false statement.    9. .................

10. The officer helped the blind man cross the street.    10. .................

11. The committee asked Arthur to sing at the banquet.    11. .................

12. The president forced the treasurer to resign.    12. .................

13. I felt the floor shake under me.    13. .................

14. I thought him to be the leader of the band.    14. .................

15. I want James to act as chairman.    15. .................

*Note: The correct answers to exercises will be found at the back of this booklet. Correct your mistakes and, if necessary, re-read the text material before going on to the next section.*

## VERB "TO BE" IN AN INFINITIVE CLAUSE

When we use the infinitive *to be* in an "infinitive clause," we have a problem in agreement of subject and complement which is often confusing. You have just learned that the subject of an infinitive is always in the objective case. This rule applies in the case of *action verbs* and *linking verbs*.

The problem arises when the infinitive is a form of a linking verb. You learned in your previous study that the noun or pronoun used after a linking verb is in the *nominative case* to agree with the subject of the sentence. Up to this point, every word used as the subject of a sentence or of a clause has been in the nominative case. In the case of the "infinitive clause" we are dealing with a subject that is in the **objective case.**

The verb *to be,* as well as other linking verbs, always takes the same case after it as it takes before it. If the case before it is the *objective case,* the *objective case* must follow it. A noun or pronoun following a linking verb must be in the same case as the subject. Since the noun or pronoun that follows a linking verb means the same person or thing as the subject, it must agree with the subject in case. Therefore, the noun or pronoun that follows the verb *to be* in an infinitive clause is in the objective case to agree with the *subject,* which is in the objective case. This is the logical agreement of *subject* and *complement* after a linking verb functioning as an infinitive in an infinitive clause.

A few illustrations will make this clear. Notice the form of the pronoun after the linking verbs in the "infinitive clauses."

I should like the chairman to be him. (*chairman*—objective case
infinitive clause               *him*—objective case)

Many of the guests thought us to be them. (*us*—objective case—
infinitive clause          *them*—objective case)

In the first sentence, the subject of the infinitive clause is *chairman,* which is in the objective case. The infinitive *to be* is followed by the predicate pronoun *him.* The pronoun used as the complement of a linking verb must agree in case with the subject. Since the subject is in the objective case, the pronoun must be in the objective case to agree with the subject.

In the second sentence, the pronoun *us* is the subject of the infinitive clause. *Us* is in the objective case. The pronoun that follows the infinitive *to be* must be in the same case as the subject. *Them* is in the objective case to agree with the case of the subject, *us.*

### EXERCISE 2

Fill in the blank space with the correct form of the **pronoun** enclosed in parentheses.

Example: I imagined it to be ............. (she)
I imagined it to be *her*.

1. The professor thought him to be ................. (I)

2. Mother wanted Jane and ................. to stay for dinner. (he)

3. My friend knew the girls to be ............ in spite of our masks. (we)

4. The committee asked Herbert and .................... to speak at the banquet. (I)

5. The officer knew the reckless driver to be ................. (she)

6. I did not know ................. to consult. (who)

7. ................. did you believe it to be? (who)

8. I believed ................. to be the artist. (he)

9. Help ................. translate this passage. (I)

10. The owner let ................. play in the vacant lot. (we)

11. Who helped ................. paint the fence? (they)

12. Do you expect ................. to come? (she)

13. The manager asked ................. girls to work overtime. (we)

14. She advised Ted and ................. to read the book. (I)

15. I thought Jerry to be ................. (he)

## THE SPLIT INFINITIVE

The parts of an infinitive (*to* with a verb form) are regarded as a unit. They should not be separated unless there is a good reason for doing so. The usual method of separating the parts of the infinitive is to place an adverb between the *to* and the *verb form.* When the parts of the infinitive are separated in this way, we refer to the infinitive as a **"split infinitive."** The adverbial modifier "splits" the infinitive.

As a rule, the infinitive should *not* be split by a modifier. Sometimes it is both desirable and effective to split the infinitive, as many authorities in grammar are pointing out. Ordinarily, it is not the best practice, as you will readily see from the following illustrations:

I asked you **to** immediately **return** my camera.
modifier

The judge was determined **to** intently and carefully **examine** the
modifier            modifier
evidence.

In the first sentence, the infinitive is *to return.* The adverbial modifier, *immediately,* is placed between the sign of the infinitive and the verb form. In this particular sentence there is no justifiable reason for splitting the infinitive. The sentence would sound much better if it were written as follows:

I asked you **to return** my camera immediately.

In the second sentence, two adverbial modifiers connected by *and* are placed between the parts of the infinitive. This sentence would sound better if the infinitive were not split in this manner:

The judge was determined **to examine** the evidence intently and carefully.

Many authorities in English call our attention to the fact that some of the best writers split infinitives. When writers do this, they have a good reason for the "split." They also know how to do it so that the sentence will not sound awkward or stilted. When a writer splits an infinitive, his purpose is to throw the emphasis in a certain direction. The following are examples of split infinitives found in good writing:

1. "I feel like inviting them to <u>first</u> consider ...."

2. "I desire to <u>so</u> arrange my affairs...."

3. .... "his ability to <u>effectually</u> carry on ...."

4. .... "to enable him to <u>properly</u> perform his work ...."

5. .... "to <u>better</u> acquaint myself with the problems ...."

6. "Our object is to <u>further</u> cement trade relations."

7. "He worked silently and swiftly, hoping to <u>speedily</u> end his patient's discomfort."

8. "All they have to do is to sit down and <u>faithfully</u> copy it."

Although there is plenty of evidence that good writers sometimes split the infinitive, ordinarily it is better practice to keep the parts of the infinitive together. A writer or speaker should certainly avoid using such awkward sentences as the following:

Edwin was eager for me to <u>especially</u> see the art exhibit. (*to see*—
        modifier
infinitive)

Eugene promised to <u>never</u> <u>again</u> be late to work. (*to be*—
        modifier  modifier
infinitive)

The committee wanted to <u>beautifully</u> decorate the hall. (*to dec-*
        modifier
*orate*—infinitive

I want to <u>next year</u> go to Europe. (*to go*—infinitive)
        modifier

In the first sentence, the infinitive *to see* is "split" by placing the adverb *especially* between the sign of the infinitive *to* and the verb form *see*. In the second sentence, two adverbial modifiers "split" the infinitive. In the third sentence, the adverb *beautifully* "splits" the infinitive. In the fourth sentence, the adverbial modifier *year* is placed between the sign *to* and the verb form, *go*. *Year* is a noun used as an adverb.

## EXERCISE 3

Underline the **split infinitives** in the following sentences. *Rewrite* the sentences without using split infinitives.

Example: The president urged him <u>to</u> immediately <u>resign</u>. (*split infinitive*)
The president urged him **to resign** immediately.

1. The manager wanted to more rapidly increase production.

2. It is annoying to in this store wait for a clerk.

3. He urged me to at once report to the draft board.

4. The immigrant did not know how to correctly sign the paper.

5. I wanted to again see the musical comedy.

6. We decided to quickly settle the matter.

7. The patient decided to promptly pay his hospital bill.

8. I expect to again see my friend when I go to New York.

9. The soldier knew how to calmly face danger.

10. You must tell him to soon make a decision.

11. I hope to tomorrow meet him.

12. You must learn how to more successfully handle your problems.

13. The workman wanted to only talk a few minutes to the manager.

14. I offered to immediately help him.

15. The farmer intends to at once buy new machinery.

## SPECIAL USES OF THE INFINITIVE

The infinitive is often used in **apposition** with a noun to explain or identify that noun. This is a very useful construction, for it enables us to explain the noun in a very few words. The infinitive used as an *appositive* is usually set off by commas. Sometimes a dash is used:

His first proposal, to borrow money, was rejected.
infinitive phrase

We were given our orders—to finish the job before ten.
infinitive phrase

In the first sentence, the infinitive phrase, *to borrow money,* is in apposition with the word *proposal.* It explains the nature of the proposal or tells what the proposal was. In the second sentence, the infinitive phrase, *to finish the job before ten,* is in apposition with the word *orders.* It explains what our orders were.

The infinitive is also used as the **delayed subject** in a sentence that begins with the introductory word *it.* In this case *it* is an **expletive.**

It always pays to tell the truth.
infinitive phrase

(It)      To tell the truth always pays.
expletive        subject

It is your duty to protect your interests.
infinitive phrase

(It)      To protect your interests is your duty.
expletive        subject

Sentences that begin with the pronoun *it* used as an expletive should always be transposed in order to see the grammatical relations more clearly.

## EXERCISE 4

Underline the *infinitive phrases* in the following sentences. On the line to the right, indicate whether the infinitive is used as the *delayed subject,* or as an *appositive.*

Example: It is advisable <u>to drive carefully.</u>          *delayed subject*
.......................

1. The manager's plan, to install new machinery, did not meet with approval.                1. .................

2. She finally achieved her goal—to become a motion picture star.                           2. .................

3. It is possible to become an excellent writer.   3. .................

4. It became a habit to accept aid.                4. .................

5. His suggestion, to interview the president, was adopted.                                 5. .................

6. John's assignment, to complete the project, kept him indoors all winter.                 6. .................

7. It is interesting to watch his reactions.       7. .................

8. He realized the grave necessity—to consult a physician at once.                          8. .................

9. It has been customary to pay on delivery.       9. .................

10. It is easy to depend on others.                10. .................

11. His main duty, to preserve harmony, was not easy.                                       11. .................

12. The warning, to beware of treachery, made us very cautious.                             12. .................

# THE THREE-SIDED CHARACTER OF THE INFINITIVE

## NOUN USES OF THE INFINITIVE

1. **Subject** of the sentence

2. **Direct object** of a verb

3. **Object** of a *preposition*

4. **Predicate noun** after a *linking verb*

5. **Appositive**

6. **Delayed subject** after an expletive

7. May take an *adjective modifier*

## THE INFINITIVE AS A MODIFIER

1. May function as an **adjective**, modifying a noun

2. May function as an **adverb** expressing purpose or degree

## VERB CHARACTERISTICS OF THE INFINITIVE

1. Expresses *action* or *state of being,* but *cannot* function as the predicate verb in a sentence

2. May take a complement: *direct object, indirect object, predicate noun,* or *predicate adjective*

3. May take modifiers: *adverbs* and *adverbial phrases*

4. May form part of an infinitive clause

## DIAGRAMMING INFINITIVES

### 1. *The infinitive used as the subject of the sentence*

*Sentence:* To drive fast is dangerous.
<u>infinitive</u>

In this sentence, *To drive* is an infinitive used as the subject of the sentence. The infinitive is modified by the adverb *fast*. In the diagram, the infinitive is raised on "stilts" so that it will be possible to show the modifiers and complements the infinitive takes in the sentence.

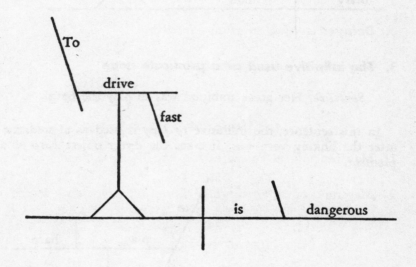

### 2. *The infinitive used as direct object of the verb*

*Sentence:* Mary likes <u>to skate</u> in the park.

In this sentence, the infinitive *to skate* is used as the direct object of the verb *likes*. The infinitive is modified by the adverbial phrase *in the park.*

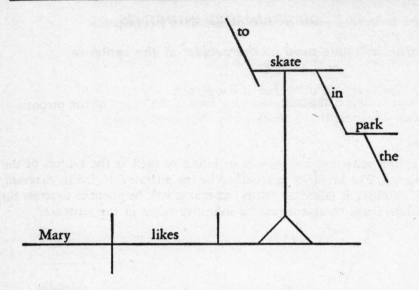

### 3. *The infinitive used as a predicate noun*

*Sentence:* Her great ambition was to play the harp.

In this sentence, the infinitive *to play* is used as a predicate noun after the linking verb *was.* It takes the direct object *harp* as a complement.

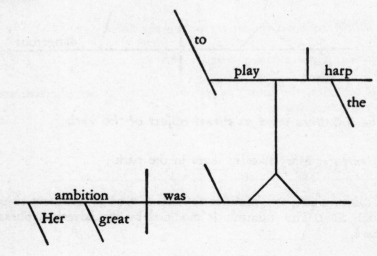

## 4. *The infinitive used as the object of a preposition*

*Sentence:* The dog did nothing but (to) bark loudly.

In this sentence, the infinitive *(to) bark* is the object of the preposition *but*. The infinitive is modified by the adverb *loudly*.

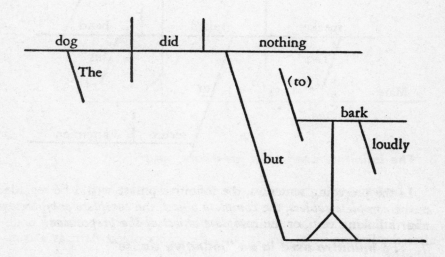

## 5. *The infinitive used as an adjective modifier*

*Sentence*: Apartments to rent are very scarce.

In this sentence, the infinitive *to rent* is used as an adjective and modifies the noun *Apartments*.

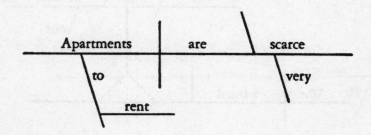

## 6. *The infinitive used as an adverbial modifier*

*Sentence:* The speaker raised his hand to secure attention.

In this sentence, the infinitive *to secure* is used as an adverb. It modifies the verb *raised* and expresses purpose. The infinitive *to secure* takes the object *attention.*

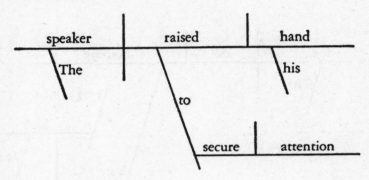

In the preceding sentences, the infinitive phrase would be regarded as the *complete subject,* the *complete object,* the *complete complement* after a linking verb, or the *complete object of the preposition.*

## 7. *The infinitive used in an "infinitive clause"*
*Sentence:* We wanted her to be our director.
infinitive clause

## 8. *The infinitive used as the delayed subject after "it"*

*Sentence:* It is interesting <u>to watch his reactions.</u>
delayed subject

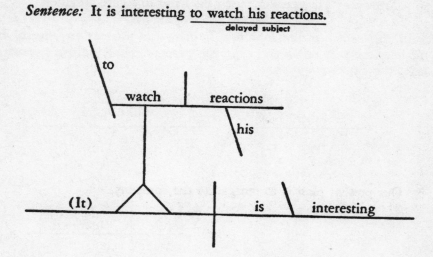

### EXERCISE 5

Diagram the following sentences using the methods of diagramming that have been presented in this unit.

1. The firm wants me to stay in Chicago.

2. To become a director was his great ambition.

3. Our present plan is to reorganize the company.

4. The old man did nothing but (to) complain.

## SUMMARY OF GRAMMAR UNIT TWENTY-FIVE

An **infinitive** is often found in a construction which is commonly called the *"infinitive clause."* This construction is called a clause because the infinitive has a *subject,* and the entire expression is the equivalent of a noun clause. *The infinitive clause is not a true clause* because an infinitive cannot function as a predicate verb.

The **subject** of an infinitive in an infinitive clause is always in the **objective case.** This presents a problem in agreement when we are dealing with verbs like the verb *to be.* A linking verb always takes the same case after it as before it. If the subject is in the *objective case,* the noun or pronoun that follows the linking verb must also be in the *objective case.* This is the logical agreement of subject and predicate noun or pronoun. The pronoun that follows a linking verb in an infinitive clause must be in the objective case. Example: I knew it to be him. *Him* is in the objective case to agree with the pronoun *it.*

An *infinitive* is often **"split"** by placing an adverbial modifier between the sign (to) and the verb form. The parts of an infinitive are regarded as a unit and should not be split unless there is a good reason for doing so. But there are times when it is desirable to split an infinitive. Examples of *split infinitives* are found in good modern prose. Ordinarily, it is not the best practice to split an infinitive because it often results in an awkward or unnatural expression.

The infinitive is often used as the **delayed subject** in a sentence that begins with the introductory word "it." In such cases, the word *it* is used as an **expletive** and the infinitive is the logical subject of the sentence. Example: It is his duty to check the accounts. The true subject of the sentence is the infinitive *to check.*

## SELF-GRADING ASSIGNMENT 1

The purpose of this assignment is to determine whether you are familiar with the following uses of the infinitive and the infinitive phrase:

| | |
|---|---|
| **subject** | **appositive** |
| **direct object** | **delayed subject after "it"** |
| **predicate noun** | **adjective modifier** |
| **object of a preposition** | **adverbial modifier** |

Directions: Underline the **infinitive** or the **infinitive phrase** in each of the following sentences. On the line to the right, indicate how the infinitive or the infinitive phrase is used.

Example: Irene wanted <u>to be a hostess.</u>     *direct object*
.........................

1. Dolores didn't have time to argue.     1. ...................

2. The manager promised to reserve our seats.     2. ...................

3. It was our intention to remodel the house.     3. ...................

4. She did nothing but wring her hands.     4. ...................

5. He stopped the car to avoid an accident.     5. ...................

6. Her ambition, to swim the channel, was realized.     6. ...................

7. To buy fruit out of season is extravagant.     7. ...................

8. Her sole desire was to help others.     8. ...................

9. I dare not venture into the forest.     9. ...................

10. The company's aim is to please the customers.     10. ...................

11. To show their displeasure, many left the meeting.     11. ...................

12. Attempts to expose the culprit failed.     12. ...................

*Caution: Check your answers to each assignment with the answer key at the back of the booklet before proceeding with the next assignment.*

## SELF-GRADING ASSIGNMENT 2

This assignment will show whether you can supply the correct form of the pronoun in an infinitive clause. Keep in mind these two facts: (1) The *subject* of an infinitive is in the *objective case;* (2) the verb *to be* takes the same case after it as it takes before it.

Directions: Fill in the blank with the *correct form* of the **pronoun** in parentheses.

Example:  I want ............... to go. (he)   I want *him* to go.

1.  We believed ............... to be reliable. (she)

2.  We expect ............... to return tonight. (they)

3.  I imagined it to be ............... (he)

4.  We thought the culprits to be ............... (they)

5.  They believed the applicant to be ............... (she)

6.  ............... did you want to lead the singing? (who)

7.  She mistook ............... to be ............... (they, we)

8.  Why did you want the ushers to be ...............? (they)

9.  The chairman asked Herbert and ............... to serve on the committee. (he)

10.  The guests thought ............... to be ............... (she, I)

11.  ............... do they consider to be the best musician? (who)

12.  Let Jerry and ............... make the arrangements. (I)

13.  ............... do you want to make the speech? (who)

14.  I considered ............... to be honest. (he)

15.  They expected ............... to favor ............... (we, she)

## SELF-GRADING ASSIGNMENT 3

Directions: Underline the word or words that split the infinitives in the following sentences. Rewrite the sentences without splitting the infinitives.

Example: The president intends to <u>immediately</u> discuss the matter with you.

The president intends *to discuss* the matter with you immediately.

1. The agent promised to promptly ship the order.

2. The building was ready to almost fall.

3. The prisoner desired to only talk a minute.

4. Ellis wanted to quickly learn to fly a plane.

5. We were fortunate to early secure passage.

6. The plan was to immediately raise funds.

7. The manager intends to privately discuss the matter with you.

8. We invited them to every summer stay at the lodge.

9. To learn to correctly speak is not difficult.

10. The attempt to suddenly block the enemy failed.

11. She liked to often visit the art galleries.

12. We decided to quickly sell the house.

13. She began to carefully read the letter.

14. The clerk tried to efficiently keep the records.

15. Mother tries to economically plan the meals.

## PROGRESS TEST TWENTY-FIVE

This test will show whether you are able to distinguish between infinitive, participial, and gerund phrases. It will also show whether you are familiar with the use of the infinitive clause.

Directions: Underline the *infinitive,* the *participial,* and the *gerund phrases.* Underline the *infinitive clauses.* On the line to the right, indicate how the phrase or the infinitive clause is used in the sentence. (*44 points*)

Examples: I did not want <u>him to speak at the meeting.</u> *direct object*
<small>infinitive clause</small>

The boys, <u>covered with snow,</u> stopped at the inn.    modifies *boys*
<small>part. ph.</small>

1. I have written the letter without making a mistake.     1. ...................

2. The house, hidden by tall trees, was very beautiful.     2. ...................

3. After thinking about the position, I decided I did not want it.     3. ...................

4. They planned to spend the winter in Florida.     4. ...................

5. Born in Mexico, he learned to speak two languages — Spanish and English.     5. ...................

6. Soaring above the high buildings, the birds soon disappeared from sight.     6. ...................

7. Before starting for Europe, my cousin sold his business.     7. ...................

## PROGRESS TEST TWENTY-FIVE (continued)

8. It is a pleasure to know such a talented person.    8. ..................

9. The manager is the one to interview today.    9. ..................

10. Clark heard him mutter a strange name.    10. ..................

11. Identifying the witnesses was Allen's job.    11. ..................

12. Entering the office, Raymond found everything in disorder.    12. ..................

13. Discouraged by his failure in business, Anthony left the city.    13. ..................

14. Refusing to answer was Marvin's way of coping with the situation.    14. ..................

15. His greatest pleasure was reading good books.    15. ..................

16. I did not like his signing the petition.    16. ..................

17. She had time to interview all the candidates.    17. ..................

18. Carpenters called to the scene built temporary shelters.    18. ..................

19. The fireman climbed a ladder to reach the injured man.    19. ..................

20. They expect Gerald to leave at once.    20. ..................

## ANSWER KEY

for

## EXERCISES, ASSIGNMENTS, AND PROGRESS TEST

### Grammar Unit Twenty-five

---

## CORRECT ANSWERS TO EXERCISE 1

|    |                                                              | Subject of Infinitive |
|----|--------------------------------------------------------------|----|
| 1. | We invited **them to stay at the lodge.**                    | 1. them |
| 2. | I knew **it to be true.**                                    | 2. it |
| 3. | Robert expects **Mary to go to the dance.**                  | 3. Mary |
| 4. | The manager urged **Norman to remain with the firm.**        | 4. Norman |
| 5. | We believed **Jack to be the best tennis player.**           | 5. Jack |
| 6. | The professor advised **me to study Spanish.**               | 6. me |
| 7. | I mistook **Florence to be my sister.**                      | 7. Florence |
| 8. | I considered **her to be my best friend.**                   | 8. her |
| 9. | I never heard **him (to) make a false statement.**           | 9. him |
| 10. | The officer helped **the blind man (to) cross the street.** | 10. man |
| 11. | The committee asked **Arthur to sing at the banquet.**      | 11. Arthur |
| 12. | The president forced **the treasurer to resign.**           | 12. treasurer |
| 13. | I felt **the floor (to) shake under me.**                   | 13. floor |
| 14. | I thought **him to be the leader of the band.**             | 14. him |
| 15. | I want **James to act as chairman.**                        | 15. James |

## CORRECT ANSWERS TO EXERCISE 2

1. The professor thought him to be **me.**
2. Mother wanted Jane and **him** to stay for dinner.

3. My friend knew the girls to be **us** in spite of our masks.

4. The committee asked Herbert and **me** to speak at the banquet.

5. The officer knew the reckless driver to be **her.**

6. I did not know **whom** to consult.

7. **Whom** did you believe it to be?

8. I believed **him** to be the artist.

9. Help **me** (to) translate this passage.

10. The owner let **us** (to) play in the vacant lot.

11. Who helped **them** (to) paint the fence?

12. Do you expect **her** to come?

13. The manager asked **us** girls to work overtime.

14. She advised Ted and **me** to read the book.

15. I thought Jerry to be **him.**

## CORRECT ANSWERS TO EXERCISE 3

1. The manager wanted **to increase** production more rapidly.

2. It is annoying **to wait** for a clerk in this store.

3. He urged me **to report** to the draft board at once.

4. The immigrant did not know how **to sign** the paper correctly.

5. I wanted **to see** the musical comedy again.

6. We decided **to settle** the matter quickly.

7. The patient decided **to pay** his hospital bill promptly.

8. I expect **to see** my friend again when I go to New York.

9. The soldier knew how **to face** danger calmly.

10. You must tell him **to make** a decision soon.

11. I hope **to meet** him tomorrow.

12. You must learn how **to handle** your problems more successfully.

13. The workman wanted **to talk** to the manager only a few minutes.

14. I offered **to help** him immediately.

15. The farmer intends **to buy** new machinery at once.

## CORRECT ANSWERS TO EXERCISE 4

1. The manager's plan, **to install new machinery,** did not meet with approval.
       1. *appositive*

2. She finally achieved her goal — **to become a motion picture star.**
       2. *appositive*

3. It is possible **to become an excellent writer.**
       3. *delayed subject*

4. It became a habit **to accept aid.**
       4. *delayed subject*

5. His suggestion, **to interview the president,** was adopted.
       5. *appositive*

6. John's assignment, **to complete the project,** kept him indoors all winter.
       6. *appositive*

7. It is interesting **to watch his reactions.**
       7. *delayed subject*

8. He realized the grave necessity — **to consult a physician at once.**
       8. *appositive*

9. It has been customary **to pay on delivery.**
       9. *delayed subject*

10. It is easy **to depend on others.**
        10. *delayed subject*

11. His main duty, **to preserve harmony,** was not easy.
        11. *appositive*

12. The warning, **to beware of treachery,** made us very cautious.
        12. *appositive*

## CORRECT ANSWERS TO EXERCISE 5

1. The firm wants me to stay in Chicago.
   <u>infinitive clause</u>

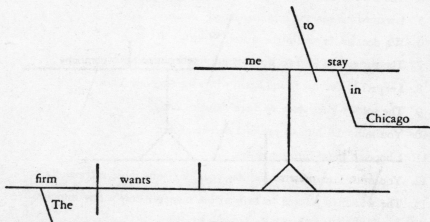

The infinitive clause, *me to stay in Chicago,* is used as the object of the verb, *wants.*

2. <u>To become a director</u> was his great ambition.
infinitive phrase

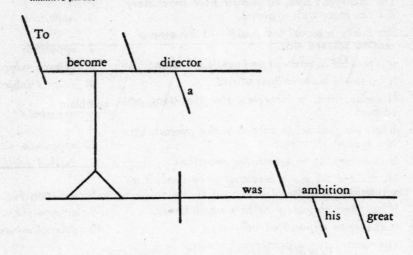

The infinitive phrase, *To become a director,* is used as the subject of the sentence.

3. Our present plan is <u>to reorganize the company.</u>
infinitive phrase

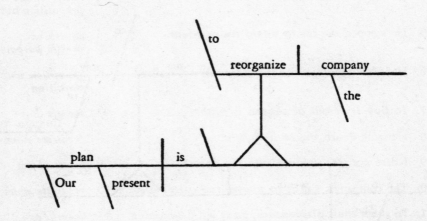

The infinitive phrase, *to reorganize the company,* is used as a predicate noun after the linking verb *is.*

4. The old man did nothing but (to) complain.
infinitive

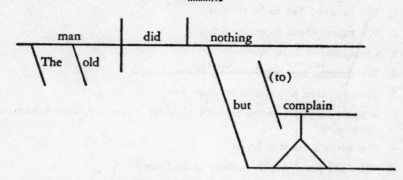

The infinitive *(to) complain* is used as the object of the preposition *but.*

## CORRECT ANSWERS TO ASSIGNMENT 1

| | |
|---|---|
| 1. Dolores didn't have time **to argue.** | 1. *adjective* |
| 2. The manager promised **to reserve our seats.** | 2. *direct object* |
| 3. It was our intention **to remodel the house.** | 3. *delayed subject* |
| 4. She did nothing but *(to)* **wring her hands.** | 4. *object of the preposition* **but** |
| 5. He stopped the car **to avoid an accident.** | 5. *adverb, expresses purpose* |
| 6. Her ambition, **to swim the channel,** was realized. | 6. *apposition with* **ambition** |
| 7. **To buy fruit out of season** is extravagant. | 7. *subject* |
| 8. Her sole desire was **to help others.** | 8. *predicate noun* |
| 9. I dare not *(to)* **venture into the forest.** | 9. *direct object* |
| 10. The company's aim is **to please the customers.** | 10. *predicate noun* |
| 11. **To show their displeasure,** many left the meeting. | 11. *adverb, expresses purpose* |
| 12. Attempts **to expose the culprit** failed. | 12. *adjective* |

## CORRECT ANSWERS TO ASSIGNMENT 2

1. We believed *her* to be reliable.
2. We expect *them* to return tonight.
3. I imagined it to be *him*.
4. We thought the culprits to be *them*.
5. They believed the applicant to be *her*.
6. *Whom* did you want to lead the singing? (You did want *whom* to lead the singing?)
7. She mistook *them* to be *us*.
8. Why did you want the ushers to be *them*?
9. The chairman asked Herbert and *him* to serve on the committee.
10. The guests thought *her* to be *me*.
11. *Whom* do they consider to be the best musician?
12. Let Jerry and *me* make the arrangements.
13. *Whom* do you want to make the speech?
14. I considered *him* to be honest.
15. They expected *us* to favor *her*.

## CORRECT ANSWERS TO ASSIGNMENT 3

1. The agent promised *to ship* the order promptly.
2. The building was almost ready *to fall*.
3. The prisoner desired *to talk* only a minute.
4. Ellis wanted *to learn* to fly a plane quickly.
5. We were fortunate *to secure* passage early.
6. The plan was *to raise* funds immediately.
7. The manager intends *to discuss* the matter privately with you.
   or
   The manager intends *to discuss* the matter with you privately.
8. We invited them *to stay* at the lodge every summer.
9. To learn *to speak* correctly is not difficult.
10. The attempt *to block* the enemy suddenly failed.

11. She liked **to visit** the art galleries often.

12. We decided **to sell** the house quickly.

13. She began **to read** the letter carefully.

14. The clerk tried **to keep** the records efficiently.

15. Mother tries **to plan** the meals economically.

## CORRECT ANSWERS TO PROGRESS TEST TWENTY-FIVE

1. I have written the letter without <u>making a mistake</u>.
   ger. ph.

   1. *object of the preposition*

2. The house, <u>hidden by tall trees</u>, was very beautiful.
   part. ph.

   2. *modifies* **house**

3. After <u>thinking about the position</u>, I decided I did
   ger. ph.
   not want it.

   3. *object of the preposition*

4. They planned <u>to spend the winter in Florida</u>.
   inf. ph.

   4. *direct object*

5. <u>Born in Mexico</u>, he learned <u>to speak two</u>
   part. ph.  inf. ph.
   <u>languages</u> — Spanish and English.

   5. a) *modifies* **he**
      b) *direct object*

6. <u>Soaring above the high buildings</u>, the birds soon
   part. ph.
   disappeared from sight.

   6. *modifies* **birds**

7. Before <u>starting for Europe</u>, my cousin sold his
   ger. ph.
   business.

   7. *object of the preposition*

8. (It) <u>To know such a talented person</u> is a pleasure.
   inf. ph.

   8. *delayed subject*

9. The manager is the one <u>to interview today</u>.
   inf. ph.

   9. *adjective, modifies* **one**

10. Clark heard <u>him (to) mutter a strange name</u>.
    inf. cl.

    10. *infinitive clause object of* **heard**

## KEY TO PROGRESS TEST TWENTY-FIVE (continued)

11. <u>Identifying the witnesses</u> was Allen's job.
ger. ph.

     11. *subject*

12. <u>Entering the office</u>, Raymond found everything in
part. ph.
disorder.

     12. *modifies* **Raymond**

13. <u>Discouraged by his failure in business</u>, Anthony
part. ph.
left the city.

     13. *modifies* **Anthony**

14. <u>Refusing to answer</u> was Marvin's way of <u>coping</u>
ger. ph.
<u>with the situation.</u>
ger. ph.

     14. a) *subject*
         b) *obj. of prep.*

15. His greatest pleasure was <u>reading good books.</u>
ger. ph.

     15. *predicate noun*

16. I did not like <u>his signing the petition.</u>
ger. ph.

     16. *direct object*

17. She had time <u>to interview all the candidates.</u>
inf. ph.

     17. *adjective use—modifies* **time**

18. Carpenters <u>called to the scene</u> built temporary
part. ph.
shelters.

     18. *modifies* **carpenters**

19. The fireman climbed a ladder <u>to reach the</u>
inf. ph.
<u>injured man.</u>

     19. *adverbial modifier—expresses purpose*

20. They expect <u>Gerald to leave at once.</u>
inf. cl.

     20. *direct object*

## HOW TO OBTAIN YOUR SCORE

*The test totals 44 points. To obtain your score, divide the number of your correct answers by 44. The answer will be your score on this test. For example, if you have 40 points correct, your score is 40 divided by 44 which is 91 per cent. In other words, your score on this test is 91. You can obtain your score on any of the exercises or assignments by following the same procedure.*

## Practical English Grammar

## OUTLINE OF UNIT TWENTY-SIX

# COMPREHENSIVE REVIEW

Page

PURPOSE OF THE MASTERY TESTS........................................... 5

MASTERY TESTS:

1. PARTS OF SPEECH ................................................. 6

2. SUBJECT AND PREDICATE ..................................... 7

3. COMPLEMENTS OF VERBS ..................................... 8

4. KINDS OF SENTENCES ...................................... 9

5. VERB FORMS ........................................................ 10

6. COMPARISON OF ADJECTIVES AND ADVERBS............. 11

7. AGREEMENT OF SUBJECT AND VERB............................ 12

8. AGREEMENT OF PRONOUN WITH ANTECEDENT........ 13

9. IDENTIFYING PHRASES ...................................... 14

10. CORRECT CASE OF PRONOUNS.................................. 15

11. SUBORDINATE CLAUSES ....................................... 16

12. IDENTIFYING PARTICIPLES, GERUNDS, AND INFINITIVES ....................................................... 17

13. PLURALS OF NOUNS ........................................... 18

14. CAPITAL LETTERS ............................................... 19

15. CORRECT USAGE ................................................ 20

*Key to Correct Answers*........................................................ 23

# PURPOSE OF THE MASTERY TESTS

THE twenty-five grammar units which you have completed cover the fundamentals of grammar which everyone must understand in order to use accurate and effective English. The mastery tests in this unit are designed to show whether you can apply what you have learned, and whether you understand the principles which have been developed. These tests will also show whether you have acquired the skills which are necessary in order to use language correctly and effectively.

A careful analysis of the mistakes you make on the tests will show you the usages that still give you trouble. If you find that you have a hazy understanding of any of the problems in the tests, you should review the particular units in which those problems are presented. You will have no difficulty in finding a discussion of a construction that is similar to the one you missed in the test.

The extent of your mastery of grammar will also be revealed through your ability to deal with any language problem that may arise in speaking and in writing. It will often be necessary to make a decision regarding a question of correct usage. In most cases, you will have no difficulty in determining which is the correct form to use. However, some difficult problems will arise no matter how well you understand the fundamentals of correct usage. Even experts in grammar do not always agree in their analysis of certain constructions, or in the interpretation of the sentence in which the construction is found.

Whenever you meet such difficulties, you will find that the grammar units will serve as a convenient reference guide that will help you solve your problem. The compact presentation of each topic in a separate unit will enable you to find a discussion of the problem quickly. The reference tables and the various lists of grammatical forms will help you identify the construction.

The training provided in the grammar units of this course should enable you to express yourself clearly and accurately, and in conformity with acceptable, standard usage. Through the course you should have learned the correct forms so thoroughly that you will use them unconsciously. You should now feel at ease in almost any situation requiring the use of language.

## Mastery Test 1
### PARTS OF SPEECH

Directions: On the lines at the right, indicate the **part of speech** of each of the underlined words: *noun, pronoun, verb* or *verb phrase, adjective, adverb, preposition, conjunction, interjection.* (30 points)

1. <u>Many</u> left the game <u>early</u>.

1. .................   .................

2. I <u>should like</u> to speak to the <u>head</u> usher.

2. .................   .................

3. <u>Stop</u> that noise <u>immediately</u>!

3. .................   .................

4. The <u>other</u> men voted <u>against</u> the bill.

4. .................   .................

5. James <u>or</u> Marvin will take care of the business <u>affairs</u>.

5. .................   .................

6. Charles went to the game, <u>but</u> he did not stay <u>long</u>.

6. .................   .................

7. <u>Hurray</u>! We <u>finally</u> won a game.

7. .................   .................

8. There is an <u>apple</u> orchard <u>behind</u> the fence.

8. .................   .................

9. The prima donna sang a song <u>for</u> <u>us</u>.

9. .................   .................

10. Do not criticise him <u>if</u> he seems <u>nervous</u>.

10. .................   .................

11. We <u>shall leave</u> for Paris in two <u>days</u>.

11. .................   .................

12. The captain is <u>too</u> eager to win.

12. .................   .................

13. We walked <u>through</u> the <u>green</u> fields.

13. .................   .................

14. <u>Who</u> has the <u>courage</u> to enter the cave?.

14. .................   .................

15. <u>Well</u>! <u>What</u> did he say?

15. .................   .................

## Mastery Test 2

### SUBJECT AND PREDICATE

Directions: Write the *simple subject* and the *simple predicate* on the lines to the right. *(30 points)*

|  | Simple Subject | Simple Predicate |
|---|---|---|
| 1. In the mountains the pines are very fragrant. | 1. .................. | .................. |
| 2. There will be several applicants for the position. | 2. .................. | .................. |
| 3. Whom did you meet at the conference? | 3. .................. | .................. |
| 4. Study the illustrations carefully. | 4. .................. | .................. |
| 5. During the meeting he asked two questions. | 5. .................. | .................. |
| 6. Half of the street has been paved. | 6. .................. | .................. |
| 7. How cold the wind is tonight! | 7. .................. | .................. |
| 8. How are the men voting this time? | 8. .................. | .................. |
| 9. Working at night has become a general practice at the plant. | 9. .................. | .................. |
| 10. In the bottom drawer of the desk she found an old will. | 10. .................. | .................. |
| 11. There one can find complete rest. | 11. .................. | .................. |
| 12. Food should have been provided for the refugees. | 12. .................. | .................. |
| 13. There is no better example of modern art. | 13. .................. | .................. |
| 14. Isn't that a new Cadillac? | 14. .................. | .................. |
| 15. All of the legal papers have been returned. | 15. .................. | .................. |

### Mastery Test 3

### COMPLEMENTS OF VERBS

Directions: Underline the **complements** of the *verbs* in the following sentences. Indicate the kind of complement on the line at the right: *direct object, indirect object, predicate noun* or *pronoun, predicate adjective.* (*20 points*)

**Kind of Complement**

1. The crowd seemed restless.                          1. ...................

2. Did the bookkeeper give any reason for leaving?                                             2. ...................

3. Send her two boxes of oranges.                   3. ...................

4. Don't miss the biggest show of the year.    4. ...................

5. What a fool I have been!                             5. ...................

6. Put down that gun!                                      6. ...................

7. Which car did you finally buy?                   7. ...................

8. These apples taste sour.                              8. ...................

9. The tailor made me a new overcoat.           9. ...................

10. The captain proved a hero.                        10. ...................

11. The old soldier appears weaker today.      11. ...................

12. Was it he who offered me a seat?               12. ...................

13. Whom did they send to the meeting?         13. ...................

14. The new stenographer seems very capable.  14. ...................

15. Did the firm give you a new set of instruments?   15. ...................

## Mastery Test 4

### KINDS OF SENTENCES

#### A.

Directions: Indicate the **kind of sentence** on the line at the right: *declarative, interrogative, exclamatory, imperative.* (8 *points*)

1. Did you count the money in the cash box?    1. ...................

2. What a beautiful view this is!    2. ...................

3. There was a very heavy frost last night.    3. ...................

4. Mr. Chairman, did anyone second that motion?    4. ...................

5. For three months we traveled across the desert.    5. ...................

6. Are you going to the opera this season?    6. ...................

7. Suggest a good title for my article, Stephen.    7. ...................

8. Have you and David joined the tennis club?    8. ...................

#### B.

Directions: Indicate the **kind of sentence** on the line at the right: *simple, complex, compound.* (8 *points*)

1. You must relax, or you will become ill.    1. ...................

2. The janitor shut the door and locked it securely.    2. ...................

3. He still lives in the house where he was born.    3. ...................

4. I shall be at the station when you arrive.    4. ...................

5. The author and the producer met and discussed the play.    5. ...................

6. He liked the play; in fact, he was enthusiastic about it.    6. ...................

7. We visited Quebec, which is a very old city.    7. ...................

8. The report was that he was drowned.    8. ...................

## Mastery Test 5

### VERB FORMS

Directions: Cross out the **incorrect verb form** and write the *correct form* above it. If the sentence is correct, write the word *correct* after it. (*16 points*)

1. I seen the new cars at the exhibit.

2. We ain't going to the lake this summer.

3. When the doctor come, he asked me to park his car.

4. I wish Ned hadn't broke those records.

5. We should of spoken about the case sooner.

6. The child run out into the street and was ran over by a truck.

7. The men begun to dig the trench yesterday.

8. You should have wore a dress suit to that affair.

9. The old man lay in the shade all afternoon.

10. My brother don't play golf very well.

11. Have you ever rode in a jeep?

12. The boys have swam in the creek all afternoon.

13. The pipes in the cellar bursted during the night.

14. The letters have been laying on your desk all morning.

15. Stocks have rose several points this week.

## Mastery Test 6

### COMPARISON OF ADJECTIVES AND ADVERBS

Directions: Fill in the blanks with the correct forms of the **adjectives** and **adverbs** enclosed in parentheses. The form you select should be the *degree of comparison* required in the sentence. (*16 points*)

1. Which of the four candidates talked........................ (fluently)

2. These laws are........................than the laws passed in 1900. (just)

3. The audience listened.....................to the first of the two speakers. (intently)

4. Your writing is........................, but mine is........................ (bad)

5. Come.....................today than you did yesterday. (early)

6. I thought the last concert was the........................concert of the season. (good)

7. Father drives.....................than Alfred. (slowly)

8. James is the.....................boy in the Scout troop. (active)

9. Mr. Allen is the........................of the two lawyers. (capable)

10. Of the three children Susan speaks........................ (distinctly)

11. We chose the.....................route of the two. (long)

12. This knife is........................than the one on your desk. (good)

13. The storm broke.....................than we expected. (soon)

14. He is the.....................member of the cabinet. (brilliant)

15. The boy does the work........................than an adult. (easily)

## Mastery Test 7

### AGREEMENT OF SUBJECT AND VERB

Directions: Cross out the incorrect form of the **verb** enclosed in parentheses. On the line at the right, indicate whether the *singular* or the *plural form* of the verb should be used in the sentence. (*30 points*)

1. Neither the manager nor the supervisor (approves, approve) of the change.    1. ..................

2. The committee (is, are) in favor of the bill.    2. ..................

3. The president and the vice-president (speak, speaks) at every meeting.    3. ..................

4. A pension, together with his investments, (guarantees, guarantee) a steady income.    4. ..................

5. The scissors (was, were) found in the desk.    5. ..................

6. The news in the morning paper (is, are) alarming.    6. ..................

7. All the data (was, were) assembled by the clerks.    7. ..................

8. Jack (don't, doesn't) know the answers to the questions.    8. ..................

9. Ten dollars (is, are) the price of the lamp.    9. ..................

10. (Was, Were) you invited to the meeting?    10. ..................

11. The merger of the companies (wasn't, weren't) expected.    11. ..................

12. Half of the letters (was, were) filed.    12. ..................

13. In the park there (is, are) several pools.    13. ..................

14. A number of boxes of fruit (was, were) destroyed.    14. ..................

15. (Was, Were) either of the soldiers present at the trial?    15. ..................

## Mastery Test 8

### AGREEMENT OF PRONOUN WITH ANTECEDENT

Directions: Cross out the incorrect form of the **pronoun** enclosed in parentheses. On the line at the right, indicate whether the *singular* or the *plural form* of the pronoun should be used in the sentence. (*32 points*)

1. Either Mary or Alice left (her, their) books in the library.

1. ................

2. Every man understands what (he, they) must do.

2. ................

3. Some of the rubber has lost (its, their) elasticity.

3. ................

4. Both girls brought (her, their) swimming suits.

4. ................

5. Neither Lowell nor James has finished (their, his) assignment.

5. ................

6. Someone has left (their, his) car in the driveway.

6. ................

7. Many of the players furnished (his, their) costumes.

7. ................

8. The jury rendered (their, its) verdict.

8. ................

9. The town built a memorial to (its, their) war veterans.

9. ................

10. Everyone paid (his, their) income tax early.

10. ................

11. Neither the boy nor the men brought (their, his) birth certificates.

11. ................

12. A person always does (his, their) best when (he, they) is in good health.

12. ................

13. The secretary and the treasurer have presented (his, their) reports.

13. ................

14. The company has improved the working conditions of (its, their) employees.

14. ................

15. Many a man wishes that (he, they) had gone to college.

15. ................

## Mastery Test 9

### IDENTIFYING PHRASES

Directions: Underline the **phrases** in the following sentences. On the line at the right, identify each phrase as one of the following:

*prepositional phrase*      *participial phrase*
*gerund phrase*      *infinitive phrase*

Some sentences have two phrases to be identified. (*34 points*)

1. Having passed the examination, Jane was eligible for a teaching position.    1. ..................

2. Her ambition was to become a great actress.    2. ..................

3. The buildings along the wharf are vacant.    3. ..................

4. Building the garage was an interesting project.    4. ..................

5. The inventor obtained the right to sell his gadget.    5. ..................

6. A senator from Idaho will be the speaker    6. ..................

7. A man with a camera stood beside me.    7. ..................

8. It was difficult to hear the speaker.    8. ..................

9. His favorite diversion is playing chess.    9. ..................

10. Realizing the danger, the sailor shouted for help.    10. ..................

11. Being a counselor requires considerable tact.    11. ..................

12. David received a letter recommending him for the position.    12. ..................

13. To increase her income, Mary gives private lessons in Spanish.    13. ..................

14. Hiding his fear, Peter opened the door cautiously.    14. ..................

## Mastery Test 10
### CORRECT CASE OF PRONOUNS

Directions: Cross out the incorrect form of the **pronoun** enclosed in parentheses. On the line at the right, indicate the **case** of the *pronoun* that should be used in the sentence. (*32 points*)

1. Father gave Mary and (I, me) a car.      1. ..................

2. Do you remember (me, my) asking for your notes?      2. ..................

3. I believe it is (her, she) (who, whom) you know.      3. ..................

4. Please let Carl and (he, him) have your tickets.      4. ..................

5. They believed him to be (I, me).      5. ..................

6. (Who, Whom) did you see at the convention?      6. ..................

7. (We, Us) men are going to sign the petition.      7. ..................

8. He left the city without (their, them) knowing it.      8. ..................

9. Harris is better informed than (I, me).      9. ..................

10. Three girls—Alice, Jane, and (I, me) won the awards.      10. ..................

11. The dog lost (it's, its) collar.      11. ..................

12. Will you go with Tom and (we, us) to the game?      12. ..................

13. It was (she, her) who designed the rug.      13. ..................

14. It was difficult to decide (who's, whose) speech was the best of the four.      14. ..................

15. It must have been (they, them) who entered the hall.      15. ..................

## Mastery Test 11

### SUBORDINATE CLAUSES

Directions: Underline the **subordinate clauses.** Indicate the kind of clause on the line at the right: *adjective clause, adverbial clause,* or *noun clause,* (*30 points*)

1. The persons whom I name will receive an award.    1. .................

2. Although Albert is ill, he works every day.    2. .................

3. I do not know where Alice lives.    3. .................

4. The fact is that we do not have the equipment.    4. .................

5. When I reached the city, I registered at a famous hotel.    5. .................

6. The house which was sold yesterday was built in 1850.    6. .................

7. Tell them when the rehearsals will begin.    7. .................

8. Do you like the book that the speaker recommended?    8. .................

9. Since you object to our plan, you should suggest another.    9. .................

10. We learned how the parts of the machine were assembled.    10. .................

11. It is true that the driver was injured in the crash.    11. .................

12. The old man told his story to whomever he met.    12. .................

13. We visited the art galleries when we traveled in Europe.    13. .................

14. Adams lived in a period when travel was very slow.    14. .................

15. The day was so hot that we stayed indoors.    15. .................

## Mastery Test 12

### IDENTIFYING PARTICIPLES, GERUNDS, AND INFINITIVES

Directions: Underline the **verbals** in the following sentences. On the line at the right, indicate whether the verbal is a *participle*, a *gerund*, or an *infinitive*. (*30 points*)

1. Ellis wants to fly an airplane.    1. ..................

2. Did you read the regulations about speeding?    2. ..................

3. Having been a sailor, James liked work on boats.    3. ..................

4. We watched the artist decorate the hall.    4. ..................

5. The attempts to stop the enemy were futile.    5. ..................

6. We considered buying a home in the suburbs.    6. ..................

7. Ted went to Arizona to regain his health.    7. ..................

8. Doctors, called to the scene, examined the men.    8. ..................

9. He entered the house by breaking the lock.    9. ..................

10. Having finished our work, we left early.    10. ..................

11. You should learn to speak correctly.    11. ..................

12. Driving carefully will prevent accidents.    12. ..................

13. Esther's plan was to study music in New York.    13. ..................

14. He did everything except work.    14. ..................

15. The old manuscript was interesting.    15. ..................

## Mastery Test 13

### PLURALS OF NOUNS

Directions: Write the **plural** of each of the following *nouns* on the line at the right of the word. (*50 points*)

| | | | |
|---|---|---|---|
| 1. radio | 1. ................. | 21. Miss Smith | 21. ................. |
| 2. goose | 2. ................. | 22. man-of-war | 22. ................. |
| 3. crocus | 3. ................. | 23. saleswoman | 23. ................. |
| 4. salary | 4. ................. | 24. inquiry | 24. ................. |
| 5. Chinese | 5. ................. | 25. alumnus | 25. ................. |
| 6. spoonful | 6. ................. | 26. compass | 26. ................. |
| 7. volcano | 7. ................. | 27. Henry | 27. ................. |
| 8. calf | 8. ................. | 28. Mr. | 28. ................. |
| 9. match | 9. ................. | 29. remedy | 29. ................. |
| 10. crisis | 10. ................. | 30. knife | 30. ................. |
| 11. thief | 11. ................. | 31. alley | 31. ................. |
| 12. handkerchief | 12. ................. | 32. wolf | 32. ................. |
| 13. index | 13. ................. | 33. cupful | 33. ................. |
| 14. sheep | 14. ................. | 34. series | 34. ................. |
| 15. father-in-law | 15. ................. | 35. basis | 35. ................. |
| 16. veto | 16. ................. | 36. tomato | 36. ................. |
| 17. quantity | 17. ................. | 37. forget-me-not | 37. ................. |
| 18. belief | 18. ................. | 38. ally | 38. ................. |
| 19. banjo | 19. ................. | 39. attorney general | 39. ................. |
| 20. passer-by | 20. ................. | 40. mulberry | 40. ................. |

## Mastery Test 14

## CAPITAL LETTERS

Directions: Cross out small letters and place *capital letters* wherever needed. Cross out capital letters that are used incorrectly and write *small letters* above the capital letters. (*48 points*)

1. On tuesdays I have classes in latin, Physics, and english.

2. I received a book from my Cousin entitled "How To read A book."

3. We are going to the Lake shore club for Lunch next friday.

4. Harriet is taking mathematics 102 at Northwestern university.

5. He wrote letters to senator Lodge and to judge harmon.

6. The democrats will hold their Convention in chicago in june.

7. Her purse is made of spanish Leather and her bracelet is made of mexican silver.

8. The senior class is giving a Dance at the Hilton hotel.

9. Have you ever seen the Allegheny mountains or niagara Falls?

10. I always spend labor Day and Memorial day with my Aunt.

11. Every american should be familiar with the Declaration of independence.

12. Van gogh's picture, "Peasants digging," is very famous.

13. At the inauguration in washington, I saw both the president and vice-President.

14. There is a new woolworth store on fifth Avenue in New york.

15. The Skiers went to sun valley for the Winter sports.

## Mastery Test 15

### CORRECT USAGE

Directions: Cross out the **incorrect forms** in the following sentences. Write the *correct form* above the incorrect form. Three sentences are correct. (*55 points*)

1. Each of the oarsmen did their best.

2. The editor-in-chiefs of several newspapers met yesterday.

3. The company gave their employees a raise in salary.

4. My friend has been acting very peculiar lately.

5. Daniel lays carpets for Marshall Field and Company.

6. He sure sung that ballad remarkable well.

7. The northern lights appear frequent in Alaska.

8. Divide the fruit among the four families.

9. These lilacs smell fragrantly.

10. How long has the canoe laid on the beach?

11. The mayor greeted the visitors very cordial.

12. Prices of food are raising every day.

13. Every corporation has it's own officers.

14. The distinguished visitors might have been them.

15. The men done the job efficient.

16. At this time of the year, I wish I was in Florida.

## Mastery Test 15 (continued)

17. One likes to do what they can do good.

18. I always enjoy reading Dicken's "Christmas Carol."

19. Your car is different than mine.

20. To who did you give the supervisor's report?

21. That bell always sounds shrilly.

22. Someones coat was left in my brothers' locker.

23. The sailor jumped off of the deck.

24. This variety of flowers are rare.

25. My wife and myself attended the banquet.

26. I laid on the davenport all evening.

27. The boys have drank all the lemonade that was in the pitcher.

28. I thought the captain of the team to be he.

29. The car will cost around a thousand dollars.

30. I want you and she to help me make this dress.

31. Both brought his musical instruments.

32. This book is the most interesting of the three you sent me.

33. The number of candidates for the position are small.

## Mastery Test 15 (continued)

34. The letters were laying on his desk all week.

35. The guests have just gone in the dining room.

36. I differ from you in regard to the value of the plan.

37. The man who they are seeking must have a college degree.

38. A number of magazines was sent to the soldiers.

39. Say it like you meant it.

40. My brother, together with his wife and children, are visiting us.

41. Do you remember me speaking to you about the contest?

42. Everyone at the luncheon helped themselves.

43. All but he failed to appear at the conference.

44. Of the two hats, I bought the least expensive.

45. Was you interested in buying a new car?

46. I haven't done nothing all day.

47. I like these kind of neckties.

48. Don't you think you should of started earlier?

49. I did not like him leaving so abruptly.

50. Raymond sat besides me during the lecture.

**ANSWER KEY**

for

**MASTERY TESTS**

*Grammar Unit Twenty-six*

―――――

### KEY TO MASTERY TEST 1

1. *many*—pronoun; *early*—adverb
2. *should like*—verb phrase; *head*—adjective
3. *Stop*—verb; *immediately*—adverb
4. *other*—adjective; *against*—preposition
5. *or*—conjunction; *affairs*—noun
6. *but*—conjunction; *long*—adverb
7. *Hurray*—interjection; *finally*—adverb
8. *apple*—adjective; *behind*—preposition
9. *for*—preposition; *us*—pronoun
10. *if*—conjunction; *nervous*—adjective
11. *shall leave*—verb phrase; *days*—noun
12. *too*—adverb; *eager*—adjective
13. *through*—preposition; *green*—adjective
14. *Who*—pronoun; *courage*—noun
15. *Well*—interjection; *What*—pronoun

### KEY TO MASTERY TEST 2

|  | Simple Subject | Simple Predicate |
|---|---|---|
| 1. In the mountains the pines are very fragrant. | 1. pines | are |
| 2. There will be several applicants for the position. | 2. applicants | will be |
| 3. Whom did you meet at the conference? | 3. you | did meet |

| | | |
|---|---|---|
| 4. Study the illustrations carefully. | 4. (you) | Study |
| 5. During the meeting he asked two questions. | 5. he | asked |
| 6. Half of the street has been paved. | 6. Half | has been paved |
| 7. How cold the wind is tonight! | 7. wind | is |
| 8. How are the men voting this time? | 8. men | are voting |
| 9. Working at night has become a general practice at the plant. | 9. Working | has become |
| 10. In the bottom drawer of the desk she found an old will. | 10. she | found |
| 11. There one can find complete rest. | 11. one | can find |
| 12. Food should have been provided for the refugees. | 12. Food | should have been provided |
| 13. There is no better example of modern art. | 13. example | is |
| 14. Isn't that a new Cadillac? | 14. that | is |
| 15. All of the legal papers have been returned. | 15. All | have been returned |

## KEY TO MASTERY TEST 3

| | |
|---|---|
| 1. The crowd seemed **restless.** | 1. predicate adjective |
| 2. Did the bookkeeper give any **reason** for leaving? | 2. direct object |
| 3. Send **her** two **boxes** of oranges. | 3. *her*—indirect object *boxes*—direct object |
| 4. Don't miss the biggest **show** of the year. | 4. direct object |
| 5. What a **fool** I have been. | 5. predicate noun |
| 6. Put down that **gun!** | 6. direct object |
| 7. Which **car** did you finally buy? | 7. direct object |
| 8. These apples taste **sour.** | 8. predicate adjective |

9. The tailor made **me** a new **overcoat.**
    9. *me*—indirect object
       *overcoat*—direct object

10. The captain proved a **hero.**
    10. predicate noun

11. The old soldier appears **weaker** today.
    11. predicate adjective

12. Was it **he** who offered **me** a **seat?**
    12. *he*—predicate pronoun
       *me*—indirect object
       *seat*—direct object

13. **Whom** did they send to the meeting?
    13. direct object

14. The new stenographer seems very **capable.**
    14. predicate adjective

15. Did the firm give **you** a new **set** of instruments?
    15. *you*—indirect object
       *set*—direct object

## KEY TO MASTERY TEST 4

| A. | | B. | |
|---|---|---|---|
| 1. | interrogative | 1. | compound |
| 2. | exclamatory | 2. | simple |
| 3. | declarative | 3. | complex |
| 4. | interrogative | 4. | complex |
| 5. | declarative | 5. | simple |
| 6. | interrogative | 6. | compound |
| 7. | imperative | 7. | complex |
| 8. | interrogative | 8. | complex |

## KEY TO MASTERY TEST 5

1. I **saw** the new cars at the exhibit.

2. We **aren't** going to the lake this summer.

3. When the doctor **came,** he asked me to park his car.

4. I wish Ned hadn't **broken** those records.

5. We should **have** spoken about the case sooner.

6. The child **ran** out into the street and was **run** over by a truck.

7. The men **began** to dig the trench yesterday.

8. You should have **worn** a dress suit to that affair.

9. The old man lay in the shade all afternoon. (*correct*)

10. My brother **doesn't** play golf very well.

11. Have you ever **ridden** in a jeep?

12. The boys have **swum** in the creek all afternoon.

13. The pipes in the cellar **burst** during the night.

14. The letters have been **lying** on your desk all morning.

15. Stocks have **risen** several points this week.

## KEY TO MASTERY TEST 6

1. Which of the four candidates talked **most fluently?**

2. These laws are **more just** than the laws passed in 1900.

3. The audience listened **more intently** to the first of the two speakers.

4. Your writing is **bad,** but mine is **worse.**

5. Come **earlier** today than you did yesterday.

6. I thought the last concert was the **best** concert of the season.

7. Father drives **more slowly** than Alfred.

8. James is the **most active** boy in the Scout troop.

9. Mr. Allen is the **more capable** of the two lawyers.

10. Of the three children, Susan speaks **most distinctly.**

11. We chose the **longer** route of the two.

12. This knife is **better** than the one on your desk.

13. The storm broke **sooner** than we expected.

14. He is the **most brilliant** member of the cabinet.

15. The boy does the work **more easily** than an adult.

## KEY TO MASTERY TEST 7

1. Neither the manager nor the supervisor **approves** of the change.
      1. *singular*

2. The committee **is** in favor of the bill.
      2. *singular*

3. The president and the vice-president **speak** at every meeting.
      3. *plural*

4. A pension, together with his investments, **guarantees** a steady income.
      4. *singular*

5. The scissors **were** found in the desk.
      5. *plural*

6. The news in the morning paper **is** alarming.     6. *singular*

7. All the data **were** assembled by the clerks.     7. *plural*

8. Jack **doesn't** know the answers to the questions.     8. *singular*

9. Ten dollars **is** the price of the lamp.     9. *singular*

10. **Were** you invited to the meeting?     10. *singular or plural*

11. The merger of the companies **wasn't** expected.     11. *singular*

12. Half of the letters **were** filed.     12. *plural*

13. In the park there **are** several pools.     13. *plural*

14. A number of boxes of fruit **were** destroyed.     14. *plural*

15. **Was** either of the soldiers present at the trial?     15. *singular*

## KEY TO MASTERY TEST 8

1. Either Mary or Alice left **her** books in the library.     1. *singular*

2. Every man understands what **he** must do.     2. *singular*

3. Some of the rubber has lost **its** elasticity.     3. *singular*

4. Both girls brought **their** swimming suits.     4. *plural*

5. Neither Lowell nor James has finished **his** assignment.     5. *singular*

6. Someone has left **his** car in the driveway.     6. *singular*

7. Many of the players furnished **their** costumes.     7. *plural*

8. The jury rendered **its** verdict.     8. *singular*

9. The town built a memorial to **its** war veterans.     9. *singular*

10. Everyone paid **his** income tax early.     10. *singular*

11. Neither the boy nor the men brought **their** birth certificates.     11. *plural*

12. A person always does **his** best when **he** is in good health.     12. *singular singular*

13. The secretary and the treasurer have presented **their** reports.     13. *plural*

14. The company has improved the working conditions of **its** employees.     14. *singular*

15. Many a man wishes that **he** had gone to college.     15. *singular*

## KEY TO MASTERY TEST 9

**Kind of Phrase**

1. **Having passed the examination,** Jane was eligible **for a teaching position.**
   1. *participial phrase*
      *prepositional phrase*

2. Her ambition was **to become a great actress.**
   2. *infinitive phrase*

3. The buildings **along the wharf** are vacant.
   3. *prepositional phrase*

4. **Building the garage** was an interesting project.
   4. *gerund phrase*

5. The inventor obtained the right **to sell his gadget.**
   5. *infinitive phrase*

6. A senator **from Idaho** will be the speaker.
   6. *prepositional phrase*

7. A man **with a camera** stood **beside me.**
   7. *prepositional phrases*

8. It was difficult **to hear the speaker.**
   8. *infinitive phrase*

9. His favorite diversion is **playing chess.**
   9. *gerund phrase*

10. **Realizing the danger,** the sailor shouted **for help.**
    10. *participial phrase*
        *prepositional phrase*

11. **Being a counselor** requires considerable tact.
    11. *gerund phrase*

12. David received a letter **recommending him for the position.**
    12. *participial phrase*

13. **To increase her income,** Mary gives private lessons **in Spanish.**
    13. *infinitive phrase*
        *prepositional phrase*

14. **Hiding his fear,** Peter opened the door cautiously.
    14. *participial phrase*

## KEY TO MASTERY TEST 10

1. Father gave Mary and **me** a car.
   1. *objective*

2. Do you remember **my** asking for your notes?
   2. *possessive*

3. I believe it is **she whom** you know.
   3. *nominative*
      *objective*

4. Please let Carl and **him** have your tickets.
   4. *objective*

5. They believed him to be **me.**
   5. *objective*

6. **Whom** did you see at the convention?
   6. *objective*

7. **We** men are going to sign the petition.
   7. *nominative*

8. He left the city without **their** knowing it.
   8. *possessive*

9. Harris is better informed than **I.**
   9. *nominative*

10. Three girls—Alice, Jane, and **I** won the awards.
    10. *nominative*

11. The dog lost **its** collar.
    11. *possessive*

12. Will you go with Tom and **us** to the game?
    12. *objective*

13. It was **she** who designed the rug.
    13. *nominative*

14. It was difficult to decide **whose** speech was the best of the four.
    14. *possessive*

15. It must have been **they** who entered the hall.
    15. *nominative*

## KEY TO MASTERY TEST 11

**Kind of Clause**

1. The persons **whom I name** will receive an award.
2. **Although Albert is ill,** he works every day.
3. I do not know **where Alice lives.**
4. The fact is **that we do not have the equipment.**
5. **When I reached the city,** I registered at a famous hotel.
6. The house **which was sold yesterday** was built in 1850.
7. Tell them **when the rehearsals will begin.**
8. Do you like the book **that the speaker recommended?**
9. **Since you object to our plan,** you should suggest another.
10. We learned **how the parts of the machine were assembled.**
11. It is true **that the driver was injured in the crash.**
12. The old man told his story to **whomever he met.**
13. We visited the art galleries **when we traveled in Europe.**
14. Adams lived in a period **when travel was very slow.**
15. The day was so hot **that we stayed indoors.**

1. *adjective*
2. *adverbial*
3. *noun*
4. *noun*
5. *adverbial*
6. *adjective*
7. *noun*
8. *adjective*
9. *adverbial*
10. *noun*
11. *noun*
12. *noun*
13. *adverbial*
14. *adjective*
15. *adverbial*

## KEY TO MASTERY TEST 12

1. Ellis wants **to fly** an airplane.
2. Did you read the regulations about **speeding?**
3. **Having been** a sailor, James liked work on boats.
4. We watched the artist **(to) decorate** the hall.
5. The attempts **to stop** the enemy were futile.
6. We considered **buying** a home in the suburbs.
7. Ted went to Arizona **to regain** his health.
8. Doctors, **called** to the scene, examined the men.
9. He entered the house by **breaking** the lock.
10. **Having finished** our work, we left early.
11. You should learn **to speak** correctly.
12. **Driving** carefully will prevent accidents.
13. Esther's plan was **to study** music in New York.
14. He did everything except **(to) work.**
15. The old manuscript was **interesting.**

1. *infinitive*
2. *gerund*
3. *participle*
4. *infinitive*
5. *infinitive*
6. *gerund*
7. *infinitive*
8. *participle*
9. *gerund*
10. *participle*
11. *infinitive*
12. *gerund*
13. *infinitive*
14. *infinitive*
15. *participle*

## KEY TO MASTERY TEST 13

1. radios
2. geese
3. crocuses
4. salaries
5. Chinese
6. spoonfuls
7. volcanos or volcanoes
8. calves
9. matches
10. crises
11. thieves
12. handkerchiefs
13. indexes or indices
14. sheep
15. fathers-in-law
16. vetoes
17. quantities
18. beliefs
19. banjos
20. passers-by
21. Miss Smiths or the Misses Smith
22. men-of-war
23. saleswomen
24. inquiries
25. alumni
26. compasses
27. Henrys
28. Messrs.
29. remedies
30. knives
31. alleys
32. wolves
33. cupfuls
34. series
35. bases
36. tomatoes
37. forget-me-nots
38. allies
39. attorneys general or attorney generals
40. mulberries

## KEY TO MASTERY TEST 14

1. On Tuesdays I have classes in Latin, physics, and English.
2. I received a book from my cousin entitled "How to Read a Book."
3. We are going to the Lake Shore Club for lunch next Friday.
4. Harriet is taking Mathematics 102 at Northwestern University.
5. He wrote letters to Senator Lodge and to Judge Harmon.
6. The Democrats will hold their convention in Chicago in June.
7. Her purse is made of Spanish leather and her bracelet is made of Mexican silver.
8. The Senior Class is giving a dance at the Hilton Hotel.
9. Have you ever seen the Allegheny Mountains or Niagara Falls?
10. I always spend Labor Day and Memorial Day with my aunt.
11. Every American should be familiar with the Declaration of Independence.

12. Van **G**ogh's picture, "Peasants **D**igging," is very famous.

13. At the inauguration in **W**ashington, I saw both the **P**resident and Vice-President.

14. There is a new **W**oolworth store on **F**ifth Avenue in New **Y**ork.

15. The skiers went to **S**un **V**alley for the winter sports.

### KEY TO MASTERY TEST 15

1. Each of the oarsmen did **his** best.

2. The **editors-in-chief** of several newspapers met yesterday.

3. The company gave **its** employees a raise in salary.

4. My friend has been acting very **peculiarly** lately.

5. Daniel lays carpets for Marshall Field and Company. (*correct*)

6. He **surely sang** that ballad **remarkably** well.

7. The northern lights appear **frequently** in Alaska.

8. Divide the fruit among the four families. (*correct*)

9. These lilacs smell **fragrant**.

10. How long has the canoe **lain** on the beach?

11. The mayor greeted the visitors very **cordially**.

12. Prices of food are **rising** every day.

13. Every corporation has **its** own officers.

14. The distinguished visitors might have been **they**.

15. The men **did** the job **efficiently**.

16. At this time of the year, I wish I **were** in Florida.

17. One likes to do what **he** can do **well**.

18. I always enjoy reading **Dickens'** "Christmas Carol." (or **Dickens's**)

19. Your car is different **from** mine.

20. To **whom** did you give the supervisor's report?

21. That bell always sounds **shrill**.

22. **Someone's** coat was left in my **brother's** locker.

23. The sailor jumped off the deck. (omit **of**)

24. This variety of flowers **is** rare.

25. My wife and **I** attended the banquet.

26. I **lay** on the davenport all evening.

## KEY TO MASTERY TEST 15 (continued)

27. The boys have **drunk** all the lemonade that was in the pitcher.

28. I thought the captain of the team to be **him**.

29. The car will cost **about** a thousand dollars.

30. I want you and **her** to help me make this dress.

31. Both brought **their** musical instruments.

32. This book is the most interesting of the three you sent me. (*correct*)

33. The number of candidates for the position **is** small.

34. The letters were **lying** on his desk all week.

35. The guests have just gone **into** the dining room.

36. I differ **with** you in regard to the value of the plan.

37. The man **whom** they are seeking must have a college degree.

38. A number of magazines **were** sent to the soldiers.

39. Say it **as if** you meant it.

40. My brother, together with his wife and children, **is** visiting us.

41. Do you remember **my** speaking to you about the contest?

42. Everyone at the luncheon helped **himself**.

43. All but **him** failed to appear at the conference.

44. Of the two hats, I bought the **less** expensive.

45. **Were** you interested in buying a new car?

46. I **have** done nothing all day.
    or I haven't done **anything** all day.

47. I like **this** kind of neckties. (or *these kinds*)

48. Don't you think you should **have** started earlier?

49. I did not like **his** leaving so abruptly.

50. Raymond sat **beside** me during the lecture.


## HOW TO OBTAIN YOUR SCORE

*The test totals 55 points. To obtain your score, divide the number of your correct answers by 55. The answer will be your score on this test. For example, if you have 50 points correct, your score is 50 divided by 55 which is 91 per cent. In other words, you score on this test is 91. You can obtain your score on any of the exercises or assignments by following the same procedure.*

# OUTLINE

# PUNCTUATION REVIEW

Page

1. OPEN AND CLOSED PUNCTUATION ........................ 5

2. USE OF THE PERIOD ...................................... 6

3. USE OF THE COMMA .................................... 7

4. USE OF THE SEMICOLON ............................. 17

5. USE OF THE COLON .................................. 20

6. USE OF PARENTHESES .............................. 21

7. USE OF THE DASH .................................. 22

8. USE OF BRACKETS ............................. 25

9. USE OF THE QUESTION MARK ................ 25

10. USE OF THE EXCLAMATION MARK ........................ 26

11. USE OF QUOTATION MARKS ..................... 27

12. USE OF SINGLE QUOTATION MARKS .................... 28

13. USE OF THE APOSTROPHE ......................... 29

*Key to Correct Answers*................................................ 36

# PUNCTUATION REVIEW FOR ADULTS

THE proper placement of periods, commas, quotation marks, and other punctuation marks causes many writers more trouble than any other skill involved in composition. At Career Institute hundreds of men and women have enrolled for courses in grammar and punctuation. Many of these adults are above average in general writing ability, but weak in punctuation. Some of these persons are executives who say, "My secretary sometimes changes my punctuation, and I want to know who is right." On the other hand, a secretary may say, "I think I'm right and my boss insists he's right, and—well—I want to know exactly what is right in punctuation."

The purpose of this unit is to provide you with a complete list of punctuation rules, with practice exercises for applying the rules. You will find that this unit is a handy reference manual for use in either the home or office. Refer to it whenever a question arises about correct punctuation.

As you study the unit, keep in mind that *some sentences may be punctuated in more than one way.* Remember also that *some professions have their own style of punctuation.* A journalist, for example, omits many punctuation marks which normally should be included in a business letter. A lawyer, on the other hand, uses many more punctuation marks than are essential for most types of business writing.

## OPEN AND CLOSED PUNCTUATION

The terms *open* and *closed* punctuation apply only to the business letter and only to the heading and inside address of the letter. They do not apply to the salutation and complimentary close. If your company uses *open* punctuation, as most firms do, *omit all commas and periods at the ends of lines in the heading and inside address* unless the line ends in an abbreviation. If your firm uses *closed* punctuation, *include commas and periods at the ends of the lines in the heading and in the inside address.* The following examples illustrate the two styles of punctuation. Remember that most firms prefer open punctuation.

| Open Punctuation | Closed Punctuation |
|---|---|
| Acme Rug Cleaners, Inc. | Acme Rug Cleaners, Inc., |
| 1823 Timber Avenue | 1823 Timber Avenue, |
| Cleveland, Ohio | Cleveland, Ohio. |

The salutation and complimentary close of a business letter are usually punctuated by a colon after the salutation and a comma following the complimentary close, regardless of open or closed punctuation. Some writers, however, no longer punctuate either the salutation or the complimentary close.

## USE OF THE PERIOD

1. The period ( . ) is used after a declarative or an imperative sentence.

> She went to the office.   (declarative)
> Close the car door.   (imperative)

*Exception:* If you wish to give a declarative or an imperative sentence the force of an exclamatory sentence, use an exclamation point rather than a period.

> I was so shocked that I was speechless!   (declarative)
> Bring the Pulmotor quickly!   (imperative)

2. After requests, use a period rather than a question mark.

> May I send you a copy of our latest bulletin.   (request)
> Will you send me any further information which you have available.
>                                                      (request)

3. The period is used after abbreviations and initials.

| Dr. | Mrs. | A. M. | Jan. |
|---|---|---|---|
| Ill. | Sat. | C. I. Jones | Inc. |

*Note:* When a sentence ends with an abbreviation, one period is sufficient for both the abbreviation and the sentence.

> Mail the package to Conley and Green, Inc.

4. The period is used to indicate the omission of words in quoted passages.

(a) Repeat the period three times ( ... ) to indicate the omission of words within a quoted passage.

> "I pledge allegiance to the flag of the United States ... one nation, indivisible, with liberty and justice for all."—Francis Bellamy

(b) Repeat the period four times ( .... ) to indicate the omission of words at the end of a quoted passage.

> "Fame is the spur ...."—John Milton

## USE OF THE COMMA

1. The comma ( , ) is used after an adverbial dependent clause when the dependent clause precedes the main clause. When the dependent clause does not begin the sentence, the comma is usually unnecessary. (See Grammar Unit Twenty for a detailed discussion of adverbial clauses.)

> <u>After the director had read the minutes of the meeting</u>, he called for
> adverbial clause
> the financial report.   (comma)

> The director called for the financial report <u>after he had read the</u>
> <u>minutes of the meeting.</u>   (no comma)
> adverbial clause

2. The comma is used after a participial phrase or an absolute phrase at the beginning of a sentence. (See Grammar Unit Twenty for a detailed discussion of participial phrases and absolute constructions.)

> <u>Seeing the address across the street</u>, he wrote a note in his little book.
> participial phrase

> <u>The rain having stopped</u>, we went to lunch.
> absolute construction

3. The comma is used after an introductory infinitive phrase.

> <u>To be successful</u>, you must read widely.
> infinitive phrase

*Note:* When the subject of the sentence is an infinitive, do not separate the subject from the rest of the sentence.

> <u>To be successful</u> was his goal.
> subject

4. The comma is used to set off parenthetical expressions, whether words, phrases, or clauses.

(a) Transitional words such as *however, therefore, moreover, besides, consequently* should be set off by commas.

> Consequently, I did not receive an answer to his letter.

*Exception:* The word *also* is not set off by commas unless the writer wishes *also* to be emphasized strongly. In such a case, *also* is generally placed in an unusual position in the sentence.

> We also noticed that the salaries declined after the first of the year. (no emphasis)
> Also, we noticed that the salaries declined after the first of the year. (emphasis intended)

(b) Phrases such as *so to speak, in short, as a result, of course* should be set off by commas.

> We found, in short, many errors in his work.
> Of course, there are many ways to tackle the problem.

(c) Clauses such as *I think, we suppose, he says* should be set off by commas.

> Someone, I suppose, should check the report.

(d) Explanatory expressions, such as *and I agree with him, so far as he is concerned,* etc., which break the logical sequence of words should be set off by commas.

> The president disliked the policy, and I agreed with him, of letting all employees name their vacation time.

5. The comma is used after introductory expressions such as *yes, indeed, surely* (when it means *yes*), *well.*

> Well, the next thing we knew he had shot the deer.
> Yes, I will attend to the matter.

6. The comma is used to set off a non-restrictive clause. A non-restrictive clause is set off because *it is not essential to complete the meaning of a sentence.* A non-restrictive clause is similar to a parenthetical expression in that it gives added information about the word it modifies.

Restrictive clauses are never set off by commas. *A restrictive clause is a clause that is necessary to complete the meaning of the sentence* because the clause identifies the word it modifies. A restrictive clause *cannot* be left out of a sentence, whereas a non-restrictive clause can be. (See Grammar Unit Nineteen for further information on restrictive and non-restrictive clauses.)

> The girl who lives next door came to work in our office. (The clause *who lives next door* is restrictive because it is needed to identify the word *girl*. The clause is not set off by commas.)
> Mary Jones, who lives next door, came to work in our office. (The clause *who lives next door* is non-restrictive because it is not needed to identify the name *Mary Jones*. The name *Mary Jones* clearly identifies the person being talked about, and the clause merely gives added information about the person *Mary Jones*.)

7. The comma is used to set off words in apposition. An appositive is a word or phrase that defines or identifies another word. An appositive means the same as the word it defines.

> Jones, our office manager, is ill.
> <u>appositive</u>
>
> Reverend Brown, our minister, is an intelligent man.
> <u>appositive</u>

*Note 1:* An appositive at the end of a sentence should be preceded by a comma.

> I sent the memorandum to Jones, our office manager.

*Note 2:* Very closely related appositives do not require a comma.

> my cousin Mary                Louis the Fourth
> his friend Bill               Mary Queen of Scots

8. The comma is used to set off words used in direct address.

> We regret, Mr. Thomas, that your order was unsatisfactorily filled.
> Henry, bring me the December file.

9. The comma is used to separate a series of three or more words, phrases, or clauses.

> Alice planned to have steak, potatoes, beans, lettuce, and ice cream for dinner.
> He stalked off the stage, turned around, came back, and glared at the audience.
> At the meeting it was decided to (1) give two weeks' vacation with pay, (2) give pensions at age sixty-five, (3) establish a profit-sharing plan.

*Note 1:* A comma should always be placed before the conjunction joining the last two members of a series.

> She asked for paper, pencils, and a ruler.

*Note 2:* A comma should separate pairs of words in a series. A comma should not be placed before a conjunction joining words of a series that are considered as one unit.

> Typing and shorthand, spelling and vocabulary, grammar and punctuation are the most popular courses.   (pairs of words in a series)

> For breakfast she ordered orange juice, toast, coffee, and ham and eggs. (*Ham and eggs* is considered to be one unit.)

10. The comma is used to separate co-ordinate adjectives which modify the same noun. Adjectives are co-ordinate if the word *and* can be used between them.

> The efficient, business-like secretary received an advance in pay. (Comma—the efficient *and* business-like secretary. Both adjectives modify *secretary*.)

> The five silver spoons were very expensive.   (No comma—you would not say *five and silver spoons.*)

## EXERCISE 1

Directions: Supply the necessary punctuation in the following sentences:

1. Send this letter to Miss Alice Norcross in Harrisburg Pa

2. Before the new staff policy could go into effect the manager had to approve the changes

3. Mr Case the assistant director read a poem beginning "If you can keep your head   "

4. Regarding your letter of October 14 we are sorry to tell you that the position for which you applied has been filled

5. The filing clerk who made the error will be discharged

6. Surely I shall be glad to get the report for you

7. The advertisement moreover called for copywriters typesetters and a junior executive

8. Phyllis what did Mrs Thomas want after the meeting?

9. Our manager who had been with the company twenty years resigned yesterday

10. We do not wish of course to discourage you from applying again

## EXERCISE 2

Directions: Punctuate the following address, first in open and then in closed style of punctuation:

| Open Punctuation | Closed Punctuation |
|---|---|
| James R. Williams M D | James R. Williams M D |
| 1812 Park Boulevard | 1812 Park Boulevard |
| Washington D C | Washington D C |

Supply the necessary punctuation in the following sentences:

1. She said that she changed jobs because she was dissatisfied with the insurance system

2. The salesman who won the contest is a recent addition to our staff

3. The welcome mat so to speak was always out at the Jones' my uncle's family

4. To be acceptable for the position for which you applied you must have had at least twelve months' training

5. Any man regardless of age will be considered for the position

6. Since you cannot attend the meeting Mr Small we shall have to proceed without you

7. Upon receiving your shipment we discovered that the memorandum pads the mimeograph stencils the ink eradicator and the manila folders were missing

8. That clean-cut experienced salesman Henry Oliver was lowest in sales this month

9. My mother who lives in Omaha Nebraska came to visit me

10. No Jane you should not send every letter air mail

**EXERCISE 3**

Directions: Supply the necessary commas and periods in the following paragraphs:

Homeowners what would you do if you had a fire in your house? Unfortunately most people ask themselves this question only when it is too late By following a few suggestions however you can save yourself and your family money worry and inconvenience.

If your house should catch fire it is vitally important of course that you keep calm As a first step toward actually controlling the fire you should close all doors windows and ventilators Immediately after doing this call the fire department

While you are waiting for the firemen to arrive do what you can to put out or at least to control the fire If the fire is in draperies rugs wood or paper use water to extinguish it However when the fire is in grease oil or gasoline spread baking soda using a sweeping motion of the arm on the fire

Prompt decisive action in time of such an emergency may well determine the extent of your fire loss.

### USE OF THE COMMA (continued)

11. The comma is used in a compound sentence to separate independent clauses joined by one of the co-ordinate conjunctions *and, but, for, or, nor,* and *while* when it means the same as *but.* (See Grammar Unit Eighteen for a detailed discussion of compound sentences.)

> I dictated the letter as you ordered, but she did not transcribe it correctly.
>
> Minneapolis is a large industrial center, and it has many cultural attractions.

(a) If the clauses of a compound sentence are very short and closely connected, the comma may be omitted.

> He looked but he did not see her.

(b) Do not use a comma between two independent clauses unless a co-ordinate conjunction is used. The use of a comma without a co-ordinate conjunction between two independent clauses is called the *comma fault.* The following sentence illustrates the comma fault:

> The men in the shipping department will not follow instructions, they repeatedly make serious errors.   (Incorrect—comma should not be used without a co-ordinate conjunction.)

*Note 1:* The comma fault may be eliminated by punctuating the sentence in one of the three following ways:

(a) Use a co-ordinate conjunction after the comma:

> The men in the shipping department will not follow instructions, and they repeatedly make serious errors.   (correct)

(b) Use a semicolon between the two independent clauses:

> The men in the shipping department will not follow instructions; they repeatedly make serious errors.   (Correct—see Rule 1 under semicolons.)

(c) Punctuate the two independent clauses as two simple sentences:

> The men in the shipping department will not follow instructions. They repeatedly make serious errors.   (correct)

*Note 2:* When the independent clauses of a compound sentence are very long or have *internal punctuation,* a semicolon is generally used before the co-ordinate conjunction. Internal punctuation means that there are commas within one or both of the independent clauses.

> Copyboy, take this folder to Alan Toms, the fellow in brown over there; and be sure to come back.
> Quietly efficient, Joan continued in her position; but she never got the raise.

Both of these sentences have one or more commas in the first independent clause. Since the first clause has internal punctuation, a semicolon is used between the two independent clauses even though a co-ordinate conjunction is used. (See Rule 3 under semicolons.)

12. The comma is used to set off words or phrases expressing contrast.

> I asked you to file the contract, not destroy it.
> You may be excused from the conference this time, but never again.
> Children should be seen, not heard.

13.  The comma is used to set off a definite place, month, or year.

Cleveland, Ohio                July 12, 1922
Cook County, Illinois          the third of December, 1931

Or, in sentence form, the comma is used in the following manner:

The president was born April 8, 1872, at 1224 Elm Street, Cleveland, Ohio.

14.  The comma is used to set off a direct quotation.

The director asked, "How many of you are in favor of this change in policy?"

15.  The comma is used as a substitute for an exclamation point after a mild interjection.

Well, I'm glad that's over.
My, it's really raining.

16.  The comma is used after inverted names in lists.

Thackeray, William M.
Whittier, John Greenleaf

17.  The comma is used to indicate the omission of a word.

Fishing forms a quiet man; hunting, an eager man; racing, a greedy man.

18.  The comma is used to set off a proper name when followed by an academic degree or honorary title. The comma is used to separate two or more degrees or titles.

Philip F. Adams, A.B., M.A., Ph.D., lecturer in English.

19.  The comma is used to point off the thousands in figures of four digits or more.

1,117                   20,718                   1,817,000

*Note:* Do not use the comma in telephone, house, page, and policy numbers, or in years.

the year 1933                          Policy No. 903451
page 2348                              Arlington 7-8903
              1117 North Pensacola Avenue

20.  The comma is used to separate two sets of figures or two identical words.

John told you, you should apply immediately.
Send me 10, No. 1234 and 7, No. 138.
Since 1933, 12,000 new machines have been sold.

21. The comma is used to separate a declarative clause and an interrogative clause which immediately follows.

> The plane will arrive on time, will it not?
> Jack is to get a promotion, isn't he?

22. The comma is used to separate a phrase from the rest of the sentence when the phrase is inverted or out of its natural order.

> Like you, I think the policy is a worthwhile one.
> For me, it will mean extra work and less pay.
> In spite of his promise, he was late to work again.

## EXERCISE 4

Directions: Supply the necessary punctuation in the following sentences:

1. The head accountant and the assistant buyer read the pamphlet but found it was of little help to them

2. The typewriter needs a new ribbon space bar and roller but the repairman a slow worker will not fix the machine until tomorrow

3. Send those mimeographed statements to the home office but do not include the current balance

4. You must pay your overdue account or I shall have to take steps for collection

5. Mary not Alice was the girl who initialed the letter

6. The city was hot and humid I thought I would faint

7. More and more the middle and lower income bracket taxpayers must shoulder the burden of financing American industry

8. Do but set the example yourself and I will follow you example is the best precept

9. After he had checked his balance he found that his account was overdrawn but he lacked funds to make a deposit he therefore borrowed from his uncle a prominent man in the community

10. Collect the outgoing mail bring it to me and help me count the number of personal letters it includes

## EXERCISE 5

Directions: Supply the necessary punctuation in the following sentences:

1. Jane Pose has recently applied for a responsible position with our company and has given your name as a personal reference

2. You have our assurance that your reply will be held in strict confidence a self-addressed stamped envelope is enclosed for your convenience

3. We will greatly appreciate any information you have which will help us in considering this application

4. We are especially interested in his business ability aggressiveness honesty integrity and personal habits

5. When I arrived she left

6. I arrived and she left

7. She left when I arrived

8. I am replying to your letter of January 3 1943 from San Francisco California and I regret that I was unable to send you this information until this time

9. A handwritten copy of your father's will has been found by my investigators it is dated October 14 1863 and it was signed at Silver Creek

10. Although we double-checked the report we were unable to locate the error

## EXERCISE 6

Directions: Supply the necessary punctuation in the following sentences:

1. The entry made in 1862 stated that Emily had received the promissory note in Pittsfield Mass on July 3 1862

2. Well she soon forgot about it because she never tried to collect the inheritance

3. Betty bring me the pencils but do not sharpen them

4. Punctuate correctly the following list of names:

Dickens Charles           Rawlings Marjorie K
Wells H G                Maugham Somerset

Mary Livingstone B S M S Ph D Co-ordinator of Hearing and Audiology

5. The operator said "Dial Weather 4-1212 to find out the temperature"

6. The book your mother gave you you should read

7. Because he had been unemployed his typing speed had decreased

8. I said to tie not knot the string

9. The package contained 20 10-penny nails and 40 20-penny nails

10. Go now but come back soon

## USE OF THE SEMICOLON

The semicolon ( ; ) is used to show a stronger separation between the parts of a sentence than does a comma. In practical writing, however, avoid using the semicolon because it is generally too stiff and formal. If you use a great many semicolons, the chances are that you are either using them incorrectly, or you are writing sentences which are too long. Semicolons produce rather involved sentence patterns. Use them sparingly.

1. The semicolon is used to separate independent co-ordinate clauses closely connected in meaning when no co-ordinate conjunction is used.

The sales staff meets every other Tuesday; the production staff meets only once a month.

He would not approve the art layout as presented; he suggested several drastic changes.

*Note:* An example of this rule, as used to avoid the comma fault, was given in Rule 11 under commas.

2. The semicolon is used between co-ordinate clauses of a compound sentence when they are joined by transitional words and phrases. The following is a list of commonly used transitional words:

| | | |
|---|---|---|
| accordingly | indeed | as a result |
| afterwards | likewise | at last |
| again | meanwhile | at the same time |
| anyhow | moreover | for example |
| besides | namely | for instance |
| consequently | nevertheless | for this reason |
| doubtless | next | in any case |
| eventually | otherwise | in fact |
| evidently | perhaps | in like manner |
| finally | possibly | in short |
| furthermore | still | on the contrary |
| hence | then | on the other hand |
| however | therefore | that is |
| yet | thus | in addition |

(For further discussion of transitional words, see page 19 of Grammar Unit Eighteen.)

*Note:* You have already learned that transitional words are usually set off by commas. When you use a semicolon in place of a comma before the transitional word, you usually put a comma after the transitional word. However, when the transitional word retains its adverbial force and is not regarded as an independent element, it is seldom set off with a comma. (See Rule 4 (a) under commas and page 18 of Grammar Unit Eighteen.)

The members of the board of directors approved the change in distribution; consequently, you should appeal to them.

The weather was cold and icy; therefore we didn't go.

3. The semicolon is used before a co-ordinate conjunction (*and, but, for, or, nor*) between two independent clauses when either one or both have internal punctuation. (See Rule 11 under commas.)

The president, a well-read man, predicted a cost of living increase for the first of the year; but his prediction, which spread throughout the plant, proved to be wrong.

The staff housekeeper ordered carpets, divans, lamps, tables, and chairs; but her order was incorrectly filled.

4. The semicolon is used before such words as *for example, for instance, that is,* and *namely* that introduce an example, enumeration, or a list in a sentence. A comma is placed after such words.

> These special artist's pencils are available in three colors; namely, red, green, and blue.

> Many of our policies will be changed this year; for example, salesmen will be paid a commission instead of a salary.

5. The semicolon is used in lists where a comma is insufficient to separate the members clearly.

> Guests at the convention were Mr. Leonard Key, the past president of the corporation; Mrs. F. K. Small, the wife of the founder; and Mr. Paul Wells, the speaker of the evening.

### EXERCISE 7

Directions: Supply the necessary punctuation and capitalization in the following paragraphs:

although the weather is still cold I together with other baseball fans am turning my thoughts to the day when I can hear the umpire yell in a hoarse voice "Play ball!" and when I can shout back at his deafened ears "Kill the umpire!"

the date however is only January 29 but no matter what the time of year there are always fans who are willing to talk about the great American pastime baseball many of these fans who are self-styled experts meet in groups called "hot stove" leagues in these leagues everything about baseball is discussed nothing is accomplished the discussions however do give rabid fans a chance to argue about last year's playoff series about the world series about the "goat" of the year in baseball about players who have been traded and about trades they would like to see

several weeks ago I was in such a discussion at a friend's house Veronica one of my wife's friends called us on the telephone she said "You will come over next Sunday for supper won't you" the next Sunday over we went after supper a few more couples came in and we all exchanged a few informal remarks soon however all the men in the party were in one corner of the living-room as you know when a group of males get together their talk usually is not about the latest fashions about their wives or about the unstable situation of the world when men get together their conversation inevitably drifts to sports on this particular evening there were no preliminaries baseball was the immediate topic of conversation besides me this board of experts on the past present and future of baseball included Dan Sullivan a Sox fan from birth Carl Schultz a good fan who likes all teams Ed Reynolds who knows very little about the game and Jim Wolf a Cub follower from way back

toward the end of the evening after we had discussed possible trades this year's prospects and last year's "goat" Dan began to describe a home run he had seen DiMaggio make in the last half of the ninth inning it's hard to imagine that one run could get a man so excited but Dan was in the middle of his narration however Veronica interrupted to tell us that cake coffee and ice cream were being served in the dining-room that broke up our meeting Dan's story was never finished

over our coffee we men agreed that talking baseball was a good way to spend the evening surprisingly enough the women didn't agree!

## USE OF THE COLON

The colon (:) indicates the strongest possible break within a sentence.

1. The colon is used before a list of items or details.

> Please send out the following items: No. 378, No. 315, No. 519, and No. 570.

> His actions were as follows: He went to the drugstore, purchased a hypodermic needle, got into his car, and drove away.

*Note 1:* Capitalize the first letter of each item in a list when the list is in column form.

> You should know how to use the following office machines:
>
> 1. Typewriter
> 2. Duplicator
> 3. Dictaphone
> 4. Calculator

*Note 2:* Do not capitalize the first letter of each item in a list when the items are included in a sentence.

> You should know how to use the following office machines: typewriter, duplicator, dictaphone, and calculator.

2. The colon is used before an appositive phrase or clause.

> Our company has always had this motto: The customer is always right.
> These are your duties: Sort the mail, open all that is not personal, throw away the envelopes, and bring the letters to me.

*Note:* Capitalize the first letter of the word which follows the colon when that word introduces a complete sentence, as in the above examples.

3. The colon is used after the salutation of a business letter.

> Dear Mr. Roe:        Gentlemen:        My dear Madam:

*Note:* Never use a semicolon after a salutation. A comma may be used after the salutation of a friendly or informal letter. Some modern writers do not use any punctuation after the salutation.

> Dear Jane,        Dear Father,        Dear Jones,

4. The colon is used to divide the parts of references, titles, formulas, and numerals.

> The time was 9:15 P.M.
> He assigned Chapter XII: Section 19.
> Grammar Unit Eight: Complements of Verbs

## USE OF PARENTHESES

1. Parentheses ( ) are used to set off words, phrases, clauses, or sentences which are used by way of explanation, translation, or comment, but which are independent constructions:

> Hilda (my sister's roommate at college) is coming to visit us.
> The motto read as follows: *"De gustibus non disputandum est."* (In matters of taste there is no dispute.)

2. Parentheses are used to enclose a number, letter, or symbol when used as an appositive.

> She ordered twelve (12) night stands for the hotel.
> The bookkeeper ornamented his letterhead with the percent symbol (%).

*Note 1:* When using parentheses with other punctuation marks, punctuate the main part of the sentence as if the parenthetical portion was not there. A punctuation mark comes after the second parenthesis if the punctuation mark applies to the whole sentence and not just to the parenthetical portion.

> He analyzed and presented standards of evaluation (business and technical), but his conditions proved nothing.

*Note 2:*  Place the punctuation mark inside the second parenthesis if the punctuation mark applies only to material within the parenthetical portion.

> A simplified fire-fighting plan will help you. (See the back cover of this brochure.)

## USE OF THE DASH

The dash (—) is used to indicate an abrupt change of ideas, but should be used sparingly. Excessive use of the dash usually indicates that the writer does not know what punctuation mark to use.

There are times you may want to use the dash for visual effect or emphasis. A glance at advertisements in a newspaper shows that copy writers make frequent use of the dash. However, in business writing, such as letters, reports, minutes, and in social correspondence, use the dash with caution.

1.  The dash may be used to indicate a sudden change of thought in a sentence.

> I was certain that the manager—indeed, all of the office force—wanted John to receive the promotion.

2.  The dash may be used to indicate a summarizing thought or an afterthought added to the end of the sentence.

> I shall make out an estimate, draw up a contract, send out a man to interpret it for you—give you every help I can.

3.  The dash may be used to set off a word or phrase repeated for emphasis.

> We invited them for one meeting—one meeting only—not for the entire convention!

4. The dash may be used between numbers or dates to indicate *to* and *and*.

His chapter covered from 1860—1868.
My appointment was scheduled from 12:15—1:15.

*Note on the punctuation of parenthetical matter:* Close study of the rules on commas, parentheses, and dashes will show you that any one of the three punctuation marks may be used to set off parenthetical words, phrases, or clauses. When should you use the comma, dash, or parentheses? No strict rule can be stated. In general, follow this practice: In punctuating parenthetical matter, use dashes mainly for visual effect; use commas if the material is short; and use parentheses if the material is long.

## EXERCISE 8

Directions: Supply the necessary punctuation and capitalization in the following paragraphs:

### Safety Bulletin No. 10

since all of our machines are powered by electricity there is always the danger of shock caused by contact with an electrical circuit in case of an emergency when a person has been shocked into unconsciousness follow these steps

first eliminate the source of electricity cut the main power switch ask another employee to do the following

1. call the plant physician

2. call the power company

3. notify the department head

second if you have been successful in cutting the power find something that is dry a blanket rug or the like and cover or wrap the victim make sure the victim is kept warm and comfortable warm but not hot and perspiring

third if the victim should stop breathing or if he has difficulty in breathing apply artificial respiration continue artificial respiration until the patient is breathing normally or until the arrival of the plant physician the physician will then give instructions in a recent case one rescue worker applied artificial respiration from 2 18 3 05 p m this worker was credited with saving his fellow employee's life

in summary follow these steps in cases of electrical shock cut the source of power make the victim warm and comfortable apply artificial respiration have someone call the physician and power company

at all times KEEP CALM!

## EXERCISE 9

Directions: Supply the necessary punctuation in the following sentences. You will not need to supply any capital letters.

1. Our accountant an expert on taxes did not file his income tax report correctly and he had to fill out a second form

2. To find the error you may have to check several records for example the inventory record the accounts receivable ledger and the sales record

3. The stenographic pool included the following women Joanne Adams a girl with twelve 12 years' experience Margaret Roe a high school student who worked afternoons Phyllis Lasko a widow with three 3 children and Alice Pirk a sister of the office manager

4. We must all double our efforts if we are to meet the sales quota that is every man must sell twice as much as he did last month

5. I tried to appeal my case through your personal shopper and she directed me to you consequently I am enclosing her letter

6. You can be of help in three ways ( 1 ) by reporting changes promptly ( 2 ) by preparing your lists correctly ( 3 ) by adding new names as soon as they are sent to you

7. Dear Mrs Brown
   Your complaint is explained in the enclosed report See Chapter 1 Section 18

8. What he said was true true but completely misleading

## USE OF BRACKETS

1.  Brackets [ ] are used to enclose material added by someone other than the writer; for example, editorial additions or comments.

> The investigation [from June 1, 1950 to April 8, 1951] caused considerable speculation.

> The poet [Robert Browning] did not approve of the excessive adulation during the meeting.

2.  Brackets are used to enclose parenthetical matter within parenthetical matter.

> Your order (including items No. 391, No. 394, and No. 286 [No. 288 was out of stock]) was filled last week.

*Note:* Brackets are rarely used in business and social writing. Generally they are found only in printed material of a scholarly or technical nature.

## USE OF THE QUESTION MARK

1.  The question mark (?) is used after all interrogative sentences that ask direct questions.

> Where are the current files?
> Are you going to the next meeting of the club?

*Note:* After requests, use a period instead of a question mark. (See Rule 2 under periods.)

2.  The question mark may be used after each separate part of a sentence containing more than one question.

> Can we be sure of his willingness? his capability? his honesty?

*Note:* If the question is not complete until the end of the sentence, place a question mark at the end only.

> Will delivery be made today, tomorrow, or Friday?

3.  The question mark is used in several ways when only part of the sentence is a question. In such sentences the question is generally introduced by a comma or colon; a semicolon or dash may also be used.

> May I ask, what is his purpose?
> This is our problem: What should be done to prevent further damage?
> Our questions are, what date will you arrive? where will you stay? and, do you desire us to furnish transportation?

## USE OF THE EXCLAMATION MARK

1. The exclamation mark ( ! ) is used after all exclamatory sentences—sentences that express surprise, emotion, or deep feeling.

> Look out for that train!
> Headlines read, "Peace Treaty Signed!"
> Your answer was hard to believe!

2. The exclamation mark is used after an interjection or a word used as an interjection. At times, the sentence following the interjection may be exclamatory.

> Hurry! The train will pull out in three minutes!
> Oh! I haven't heard that before.

3. The exclamation mark is used after statements which are commands or which imply need for immediate action.

> Return the card today! Don't delay!
> Hurry! Send your order now!

4. The exclamation point is used after an interrogative sentence that is exclamatory in form or intended to be exclamatory.

> Oh, how could he say that!
> But can he be trusted!

5. The exclamation point is sometimes used to add emphasis.

> Realize what this means!
> This offer absolutely expires April 6!

## USE OF QUOTATION MARKS

1. Quotation marks (" ") are used to enclose a direct quotation. Each part of an interrupted quotation begins and ends with quotation marks.

> The inspector said, "Well, your case is not hopeless."
> "Where," he asked, "are you going to keep it?"
> "What will we do?" he asked. "Where can we raise the money?"

*Note:* Capitalize the first word of a direct quotation. Do not capitalize the first word in the second part of an interrupted quotation unless the second part begins a new sentence. Do not use quotation marks or capital letters in an indirect quotation.

> The inspector said that your case is not hopeless. (Many indirect quo-
> tations are introduced by the word *that.*)
> He asked where we would keep it.

2. Quotation marks are used to enclose the titles of magazine articles, chapters of books, names of songs, titles of poems, and other titles.

> *The New Yorker* includes a section entitled "The Talk of the Town."
> She asked Ellen to sing "Because" at her wedding.
> "Rabbi Ben Ezra" is one of my favorite poems.

*Note:* In typing or writing, underline the titles of books, magazines, operas, and any other works of art long enough to appear in book form. Underlining signifies italics for printing.

> The anthology, Toward Liberal Education, includes A. E. Housman's
> "Introductory Lecture" and S. I. Hayakawa's "Poetry and Adver-
> tising."

> The soprano sang "If Madam Should Call You" from Mozart's
> Marriage of Figaro.

3. Quotation marks are used to set off words, phrases, or sentences referred to within a sentence.

> The word "proceed" is frequently mispronounced.
> The phrase "on the other hand" is sometimes used as a transitional
> phrase.
> The sentence "Now is the time for all good men to come to the aid of
> their party" is an excellent typing exercise.

4. Quotation marks are used to set off slang words or expressions.

> She said that the office party was held at a "swank" hotel.

*Note:* Some offices prefer to use underlining instead of quotation marks in situations covered by Rules 3 and 4.

5. If several paragraphs are quoted, use quotation marks at the beginning of each paragraph, but at the end of the last paragraph only. Long quotations are usually introduced by a colon instead of a comma. Quotations of three or more lines are usually indented and set apart from the body of the text.

### USE OF QUOTATION MARKS WITH OTHER PUNCTUATION

(a) The period and comma are always placed before ending quotation marks.

> He said, "They are not here."
> "They are not here," he said.

(b) The question mark and exclamation point are placed before quotation marks when they refer only to the quoted material.

> She asked, "When are you going to be promoted?"

(c) The question mark and exclamation point follow ending quotation marks when they refer to the entire sentence.

> Did she say, "You are to be promoted next month"?

(d) The semicolon and colon follow ending quotation marks unless they are part of the quoted matter.

> She said, "You are to be promoted next month"; consequently, I expected to be promoted.

## USE OF SINGLE QUOTATION MARKS

1. Single quotation marks are used to set off a quotation within a quotation.

> "Jane," I asked, "did you tell me how to spell the word 'pathologically'?"
> The irate mother said, "You must get all of this 'junk' out of the living-room at once."

*Note:* Other punctuation marks are used with single quotation marks in the same way as with double quotation marks.

## USE OF THE APOSTROPHE

1.  The apostrophe (') is used in nouns to show possession.

*Note:* Keep in mind that the sign of the possessive case is always added to a word. It is not something that is inserted within a word.

(a) If the singular form of the noun does not end in **s** or an **s** sound, add the apostrophe and **s** (**'s**).

| Singular | Singular Possessive |
|----------|---------------------|
| boy | boy's |
| girl | girl's |
| lady | lady's |

(b) If the singular ends in **s** or an **s** sound, add the apostrophe (') or the apostrophe and **s** (**'s**) if the additional **s** sound is desired.

| Singular | Singular Possessive |
|----------|---------------------|
| boss | boss' or boss's |
| dress | dress' or dress's |
| box | box' or box's |

(c) If the plural form of the noun does not end in **s**, add the apostrophe and **s** (**'s**).

| Plural | Plural Possessive |
|--------|-------------------|
| men | men's |
| children | children's |
| mice | mice's |
| teeth | teeth's |
| geese | geese's |

(d) If the plural form of the noun ends in **s**, add the apostrophe (').

| Plural | Plural Possessive |
|--------|-------------------|
| boys | boys' |
| girls | girls' |
| ladies | ladies' |

(e) The possessives of proper nouns are formed in the same way as the possessives of common nouns. If the singular form of the name does not end in **s**, add the apostrophe and **s**. If the singular ends in **s** or an **s** sound, add the apostrophe (') or the apostrophe and **s** (**'s**). The plural possessive is always formed by adding the apostrophe to the plural form.

| Proper Noun | Singular Possessive | Plural | Plural Possessive |
|---|---|---|---|
| John | John's | Johns | Johns' |
| Phyllis | Phyllis' or Phyllis's | Phyllises | Phyllises' |
| Jane | Jane's | Janes | Janes' |

(f) Certain expressions relating to *time, distance,* and *value* are also written with an apostrophe.

| | |
|---|---|
| the day's task | five cents' worth |
| a year's time | six miles' distance |
| a minute's notice | three weeks' vacation |

(g) The singular possessive and the plural possessive of compound nouns are formed by adding the apostrophe to the end of the compound word .

| Singular | Plural |
|---|---|
| brother-in-law's | brothers-in-law's |
| father-in-law's | fathers-in-law's |

(h) Joint ownership is shown by making the last word in the series possessive. Individual ownership is shown by making both parts possessive.

Alice and Jack's apartments.   (joint ownership)
Alice's and Jack's apartments.   (individual ownership)

2.   The apostrophe is used in indefinite pronouns to show possession. The possessive case of indefinite pronouns is formed in the same way as the possessive case of nouns.

| | |
|---|---|
| everybody's duty | others' positions |
| one's coat | someone's hat |

3.   The apostrophe is used with **s** to form the plural of numbers, letters, signs, and symbols.

Your "r's" look like "n's."
He used twelve "%'s" to decorate his paper.

4.   The apostrophe is used to indicate the omission of a word, letters, or numerals.

| | | |
|---|---|---|
| don't | let's | o'clock |
| hadn't | it's | she's |
| isn't | 'tis | wouldn't |

The accident happened in '18.

## EXERCISE 10

Directions: Supply the necessary punctuation in the following sentences:

1. Where did you put the incoming correspondence

2. Bring me the file

3. Jack where is the restaurant you mentioned the other evening

4. No I dont know where you put the letters furthermore I wont look for them

5. I wonder what Alice will do now that shes finished her course

6. The three sisters Phyllis Ann and Mabel Mabel died at the age of twelve once lived in that large pale green house on the south side of Memphis Tenn

7. Ellen  the maid of honors sister sang Always an Irving Berlin composition which the bride had requested

8. The house organ The Scandal Monger included an article on keeping ones physical appearance up to par

9. The word bookkeeper is frequently misspelled by omitting one k

10. The treasurer announced all men who have been with the firm ten years or more will receive an increase in salary amounting to twenty percent or more that is at least twenty percent

## EXERCISE 11

Directions: Supply the necessary punctuation in the following business letter. Use open punctuation. Capitalize any words that should be capitalized.

chicago illinois
january 18 1952

mr r k able
1919 worthwhile avenue
toronto ontario canada

dear mr able

thank you for your inquiry about our photo service prices

to reduce our costs and to save you money weve printed our prices with an order form on the back of this letter all you need to do is to return this letter with the order form completed and your order will be shipped within ten days

when you fill out the order form youll note that all of our services are offered in special combinations if you desire most of the services in a combination but not all just cross out any unwanted services for additional services please attach a note to your order otherwise just send us your copy and mark nothing on the order except your order number and the shipping information

for open account credit if you have not previously used our services please include one banking reference and three business references a Dun and Bradstreet rating is also sufficient for open credit shipments otherwise will be made C O D to new customers

were looking forward to receiving your order our photo department will always be at your service thank you for thinking of us

sincerely yours

## EXERCISE 12

Directions: Supply the necessary punctuation in the following sentences:

1. Where on earth she asked did we get that typewriter Im used to a better machine than that

2. Did she say where she applied for her new position

3. Did she say Frances I have applied for a new position

4. She said Frances I have applied for a new position of course I wished her good luck but I really hope she is unable to find a job anywhere in Cleveland Cincinnati or Dayton

5. His Ms look like Ws whereas his Us look like Ns

6. Although Mr Jones children arent home for the summer Jones house is a young peoples entertainment center

7. The young mens girl friends mothers gave a party for the Knoxes children and the childrens friends

8. Bill and Petes car was stolen in Detroit Michigan on January 18 1952 while they were attending their companys convention

9. Hurry up well be late its eleven oclock now I hate to go into church after the bells ringing has stopped

10. The article in last weeks Time entitled What Next was informative analytical and critical

## EXERCISE 13

Directions: Supply the necessary punctuation in the following paragraphs. Do not add any capital letters.

Bill collectors in our company have a difficult job for they have many responsibilities For example each day they must call at customers homes attempt to get a payment and secure the customers promise of a future payment At the days end they must return to the office total their days collections post them to the months collection report and submit their daily collectors report

Twice a year each collectors semi-annual report is due These reports must be prepared at least fifteen days before July 1 and January 1 and they must include a summary of six months collections

In order to see customers who work during the day collectors must also call at customers homes during the evening Their working day as a result is longer than anyone elses Their pay however is not on the same salary scale as that of other employees who work in the office The manager-in-charges pay is extremely high in proportion to the small amount received by the collectors Even the salaries of new office clerks are greater than the average collectors pay In spite of apparent inequality the collectors and the assistant collectors salaries were not considered in the boards action of July 12 1951 although the board members had been requested to consider the matter

Unless some action is taken in regard to collectors salaries by January of 52 the collectors have indicated that they will either join or form a union Our new presidents proposal of a pension plan if put into effect before that date will help to prevent this occurrence The pension plan is good however salaries must also be increased

## PUNCTUATION ACHIEVEMENT TEST

Directions: Supply the necessary punctuation and capitalization in the following paragraphs:

men frequently need to be reminded of the economic strength of Americas women this strength is indeed unorganized but it is still a powerful force in the nations economy whereas men are associated with business groups concerned with making money women are members of clubs associations and similar organizations which have as their primary function social and cultural improvement rather than making money

however according to publications such as Business Week Fortune and the Wall Street Journal 70% of the countrys wealth is in the hands of women one periodical states more than 65% of the nations savings accounts are in feminine control 50% of our industrial stocks are managed by women and 44% of our utilities stocks are controlled by women

this magazine also states women pay 80% of the inheritance taxes they also buy 80% of the total consumers goods they spend 85% of the familys income women are responsible for the spending of twenty million dollars every year

womens clubs have greatly influenced the economic situation of the nation by their social improvement plans that is their conservation programs their aids to education and similar beneficial projects improvement programs not at first glance related to finance can become big business women have financed the planting of 5800 acres of trees scholarships amounting to $630000 are the result of womens efforts these projects are only two of many projects which have indirectly influenced the financial world

the modern businessman then must remember the force of his soulmate and bridge partner she is more than the passive little woman because she holds the purse zipper and the checkbook man should answer the following question which the ancients first asked Ye must know that women have dominion over you: do ye not labour and toil and give and bring all to the woman

## ANSWER KEY
### *Punctuation Review*

---

### CORRECT ANSWERS TO EXERCISE 1

1. Send this letter to Miss Alice Norcross in Harrisburg, Pa.

2. Before the new staff policy could go into effect, the manager had to approve the changes.

3. Mr. Case, the assistant director, read a poem beginning, "If you can keep your head...."

4. Regarding your letter of October 14, we are sorry to tell you that the position for which you applied has been filled.

5. The filing clerk who made the error will be discharged.

6. Surely, I shall be glad to get the report for you.

7. The advertisement, moreover, called for copywriters, typesetters, and a junior executive.

8. Phyllis, what did Mrs. Thomas want after the meeting?

9. Our manager, who had been with the company twenty years, resigned yesterday.

10. We do not wish, of course, to discourage you from applying again.

### CORRECT ANSWERS TO EXERCISE 2

**Open Punctuation**

James R. Williams, M. D.
1812 Park Boulevard
Washington, D. C.

**Closed Punctuation**

James R. Williams, M. D.,
1812 Park Boulevard,
Washington, D. C.

1. She said that she changed jobs because she was dissatisfied with the insurance system.

2. The salesman who won the contest is a recent addition to our staff.

3. The welcome mat, so to speak, was always out at the Jones', my uncle's family.

4. To be acceptable for the position for which you applied, you must have had at at least twelve months' training.

5. Any man, regardless of age, will be considered for the position.

6. Since you cannot attend the meeting, Mr. Small, we shall have to proceed without you.

7. Upon receiving your shipment, we discovered that the memorandum pads, the mimeograph stencils, the ink eradicator, and the manila folders were missing.

8. That clean-cut, experienced salesman, Henry Oliver, was lowest in sales this month.

9. My mother, who lives in Omaha, Nebraska, came to visit me.

10. No, Jane, you should not send every letter air mail.

## CORRECT ANSWERS TO EXERCISE 3

Homeowners, what would you do if you had a fire in your house? Unfortunately, most people ask themselves this question only when it is too late. By following a few suggestions, however, you can save yourself and your family money, worry, and inconvenience.

If your house should catch fire, it is vitally important, of course, that you keep calm. As a first step toward actually controlling the fire, you should close all doors, windows, and ventilators. Immediately after doing this, call the fire department.

While you are waiting for the firemen to arrive, do what you can to put out (*or,*) or at least to control (*or,*) the fire. If the fire is in draperies, rugs, wood, or paper, use water to extinguish it. However, when the fire is in grease, oil, or gasoline, spread baking soda, using a sweeping motion of the arm, on the fire.

Prompt, decisive action in time of such an emergency may well determine the extent of your fire loss.

## CORRECT ANSWERS TO EXERCISE 4

1. The head accountant and the assistant buyer read the pamphlet but found it was of little help to them.

2. The typewriter needs a new ribbon, space bar, and roller; but the repairman, a slow worker, will not fix the machine until tomorrow.

3. Send those mimeographed statements to the home office, but do not include the current balance.

4. You must pay your overdue account, or I shall have to take steps for collection.

5. Mary, not Alice, was the girl who initialed the letter.

6. The city was hot and humid; I thought I would faint.
   *or* The city was hot and humid. I thought I would faint.

7. More and more, the middle and lower income bracket taxpayers must shoulder the burden of financing American industry.

8. Do but set the example yourself, and I will follow you. Example is the best precept. *or* Do but set the example yourself, and I will follow you; example is the best precept.

9. After he had checked his balance, he found that his account was overdrawn, *(or;)* but he lacked funds to make a deposit. He, therefore, borrowed from his uncle, a prominent man in the community.

10. Collect the outgoing mail, bring it to me, and help me count the number of personal letters it includes.

## CORRECT ANSWERS TO EXERCISE 5

1. Jane Pose has recently applied for a responsible position with our company and has given your name as a personal reference.

2. You have our assurance that your reply will be held in strict confidence. A self-addressed, stamped envelope is enclosed for your convenience. *or* You have our assurance that your reply will be held in strict confidence; a self-addressed, stamped envelope is enclosed for your convenience.

3. We will greatly appreciate any information you have which will help us in considering this application.

4. We are especially interested in his business ability, aggressiveness, honesty, integrity, and personal habits.

5. When I arrived, she left.

6. I arrived, and she left. *or* I arrived and she left. (Sentence is so short that the comma may be omitted.)

7. She left when I arrived.

8. I am replying to your letter of January 3, 1943, from San Francisco, California; and I regret that I was unable to send you this information until this time.

9. A handwritten copy of your father's will has been found by my investigators; it is dated October 14, 1863, and it was signed at Silver Creek.
*or* A handwritten copy of your father's will has been found by my investigators. It is dated October 14, 1863, and it was signed at Silver Creek.

10. Although we double-checked the report, we were unable to locate the error.

## CORRECT ANSWERS TO EXERCISE 6

1. The entry, made in 1862, stated that Emily had received the promissory note in Pittsfield, Mass., on July 3, 1862.

2. Well, she soon forgot about it because she never tried to collect the inheritance.

3. Betty, bring me the pencils, but do not sharpen them. *or* Betty, bring me the pencils; but do not sharpen them.

4.          Dickens, Charles                    Rawlings, Marjorie K.
            Wells, H. G.                        Maugham, Somerset

Mary Livingstone, B.S., M.S., Ph.D., Co-ordinator of Hearing and Audiology

5.  The operator said, "Dial Weather 4-1212 to find out the temperature."

6.  The book your mother gave you, you should read.

7.  Because he had been unemployed, his typing speed had decreased.

8.  I said to tie, not knot, the string.

9.  The package contained 20, 10-penny nails and 40, 20-penny nails.

10. Go now but come back soon. *or* Go now, but come back soon. (Sentence is so
    short that the comma may be omitted.)

## CORRECT ANSWERS TO EXERCISE 7

Although the weather is still cold, I, together with other baseball fans, am
turning my thoughts to the day when I can hear the umpire yell in a hoarse voice,
"Play ball!" and when I can shout back at his deafened ears, "Kill the umpire!"

The date, however, is only January 20. (*or, or;*) But no matter what the time of
year, there are always fans who are willing to talk about the great American pastime, baseball. Many of these fans, who are self-styled experts, meet in groups
called "hot stove" leagues. In these leagues everything about baseball is discussed;
nothing is accomplished. The discussions, however, do give rabid fans a chance to
argue about last year's playoff series, about the world series, about the "goat" of the
year in baseball, about players who have been traded, and about trades they would
like to see.

Several weeks ago, I was in such a discussion at a friend's house. Veronica, one of
my wife's friends, called us on the telephone. She said, "You will come over next
Sunday for supper, won't you?" The next Sunday, over we went. After supper a
few more couples came in, and we all exchanged a few informal remarks. Soon,
however, all the men in the party were in one corner of the living-room. As you
know, when a group of males get together, their talk usually is not about the latest
fashions, about their wives, or about the unstable situation of the world. When
men get together, their conversation inevitably drifts to sports.

On this particular evening, there were no preliminaries. (*or;*) Baseball was the
immediate topic of conversation. Besides me, this board of experts on the past,
present, and future of baseball included Dan Sullivan, a Sox fan from birth; Carl
Schultz, a good fan who likes all teams; Ed Reynolds, who knows very little about
the game; and Jim Wolf, a Cub follower from way back.

Toward the end of the evening, after we had discussed possible trades, this year's
prospects, and last year's "goat," Dan began to describe a home run he had seen

DiMaggio make in the last half of the ninth inning. It's hard to imagine that one run could get a man so excited, but Dan was. In the middle of his narration, however, Veronica interrupted to tell us that cake, coffee, and ice cream were being served in the dining-room. That broke up our meeting; (*or.*) Dan's story was never finished.

Over our coffee, we men agreed that talking baseball was a good way to spend the evening. Surprisingly enough, the women didn't agree!

## CORRECT ANSWERS TO EXERCISE 8

### *Safety Bulletin No. 10*

Since all of our machines are powered by electricity, there is always the danger of shock caused by contact with an electrical circuit. In case of an emergency, when a person has been shocked into unconsciousness, follow these steps:

First, eliminate the source of electricity; (*or.*) cut the main power switch. Ask another employee to do the following:

1. Call the plant physician.

2. Call the power company.

3. Notify the department head.

Second, if you have been successful in cutting the power, find something that is dry—(*or,*) a blanket, rug, or the like—(*or,*) and cover or wrap the victim. Make sure the victim is kept warm and comfortable—warm, but not hot and perspiring.

Third, if the victim should stop breathing or if he has difficulty in breathing, apply artificial respiration. Continue artificial respiration until the patient is breathing normally or until the arrival of the plant physician. The physician will then give instructions. In a recent case, one rescue worker applied artificial respiration from 2:18—3:05 P.M. This worker was credited with saving his fellow employee's life.

In summary, follow these steps in cases of electrical shock: Cut the source of power, make the victim warm and comfortable, apply artificial respiration, have someone call the physician and power company.

At all times, KEEP CALM!

## CORRECT ANSWERS TO EXERCISE 9

1. Our accountant, an expert on taxes, did not file his income tax report correctly; and he had to fill out a second form.

2. To find the error, you may have to check several records; for example, the inventory record, the accounts receivable ledger, and the sales record.

3. The stenographic pool included the following women: Joanne Adams, a girl with twelve (12) years' experience; Margaret Roe, a high school student who worked afternoons; Phyllis Lasko, a widow with three (3) children; and Alice Pirk, a sister of the office manager.

4. We must all double our efforts if we are to meet the sales quota; that is, every man must sell twice as much as he did last month.

5. I tried to appeal my case through your personal shopper, and she directed me to you. (*or;*) Consequently, I am enclosing her letter.

6. You can be of help in three ways: (1) by reporting changes promptly, (2) by preparing your lists correctly, (3) by adding new names as soon as they are sent to you.

7. Dear Mrs. Brown:
   Your complaint is explained in the enclosed report. (See Chapter 1: Section 18.)

8. What he said was true—true, but completely misleading. *or* What he said was true, true but completely misleading.

## CORRECT ANSWERS TO EXERCISE 10

1. Where did you put the incoming correspondence?

2. Bring me the file.

3. Jack, where is the restaurant you mentioned the other evening?

4. No! (*or,*) I don't know where you put the letters. (*or;*) Furthermore, I won't look for them.

5. I wonder what Alice will do now that she's finished her course.

6. The three sisters, Phyllis, Ann, and Mabel (Mabel died at the age of twelve), once lived in that large, pale green house on the south side of Memphis, Tenn. (*Note:* Dashes could be used instead of parentheses.)

7. Ellen, the maid of honor's sister, sang "Always," an Irving Berlin composition (*or,*) which the bride had requested.

8. The house organ, The Scandal Monger, included an article on keeping one's physical appearance up to par. (*or* "up to par.")

9. The word "bookkeeper" is frequently misspelled by omitting one "k."

10. The treasurer announced, "All men who have been with the firm ten years or more will receive an increase in salary amounting to twenty percent or more; that is, at least twenty percent."

## CORRECT ANSWERS TO EXERCISE 11

Chicago, Illinois
January 18, 1952

Mr. R. K. Able
1919 Worthwhile Avenue
Toronto, Ontario, Canada

Dear Mr. Able:

Thank you for your inquiry about our photo service prices.

To reduce our costs and to save you money, we've printed our prices with an order form on the back of this letter. All you need to do is to return this letter with the order form completed, and your order will be shipped within ten days.

When you fill out the order form, you'll note that all of our services are offered in special combinations. If you desire most of the services in a combination, but not all, just cross out any unwanted services. For additional services, please attach a note to your order.* Otherwise, just send us your copy and mark nothing on the order except your order number and the shipping information.

For open account credit, if you have not previously used our services, please include one banking reference and three business references. A Dun and Bradstreet rating is also sufficient for open credit. Shipments, otherwise, will be made C.O.D. to new customers.

We're looking forward to receiving your order.* Our photo department will always be at your service. Thank you for thinking of us.

Sincerely yours,

*You may have used a semicolon at these points. If you did, your sentences are too long, and not so effective as the shorter sentences. Keep in mind that the semicolon is too stiff and formal for most business writing.

## CORRECT ANSWERS TO EXERCISE 12

1. "Where on earth," she asked, "did we get that typewriter? I'm used to a better machine than that."

2. Did she say where she applied for her new position?

3. Did she say, "Frances, I have applied for a new position"?

4. She said, "Frances, I have applied for a new position." Of course, I wished her good luck; (or,) but I really hope she is unable to find a job anywhere in Cleveland, Cincinnati, or Dayton.

5. His M's look like W's, whereas his U's look like N's.

6. Although Mr. Jones' children aren't home for the summer, Jones' house is a young people's entertainment center.

7. The young men's girl friends' mothers gave a party for the Knoxes' children and the children's friends.

8. Bill and Pete's car was stolen in Detroit, Michigan, on January 18, 1952, while they were attending their company's convention.

9. Hurry up! We'll be late. (; or !) It's eleven o'clock now. I hate to go into church after the bell's ringing has stopped.

10. The article in last week's <u>Time</u> entitled "What Next?" was informative, analytical, and critical.

## CORRECT ANSWERS TO EXERCISE 13

Bill collectors in our company have a difficult job, for they have many responsibilities. For example, each day they must call at customers' homes, attempt to get a payment, and secure the customer's promise of a future payment. At the day's end, they must return to the office, total their day's collections, post them to the month's collection report, and submit their daily collector's report.

Twice a year, each collector's semi-annual report is due. These reports must be prepared at least fifteen days before July 1 and January 1, and they must include a summary of six months' collections.

In order to see customers who work during the day, collectors must also call at customers' homes during the evening. Their working day, as a result, is longer than anyone else's. Their pay, however, is not on the same salary scale as that of other employees who work in the office. The manager-in-charge's pay is extremely high in proportion to the small amount received by the collectors. Even the salaries of new office clerks are greater than the average collector's pay. In spite of apparent inequality, the collectors' and the assistant collectors' salaries were not considered in the board's action of July 12, 1951, although the board members had been requested to consider the matter.

Unless some action is taken in regard to collectors' salaries by January of '52, the collectors have indicated that they will either join or form a union. Our new president's proposal of a pension plan, if put into effect before that date, will help to prevent this occurrence. The pension plan is good; (or.) however, salaries must also be increased.

## CORRECT ANSWERS TO PUNCTUATION ACHIEVEMENT TEST

Men frequently need to be reminded of the economic strength of America's women. This strength is, indeed, unorganized, (*or* ;) but it is still a powerful force in the nation's economy. Whereas men are associated with business groups concerned with making money, women are members of clubs, associations, and similar organizations which have as their primary function social and cultural improvement rather than making money.

However, according to publications such as Business Week, Fortune, and the Wall Street Journal, 70% of the country's wealth is in the hands of women. One periodical states, "More than 65% of the nation's savings accounts are in feminine control, 50% of our industrial stocks are managed by women, and 44% of our utilities' stocks are controlled by women."

This magazine also states, "Women pay 80% of the inheritance taxes. They also buy 80% of the total consumers' goods. (*or* ;) They spend 85% of the family's income. Women are responsible for the spending of twenty million dollars every year." (*or* !)

Women's clubs have greatly influenced the economic situation of the nation by their social improvement plans; that is, their conservation programs, their aids to education, and similar beneficial projects. Improvement programs, not at first glance related to finance, can become big business. Women have financed the planting of 5,800 acres of trees. Scholarships amounting to $630,000 are the result of women's efforts. These projects are only two of many projects which have indirectly influenced the financial world.

The modern businessman, then, must remember the force of his soulmate and bridge partner. She is more than the passive "little woman" because she holds the purse zipper and the checkbook. Man should answer the following question which the ancients first asked: "Ye must know that women have dominion over you: do ye not labour and toil, and give and bring all to the woman?"